Charles Mackay

Through the long day

Memorials of a literary life during half a century. Vol. I

Charles Mackay

Through the long day
Memorials of a literary life during half a century. Vol. I

ISBN/EAN: 9783744741019

Printed in Europe, USA, Canada, Australia, Japan

Cover: Foto ©ninafisch / pixelio.de

More available books at **www.hansebooks.com**

THROUGH THE LONG DAY.

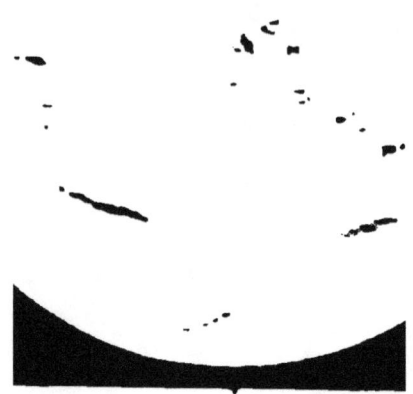

CHARLES MACKAY. 1852.
From a Medallion by Alexander Munro.

THROUGH THE LONG DAY,

OR,

MEMORIALS OF A LITERARY LIFE DURING HALF A CENTURY.

BY

CHARLES MACKAY, LL.D.,

FELLOW OF THE ROYAL ANTIQUARIAN SOCIETY OF DENMARK.
AUTHOR OF
"EGERIA," "STUDIES FROM THE ANTIQUE," "A MAN'S HEART,"
"VOICES FROM THE CROWD," ETC.

Vol. I.

LONDON:
W. H. ALLEN & CO., 13 WATERLOO PLACE,
PALL MALL. S.W.

1887.

(All rights reserved.)

LONDON:
PRINTED BY W. H. ALLEN AND CO., 13 WATERLOO PLACE.

PREFACE.

An autobiography is of necessity egotistical, but the egotism need not be aggressive or overweening. I have striven in the following pages to avoid falling into the error of making too much of myself, and have rather chosen to consider my own personality as a mere shelf in a book-case on which I might range the volumes of my experience, and the records of my intercourse with the once celebrated people who, in their day, ranked among the lights of the age in which my lot and theirs was cast. I have, as far as possible, avoided speaking of the living.

The work may be looked upon as a supplement to another, written nearly eleven years ago, entitled, *Forty Years' Recollection of Life, Literature, and Politics*, breaking new ground and going over the old ground, with fuller details of events than at that time would have been either judicious or profitable. It forms a faithful record of a literary career that has yielded me enjoyment in the pursuit, and, I am fain to hope, the respect of my contemporaries, without securing to me the worldly advantages which might have been mine, if I had been prudent enough in my youth to devote my energies to a more lucrative, though I will not say a more honourable profession. I leave my works —such as they are—and my reputation—such as it is—to the charitable judgment of posterity, if my name should reach it, as I cannot help hoping that it may.

December, 1886.

CONTENTS OF VOL. I.

	PAGE
CHAPTER I.—MY CHILDHOOD AND YOUTH	1
CHAPTER II.—THE "MORNING CHRONICLE" AND THE NEWSPAPER PRESS HALF A CENTURY AGO	49
CHAPTER III.—THE EGLINTON TOURNAMENT—ASCENT OF GOATFELL, IN ARRAN	68
CHAPTER IV.—A CHARGE OF PLAGIARISM	91
CHAPTER V.—OLD LONDON LIFE AND MANNERS	111
CHAPTER VI.—MUSICAL EPIDEMICS IN LONDON	127
CHAPTER VII.—THE SCOTT MONUMENT AT EDINBURGH	143
CHAPTER VIII.—THE DOUBLEDAY THEORY OF POPULATION	181
CHAPTER IX.—BREAKFASTS WITH SAMUEL ROGERS	199
CHAPTER X.—A CASE OF ARBITRATION	340
CHAPTER XI.—PATRIC PARK AND CELEBRATED MODERN SCULPTORS	366
CHAPTER XII.—THEODORE VON HOLST	388

THROUGH THE LONG DAY.

CHAPTER I.

MY CHILDHOOD AND YOUTH.

That "the child is father of the man" has been said so often as to have degenerated into a truism. What sort of a father, as a child, I was to the man that I have long been, I do not well know, though I would fain inquire of my conscience and my memory. I fear, however, that such knowledge as I may seek to obtain through the mist of bygone years may be imperfect or misleading, and that, neither as a child nor as a man, have I been enabled to reach to the height of the great wisdom inculcated by the Greek sage in the two famous words, "Know thyself." But I will do my best to discover, not only what I was, but what I am, and grope my way on the dim and hazy, though in some respects familiar road, from the starting-point of the cradle to the not now distant goal of the grave.

My earliest recollections go back to the time when I must have been three or four years old, and lived with my kind-hearted and excellent father at a lonely house on the southern shore of the Frith of Forth, near the little fishing-village of Newhaven. Having unfortunately lost my mother, I was under the charge of a careful nurse—a bonnie and buxom lass of Falkirk—who was very fond of me, and sang Scottish songs to amuse herself and me. Their melodies haunt me still, and will continue to do so while memory lasts, and the love of the beautiful has a home in my heart. She had also a great store of fairy-tales, which I was never tired of hearing her repeat. I wandered with her on the sea-shore, and picked up pebbles, sea-weed, and shells, and endeavoured—most frequently in vain—to detach the limpets from the rocks, greatly perplexed at the pertinacious hold which the creatures took when I tried to dislodge them. I could see the pier of Leith, which seemed to my infant eyes to stretch across an all but illimitable ocean.

I had another companion on the shore—a pug dog named "Smut," a very intelligent animal—more intelligent, perhaps, than myself, for he was in the maturity of his age and wisdom, and I was but an infant. Smut was very fond of music, and, when my father played Scottish airs on the flute—which he did with great taste and feeling—would jump on a chair, hold up his ugly but knowing head ceiling-wards, and howl in evident delight by way of accompaniment to the melody. This my father, more or less amused, endured until human nature could hold out no longer, and Smut was turned ignominiously into the garden.

The dog was not only intelligent, but adventurous, and had a strong will of his own. I have often heard the story that my father had occasion to go to London, by the Leith smack to Wapping, and that Smut, being determined to go with him, followed him unbidden to the wharf, and got stealthily on board. When discovered, as he speedily was, he was put on shore, with a reprimand, and possibly a chastisement for his impudence. But Smut was undaunted and pertinacious. The next smack sailed for Wapping a week afterwards, and was boarded by the sagacious animal, who concealed himself like a stow-away until the vessel was at sea. The captain knew my father, and knew Smut, and, there being no help for it, treated the poor animal kindly, and put him ashore on arrival at Wapping. Smut remained on the wharf for a day and night, watching the smack, and when the captain had concluded his business on the ship, followed him to his lodgings in Stepney or Poplar, I forget which. The captain knew where my father stayed in London, and took an early opportunity to deliver the intelligent and adventurous dog to his surprised owner.

Smut died at a good old age, very sincerely lamented, and my father buried him in his garden at Newhaven, with a tablet of slate over his grave, inscribed with an affectionate but cynical epitaph, which, of course, I could not read, but which I learned in after years was as follows:—

> Near this Tree
> are deposited the remains
> of one
> Who during life evinced gratitude,
> genuine attachment,
> and
> unqualified fidelity.
> Peruse this epitaph, you
> self-styled Christians,
> and Blush.
> For know that the poor inhabitant below,
> Who possessed these virtues
> of which you are deficient,
> was not a Christian,
> but a
> D O G.

This epitaph was a favourite with my father, who doubtless took pains over its composition. Many years afterwards, in 1838, when he was a resident in Brussels, he buried another dog, which he had received as a present from Baron Stein von Altenstein during a visit to Spa. The place of sepulture was in the back garden of a house, since demolished in the improvements of the city consequent upon the removal of the old boundary-wall that formerly encircled the Boulevards; and the identical epitaph did duty a second time.

Among the many Scotch songs which my kindly nurse often sang to me was "Maggie Lauder"—represented as a saucy lass, with her bare arms akimbo, who captivated by her too aggressive charms the susceptible heart of a wandering bagpiper. I remember one day, when the nurse took me to Leith, that my observant eyes caught sight of a young girl of fourteen or fifteen years of age playing in the streets with her companions. She so impressed my juvenile fancy with the idea that she was Maggie Lauder herself, that I called out loud enough to be heard by all her comrades, "Maggie Lauder! Maggie Lauder!" The young lady took the cry as a personal insult, and, darting out from the little crowd of her playmates, seized me by the collar, and administered with right good will two or three boxes on the ear, calling me at the same time a "deevil's buckie." My nurse was highly indignant, and a war of words ensued between the two. I believe the war had no physical results affecting either of the fair combatants, and only remember that I was led off "blubbering," or, as the Scotch say, "greetin." Such was my first attempt at criticism, and such was its reward!

I have been told that when I was about four years old I often contrived to get hold of a book, and, opening it out before me on a chair, would pretend to read aloud, uttering words that sometimes, but not always, seemed to have a meaning; that after a while I would look up with the appealing question, "Is na that bonnie readin'?" Whether the child was acting in this a paternal part towards the man into which Time was to develop it, I know not; but I incline to a vague belief that the germs of a literary taste were somehow or other inherent in the performance.

Another idiosyncrasy, if I may so call it, that dates from my early childhood, and has possessed me through life, and still remains as strong as ever in my mind, is a love, combined with a reverential awe wholly devoid of terror, for a thunder-storm. I was fascinated with the solemn peals that seemed to shake the skies, because I had been told that it was the voice of God speaking to the wicked. I never imagined that I myself could be one of those to whom the warning of God's displeasure was addressed. A few years later, I came to the conclusion that thunder was not the voice of God, but the rumbling of his chariot-wheels over the sky, and that the lightnings were the arrows with which He slew the wicked. The little imaginative child did not understand poetry, and had no acquaintance with the word; but the man learned in due time that in the childhood of civilisation a similar idea gave birth to some of the fables in the Greek mythology.

I have but one other remembrance of Scotland at this early time. My father was a temporary resident of Dunkeld, and sometimes talked of going to see the " Deuk," meaning the Duke of Athol; and as in broad Scotch—which my father usually spoke to me, with the notion that I would understand it better, as the language of the nurse and the servants with whom I had most intercourse, than I would have done plain English—the words " Duke " and deuk, a " duck," are almost identical in sound, I imagined that it was a "duck" he was going to visit. I did not know what a "duke" was, but a " deuk " I knew full well, and did not consider it at all extraordinary that my father should have a kind of friendship, or at least intimacy with a bird of that species. The belief was no doubt to be attributed to the influence of the fairy-tales which the nurse never tired of telling me, and which I was never tired of listening to. When I was taken to the Duke's palace, I wondered why a duck should be so splendidly housed, and thought that the " deuk " was in reality a fairy prince. And when I was led to the library, and the Duke placed me on his knee, and gave me a kiss and a bright new sixpence to buy " sweeties " with, my belief in fairyland was, if possible, strengthened. I thought that the " deuk " had suddenly become a prince, and that the prince would as suddenly become a "deuk" again, and fly off to the water with a loud whirr of his wings and the well-known cry of "quack, quack!"

My only playfellow at Newhaven, besides Smut, was a boy of my own age, the son of the man who kept the toll-gate on the Leith road. This youth's ambition was to save up his money—like myself, he had seldom possessed more than a penny—and buy a pony. Mine was to buy a violin; an instrument, however, which, in the coming years, I never learned or attempted to learn. But there was music in my soul nevertheless, though it never came into my fingers on a stringed instrument, or into my breath on fife or flute, flageolet, or hautboy, or any other wind instrument.

I have no recollection of the year when I was conveyed to London by a Leith smack, which, owing to adverse winds, took eleven days to complete the voyage. At the end of that time I found my father waiting for me at Wapping, released from all his fears for my safety and that of the smack. I had no opportunity of making an acquaintance with London or its busy streets, even had my age allowed me to do so; for, after a very short stay, I was transferred to Woolwich, not then a mere suburb of the great capital, as it has now become—but a distant and almost rural village. Here I passed two or three years under the care of a worthy couple named Threlkeld— the husband a sturdy Cumbrian, and the wife a winsome Scottish woman from my native city of Perth.

Here I remained for two or three years, and learned to read, I do not exactly know how, but certainly without finding the first steps up the hill of knowledge a pain or trouble, or experiencing any repugnance to or difficulty in climbing them. I took far more pleasure in fairy-tales than in the sports of childhood, or the society of boys of my own age; though I did not disdain an occasional game at leap-frog, blind-man's buff, or hop-scotch, or the delights of a peg-top or humming-top, a battle-door and shuttlecock, and cricket. But I found greater pleasure on the parade in front of Woolwich barracks, in listening to the band of the Royal Artillery, and thinking what a grand thing it would be to become a soldier, as my father and grandfather had been before me. Before I was ten years of age, I had read *Robinson Crusoe*, a juvenile edition of the *Arabian Nights, Sandford and Merton, Jack the Giant Killer, The Babes in the Wood, Little Red Riding Hood, Gulliver's Travels*, and *The Seven Champions of Christendom*. I had also gone through the Bible in search of such stories as Joseph and his Brethren, Esther and Ahasuerus, Saul and David, and Daniel in the Lion's Den. All the rest of the

Bible was imperfectly known to me, or beyond my comprehension.

I was removed from Woolwich in my eleventh year, and placed under the care of the Rev. John Lees, a minister of the Church of Scotland, who had no cure of souls. He only preached to a very small congregation, in the Gaelic language, and derived but scanty emolument for the performance of this duty from the interest of a bequest made by a rich and patriotic Highlander, to keep up the love of the native language of the Gael. Mr. Lees was a native of Stornoway in the island of Lewes, in the outer Hebrides, and in after life was appointed to the incumbency of that town by my relative, Sir James Matheson, who had made a magnificent fortune in China, and purchased the whole island, at a large price, from the then proprietor, the Hon. Mrs. Stewart Mackenzie of Seaforth. Mr. Lees grounded me in Latin and Greek, though the seeds which he planted never took root or flourished. He soon discovered that my *forte*, as he called it, was for mathematics, conjoined with a still more decided *forte* for poetry.

These two *fortes* are commonly considered to be antagonistic, and mutually destructive of each other, though in my case they did not prove to be so. I became the acknowledged dux of my school in all mathematical exercises, but never wavered in my love of imaginative literature, and especially of poetry. Beattie's *Minstrel*, the poems of Henry Kirk White, of Thomas Campbell, and of Lord Byron, were my especial delights; and as early as my thirteenth year, I committed the sin of rhyme, and revelled in the iniquity. My kind preceptor first winked at my transgressions, and ended by encouraging them. He ultimately endeavoured to guide me in the choice of books, referring me to, and making me a present of, a small volume of Dodd's *Beauties of Shakepeare*. This, however, I did not find, at the time, to possess so many attractions for my youthful mind as the lyrical poems of Milton, such as "L'Allegro," "Il Penseroso," and "Lycidas," the old ballads in Percy's *Reliques of Ancient English Poetry*, some few pieces of Oliver Goldsmith's, and, above all else, the inimitable war odes of Thomas Campbell. At this time there was published in London a little penny periodical, that appeared weekly under the title of the *Casket*, to which I timidly sent one of my juvenile productions. Much to my delight, it found favour in the eyes of the editor, and was published in due course. I was in my fourteenth year at the time, and never, I think, during the whole period of my after life, have I experienced such joy as I experienced on opening the pages of the *Casket*, and discovering my rhymes in print, with my name appended. It was the first kiss of love that my mistress, my nymph, my bride, my goddess, Literature, had given me, and the rapture it afforded me was indescribable. I contributed several other poems—so I thought them—to the *Casket*, the only one of which I can recall to memory, and that simply by its title, was an "Ode on the Death of Canning"; a very ambitious subject for a boy, who knew nothing of politics or contemporary history, and very little of ancient history, except the smattering derived from school-books. It was doubtless very great trash, but it found acceptance with the editor of the *Casket*, if not with his readers, and sufficed to give me encouragement to presevere in the disappointing career of authorship, not then so overcrowded with eager competitors as it is now.

At this time my half-holidays, twice a week, were usually spent in the Poets' Corner of Westminster Abbey, or in St. Paul's Cathedral, where it was my pleasure to study the monuments erected to the memory of the illustrious dead, and debating in my own mind whether it were possible that I, too, small and of no present account as I was, might hereafter be enabled to tread in their footsteps, and make myself a name among those of the worthies of my country. Thus early did I feel the spur of ambition or of emulation—or perhaps it was only vanity and conceit? But, whatever it may have been, it had possession of my mind, and I could not help thinking that I also had a little spark in my bosom, that might grow into a flame when I was older. Though I seemed to be destined by my father and his uncle—General Robert Mackay, of the East India Company's Service—for a military life, and fully expected, on attaining the age of sixteen, to be sent out to India as a cadet, I built but faint hopes of distinction in that career. I had no prejudice against it, and would have done my best to pass creditably through it; but my thoughts, in spite of myself, dwelt far more upon literary than upon military renown, and I looked with more satisfaction upon the marble effigies of poets and renowned authors, in the two national temples, than upon those of renowned naval and military heroes who had deserved well of their country.

During this period of my boyhood, I was a very unwilling slave to long sermons. The preacher to whom I was condemned to listen twice every Sunday, at his chapel in Cross Street, Hatton Garden, was one of the most eloquent pulpit orators of his time. All the fashion and intellect of London congregated to hear the Rev. Edward Irving, who preached like one inspired, and who fascinated not only the women, but, in a minor degree, the men who listened to him, by the wild and picturesque beauty of his personal appearance. They came in such throngs as to be unable to find even standing-room in his chapel. Enthusiasts were often known to climb to the window-sills of the chapel, and break the panes of glass so that they might see and hear him—perhaps more from vulgar curiosity and the contagious influence, or rage of the fashion, than from any real appreciation of his doctrine or his eloquence.

Mr. Irving's discourses were far above my comprehension, and I usually took refuge from the depressing monotony of his Calvinistic theology in the reading of the Old Testament and the Apocrypha, and in endeavouring to turn the Song of Solomon and the Psalms of David into rhyme and rhythm, to while away the time that hung so heavily upon me, and to prevent myself from going to sleep. If I now and then, in the rare intervals when I attended to the discourse, heard and understood his assertion that endless torments of fire and brimstone were mercilessly inflicted upon the wicked, and that good works and a blameless life were of no avail in the sight of God, if they were unaccompanied by belief in the doctrines inculcated in the Catechism of the Scottish Church, and that only a few of the human creatures born upon this miserable earth were the elect of Heaven from all eternity, and that the immense majority of the non-elect, however pure and holy their lives might be, were doomed to eternal perdition—I felt growing up in my mind an intellectual wrath and intolerance, such as might have taken possession of it if any daring disputant had maintained in my despite, as an arithmetician and a mathematician, that two and two made five, or that two parallel lines, continued *ad infinitum*, could be contained in a circle, however immense the circle might be.

I certainly derived neither moral nor intellectual benefit from the eloquent and earnest preaching of Mr. Irving, and the strong armour of my unbelief in the doctrines of his sect—as far as I was able to comprehend them—prevented his vigorous sword-thrusts, his sharp arrows, and his fiery artillery, from reaching either my heart or my brain, or converting me, even in the slightest degree, to the belief that the merciful God was unmerciful, that the God of Love and Justice was the God of Hate and Vengeance, or that the Eternal, the Infinite, the Immaculate Being, could be as like to a man in passions as Moses in the Old Testament, but not Jesus Christ in the New, had represented Him to be.

During the three years of my attendance on the ministrations of Mr. Irving, I only remember the general teaching of his frightful Calvinism, and two little incidents that occurred in his pulpit. The first was the impressive and touching manner in which he told the well-known story of St. Augustine and the angel, amid a silence that was positively felt, and that appeared to drop upon the whole congregation as if it had been a garment or a pall, or the sudden cessation of all power to move or to breathe, on the part of the listeners, until the story was ended. The second was an interlude—caused by the rush of a considerable portion of the congregation to the doors, when the sermon, extending to what they seemed to consider an intolerable length, filled them with apprehension that their dinners might be spoiled if they remained in church any longer. This excited the displeasure—I will not say the wrath—of the preacher. Suddenly arresting the torrent of his eloquence, snapping the thread—or, I may call it, the cable—of his discourse, he called to the door-keeper in a familiar tone, but with a loud emphasis, to shut and fasten the doors, so that nobody might quit the building. He then addressed himself to the congregation: "You seem to prefer your dinners to the word of God—at least some of you do; and, though you treat the Gospel with disrespect, which I cannot help, you shall not treat *me* with disrespect, and shall hear me out, whether you like it or not. I have ordered the doors to be shut, and they shall not be opened again until the service is concluded." The congregation was overawed, as sheep are at the bark of the collie, and, without resuming their places in the pews which they had quitted, stood near the door, and made no further attempt to resist the imperious mandate of the pastor.

In private life Mr. Irving was highly esteemed

and beloved by all who knew him. He was courteous and fascinating in his manners, and bore no trace of the Boanerges of the pulpit, or of the haughty and intolerant spirit of Calvin and John Knox, all displays of which he seemed to reserve for Sundays in the exercise of his vocation. He had a love for literature, especially for poetry, and formed an intimate friendship with Samuel Taylor Coleridge.

On the attainment of my fourteenth year, I was transferred to my father's care in Brussels, and was placed at school on the Boulevard de Namur, under the care of a Mr. Jay, who was afterwards succeeded by the Rev. Dr. Drury. Under their superintendence I made but slight progress in Greek and Latin, though I rapidly became proficient in French and German, and, in less than a twelvemonth, was able to speak and write in the former language as fluently and correctly as in English. My German was less perfect, for want of opportunity to speak it in a country where French was principally, and Flemish was partly, the language of the people. I feel myself justified in saying that these acquirements were of far more value to me in after life than any amount of Greek and Latin would have been, though I am far from ignoring the benefits derivable from a thorough acquaintance with the ancient classics, to which neither my tastes nor my opportunities inclined me. In addition to the pleasure I derived from a knowledge of French and German—to which I afterwards added an acquaintance more or less intimate with Italian and Spanish—there was daily bread for me in the mastery of the modern languages, which there might not have been in the command of Greek and Latin; for, after the age of sixteen, when I left school, and the opportunity of going out to India as a cadet had been lost—through no fault of mine, but solely in consequence of a misunderstanding (or perhaps it was a quarrel) between my poor, proud father, the half-pay lieutenant, and his rich, proud uncle, the General—I, who was as proud as either of them—or as both of them combined—determined, if possible, to earn my own livelihood, and, if I could not cease altogether to be a burthen upon my father's resources, to contribute something towards my own support. I felt myself to be a man, although only a growing lad in my teens, and had an idea that I was strong enough for anything. I was certainly ambitious enough for anything, and was in happy ignorance of the difficulties that encumbered the ascent of the hill of life—of the bogs, the rocks, the pits, and the precipices, that either yawned at the feet or bristled in the pathway of the climber.

That "Fortune favours the bold," the Roman poet has informed us, and the moderns would have known the fact from their own experience, if the ancients had not told them of it. But whether I was bold or not bold at this period of my adolescence, Fortune certainly favoured me. My father was well acquainted with Mr. William Cockerill, a venerable gentleman in weak health, who had long been a resident in Brussels. Mr. Cockerill was a Lancashire man, a working engineer and machinist, who shortly before the outbreak of the French Revolution in 1789 had betaken himself to the Continent, with the hope of making the continental people better acquainted with the construction and the uses of English machinery. He first went to St. Petersburg, where he managed to secure the patronage of the semi-lunatic Emperor Paul, who entrusted him with the construction of several important public works. While thus engaged he narrowly escaped being sent to Siberia by the eccentric Czar, because, through no fault of his own, he had failed to complete a lucrative contract within a few days of the stipulated time. Being forewarned, he managed to escape to the Netherlands, whither he had previously transmitted his earnings. He turned his knowledge, his enterprise, and his capital to profitable account, and, prospering more or less in his many undertakings, was ultimately enabled to establish the great iron and machine works at Seraing, near Liège. He had for several years withdrawn from business on account of old age and failing health before my father knew him, and had made over to his sons, James and John, the establishment at Seraing, and all others in which he was interested. He lived very quietly at Brussels, a prosperous gentleman, deriving but little pleasure from his wealth, except the one pleasure—great to him—of being enabled to purchase the finest horses in the market, and of taking daily drives in the handsomest and most commodious carriages that were ever seen on the Boulevards of Brussels.

One day when my father happened to call upon him, the old gentleman, sitting in his arm-chair, from which he could not rise without assistance, asked him if among the English colony at Brussels he knew of any young gentleman who could speak French and German, keep accounts, and act generally as his secretary. The reason of his asking was that the middle-aged gentleman whom for two or three years he had employed in that capacity had given way to habits of intemperance, which had grown upon him so rapidly, and had taken such firm possession of him, that—after repeated trials, and patient condonation of his faults in the hope that, as his daily bread was in peril, he would amend his life—Mr. Cockerill had been reluctantly compelled to dismiss him. My father, agreeing apparently in the Scriptural text that the man who provided not for those of his own household "denied the faith and was worse than an infidel," bethought himself of me. He had a misgiving that I might be too young for the post, and mentioned to Mr. Cockerill my qualifications and my age, though with but slight hopes that I might be considered suitable. Somewhat to his surprise and greatly to his satisfaction, Mr. Cockerill did not find my age to be an objection, but, on the contrary, an advantage, because, he said, a youth in his seventeeth year was not likely to be a drunkard, as his previous secretary had been. Provided my lingual and clerical qualifications were up to the mark, and my general character for diligence and good conduct would bear investigation, he expressed his willingness to make trial of me. I was to board but not to lodge with him, and to receive an annual salary of 1,200 francs. The terms were considered liberal by my father, magnificent by me, and the work was light.

Within two days I was installed in office, resolved to do my best to give satisfaction. I succeeded beyond my father's hopes, but not beyond my own expectations, and managed to make myself a pleasant companion both indoors and out of doors to the excellent old gentleman.

Mr. Cockerill had been but imperfectly educated as a boy, and had never cultivated his intellectual tastes. He knew nothing or next to nothing of literature, except that which might be drawn out of newspapers, but he had an inquiring mind, strong common sense, and a keen appreciation of wit and humour. The oldest jokes were always new to him, and his laugh was as ready and as hearty at the *crambe recocta* of any of Joe Miller's jests as at the first hearing. He bore his infirmities with the greatest patience and good humour; and now and then allowed himself to be seduced into singing a song to please his son James of Aix-la-Chapelle, his particular favourite, who shared with him his passionate love of horses, and was the fortunate possessor of the once famous horse Smolensko—well known in the annals of English sport—and which he had purchased at a very large price. The old gentleman's song, very popular in the days when Nelson was the national hero of Great Britain, and still occasionally sung by sailors in the forecastle, was—

> The rough old Commodore,
> The tough old Commodore,
> The fighting old Commodore, he—

whose great sorrow was that

> The bullets and the gout
> Had so knocked his hull about,
> That he'd never more be fit for sea.

Mr. Cockerill had decided political opinions; and though by birth and training a man of the people, he remained a sturdy old English Tory to the end of his days; though he had never set foot in

England since his early manhood, always spoke of the Great Napoleon as "Boney" and a tyrant; and whenever Daniel O'Connell was mentioned, declared that " hanging was too good for him."

The principal English physician in Brussels in those days was one Dr. Tobin, an Irishman, who had been in the army in his youth, and who paid Mr. Cockerill a daily visit for a fee of five francs. On one occasion, I remember, he called in company with a fresh handsome-looking young man, who was on his way to some German university, and whom he introduced as Mr. Charles Lever, a countryman of his own, and a medical student. I did not suspect at the time—how could I?—that this Charles Lever was destined to become in after years a great literary character, to write *Harry Lorriquer*, *Charles O'Malley*, and half-a-score of other excellent novels, full of wild Irish fun and humour, which threw all previous Irish novels into the shade. This was the only time that I met Charles Lever, though if chance had ever thrown him in my way, I should not have failed to remind him of our slight foregathering in the house of Mr. Cockerill. A few years afterwards, when I was no longer a resident in Brussels, but had taken up my abode in London, I heard that Mr. Lever had succeeded to the practice of Dr. Tobin, and acted as physician to the British Embassy.

While in the service of Mr. Cockerill, I had a

dream, which I have never since forgotten, that I had written a great book, under the title of "The Political History of Hunger." I thought at the time that the title and the subject were alike good, and I think so still, after the lapse of nearly half a century. I could not refrain from mentioning this dream to Mr. Cockerill, who was by no means of a literary turn of mind, but who, as I have said, was a keen politician in a rough way. He expressed his opinion that nations, like individuals, were more or less governed by "the belly," and that hunger was at the bottom of nearly all the popular revolutions that had taken place in the government of nations; and that such a book as that of which I had dreamed, would be both interesting and instructive, if truly written. "But it would not be worth your while to write it, even if you were able to do so," he added. "Better to keep a shop than write a book. Books don't pay; a shop does." The advice given was lost upon me; for though I never wrote the book referred to, or thought, at the time, of writing any other than a book of poems, I never wavered in my love for literature, or in my determination to adopt it as a profession.

I was but a poor moth, fluttering about in riotous freedom, in the light and blaze of hope and fancy, and literature was a lamp burning and shining above me; and, mothlike, I was attracted towards it, neither knowing nor heeding, in its transcendant attraction, that my wings might be scorched, or that my life might be lost if I yielded to its too powerful, or, it might be, its fatal, fascination. I sketched out some sort of a plan for the " Political History of Hunger," which I resolved to commence with the emigration of the patriarch Jacob and his children, seeking the corn in Egypt with which he could not provide himself in his native country, and ending the book with the great Revolution of 1789. But the work never went further than the first rough skeleton, and the catalogue of the main incidents which it would be necessary to include in a comprehensive treatment of the subject. The idea at last appalled me by its vastness, and, although I never wholly abandoned it, was consigned for its completion, and even for its serious commencement, to the " Greek Kalends."

While in Brussels I was an occasional contributor, in the French language, to the *Courier Belge*, of which M. Sylvain Van de Weyer, afterwards, and for many years, Belgian Minister in London, was one of the editors. I also contributed to the *Telegraph*, an English newspaper, established as a rival to a pre-existing journal called *News from Home*. I had been reading, for the first time, Coleridge's wild and fascinating poem, "The Ancient Mariner," and signed my contributions, that were exclusively in verse, and which I fondly imagined to be poetry, with the pseudonym of "Albatross." These contributions excited some little curiosity, and my father, who was not in the secret of the authorship, involuntarily hurt my feelings, when he said, in talking on the subject in my presence, that "Albatross" was synonymous with "*Great Goose.*" This accidental remark put me out of conceit with my adopted signature, and "Albatross" forthwith disappeared from the poet's corner of the Brussels *Telegraph*. The editor did the "Great Goose" the honour, in a notice to correspondents, to inform him that his contributions would always be acceptable. The future contributions of "Albatross" appeared with the initials "C. M.," and to this extent only was the English colony of Brussels admitted to the unimportant secret of the authorship of these, happily, dead and forgotten versicles.

Early in 1830, Mr. Cockerill, though seventy-five years of age, and scarcely able to endure the fatigue of the journey, visited Paris, accompanied by his niece and myself. His object was to consult a famous oculist, from whom, however, he failed to derive any benefit. We were eight days on the road, travelling leisurely, with our own horses, in a comfortable landau, driven by Mr. Cockerill's favourite coachman, a Walloon, named Antoine, recommended to his father by Mr. James Cockerill of Aix-la-Chapelle. To my young mind, the visit to the great historical city was one of extreme pleasure, only alloyed by the fact that the manifold enjoyments of the gay and brilliant capital were alike beyond the reach of my age and my pecuniary resources, and that Fate and circumstances persisted in considering me to be a boy, when I felt myself to be a man. I should have liked to have given a dinner at the famous restaurant of the *Trois frères Provençaux*, in the Palais Royal, to the three poets, Beranger, Victor Hugo, and Casimir Delavigne, who were, at that time, the literary gods of my idolatry. But I had no personal acquaintance with either of them, and no certainty that any overtures I, an unknown youth, might venture to make, would be favourably entertained. Worse than all, I had not the half, the quarter, the tenth, or the twentieth part of the money that so grand a symposium would have cost me; and so, like the "Political History of Hunger," it remained a dream, that never hardened into reality.

The symptoms of political convulsion that, in the course of this year, drove Charles X. and the elder branch of the Bourbons from the throne that they were unworthy to occupy, were apparent during my stay in Paris; but I was too young to fully appreciate their gravity, or to suspect that the revolutionary fires about to be kindled in Paris, would end in a conflagration that would embrace nearly the whole of Europe. Mr. Cockerill, however, saw farther before him, and read, more correctly than I could do, the signs of the times. These signs seemed to him to be so ominous of impending calamity, that he expedited the transaction of the little business which he had in Paris, lest, as he said, another Robespierre and a new Convention should arise to institute a second reign of terror, and all the wild beasts of ultra democracy should be let loose in Paris. He, therefore, determined to leave the country, while there was yet time; much to my disappointment, for I must confess that I was foolish and ignorant enough to wish to stay in the midst of the anticipated commotion, if I might thereby witness so great and historical an event as a new French Revolution and the downfall of a monarchy.

We left Paris by slow stages, as we had entered it, and had not been re-installed in Brussels more than a few months, when the storm burst over Paris in all its fury, astonishing all Europe, and justifying alike Mr. Cockerill's alarm and his foresight. It was not long before the storm extended to Brussels, where the materials for an explosion had long been accumulating and fermenting, and where the destined leaders had been diligently, though secretly, preparing to apply the lighted match to the powder magazine of popular discontent. The French Revolution of July 1830 was entirely political; that of Belgium, which broke out in September, was not only political but religious, and was aggravated by questions of race and language, as well as of theology.

Holland, with which Belgium was yoked in ill-assorted union, was Protestant, and spoke Dutch; Belgium was Catholic, and for the most part spoke French and Walloon. William I., the King of the Netherlands, who was in the main a well-meaning man, was ill-advised enough to attempt to supersede the French language by the Dutch in all legal and official proceedings, and to disqualify every schoolmaster for the exercise of his profession, who was not able to teach the language of Holland as well as that of France.

Mr. Cockerill was greatly alarmed at the outbreak in Brussels, and lost no time in deciding to take refuge with his son James in Aix-la-Chapelle. His niece had packed up. I had received instructions to accompany him, and he was ready to depart, when the alarming news was received that the mob of Aix-la-Chapelle had caught the infection of rebellion against constituted authority, and had risen in insurrection. But its ill-will was not political, as in Paris, or half political, half religious as in Brussels, but wholly socialistic, and directed exclusively against the rich. Mr. James Cockerill was the richest man in Aix-la-Chapelle, lived in the grandest style, and was in all respects the most prominent citizen. Against him, therefore, the first unreasonable fury of the mob was directed and spent itself. His splendid house was sacked, his pictures, works of art, and furniture destroyed, his cellars broken into, and his wines consumed by the thirsty and outrageous populace. In the helpless state of intoxication to which the majority reduced themselves, they speedily succumbed to the police and other legal authorities that were brought to oppose them; and order was restored without much difficulty or any loss of life. The riots had no support whatever among the middle classes, and comparatively little among the lowest; they were neither so obstinate nor so dangerous as they might have been in a more densely populated city.

Mr. Cockerill was ready to receive his father within a week, at a new and more spacious house than that which had been wrecked by the insurgents, and at the end of the week, Brussels still remaining in the hands of the revolutionists, at the head of whom were the magistracy and all the municipal authorities; old Mr. Cockerill, his niece, and myself set out by slow stages for Aix-la-Chapelle. Our first halting-place was at Louvain, where we remained a week at a comfortable hotel on the banks of the Dyle. Here I had the pleasure of making the acquaintance of Lady Blantyre and her children, who had taken refuge in that town from Brussels. Lord Blantyre's house in the Rue Royale at Brussels, which overlooked the Park, was the property of Mr. Cockerill; and, as future events unfortunately proved, was situated in the very centre of the sanguinary conflicts that afterwards arose between the insurgents and the Dutch troops which the King of the Netherlands had sent against them. Lady Blantyre and her family did not stay many days in Louvain, but returned to Brussels, thinking that all danger was over. Unfortunately she miscalculated. The Dutch troops, under the command of Prince Frederick of Holland, shortly after besieged and entered the city, no longer fortified as it once had been, and succeeded in entering by the Scharbeck end of the Rue Royale, and, after some resistance, effected a lodgment in the Park, midway between the Royal Palace and the Legislative Chambers. In one of the struggles by which the insurgents and the Civic Guard of Brussels attempted to expel them, Lord Blantyre, whose house abutted on the scene of conflict, unfortunately looked out of an upper window and was wounded in the neck by a random shot, and fell back dying into the arms of his wife who stood behind him. It was never ascertained whether the fatal shot proceeded from a Dutch or Belgian belligerant, but suspected that it was fired out of pure mischief and malice by some recklessly wicked scoundrel in the Belgian ranks, who could have had no necessity, while there were enemies in front of him in the park, to take aim at the fourth-floor window of a house not occupied by a military enemy.

While we were at Louvain, the alarm was raised that the town was to be attacked by Prince Frederick, and a call was made by the municipality on all the able-bodied inhabitants to arm themselves in its defence.

I was one of those who responded to the summons, and for the first and last time in my life shouldered a musket, and proceeded with some hundreds of others to the ramparts. The scene was highly picturesque when we assembled in the Grande Place in front of the Hotel de Ville. A bright full moon was shining in a cloudless sky, and, as a total eclipse had been predicted, a vast crowd had gathered, composed of women, children, and other non-combatants, to witness its commencement and its progress. To my young mind the spectacle was a sublime one; and to my excited imagination appeared still more sublime when a wild-looking man, bare-headed, with long dishevelled hair, suddenly pierced through the crowd, holding aloft a drawn sword, and took up a position within a few paces of the spot where I and the other volunteers were drawn up in marching order, ready to start to the ramparts. Pointing his sword to the moon, already in the earth's shadow, he exclaimed in a clear, sonorous voice, that all the signs and portents of the heavens were in favour of Belgium, and that the moon in dark eclipse represented Holland! The rumour prevailed in the crowd that the wielder of the sword was a priest. The rumour seemed to be confirmed when he knelt down before the assembled volunteers and invoked the blessings of Almighty God upon their efforts to repel the Protestant invader.

Their services, however, were not called into requisition. Prince Frederick made no attempt to enter Louvain, but, after showing himself at a distance of five or six miles, turned off towards Brussels, and so relieved the volunteers of Louvain of all present opportunity of distinguishing themselves by their valour.

Mr. Cockerill was highly pleased at the result for its own sake, as well as for the excuse which it afforded him of making merry at the expense of what he was pleased to consider the premature and, as he hoped, the final close of my career as a revolutionary warrior.

All was quiet when we arrived at Aix-la-Chapelle, and no further attempt was made by the Socialist malcontents to disturb the peace of the city. Political disaffection was scarcely, if at all, existent in any part of the Prussian dominions, and all the ill-will that manifested itself overtly or covertly in this small frontier city was that of the "have nots" against the "haves," of the hungry against the well-fed, and who all stood in such salutary terror of the civil power as to beware of braving it a second time so very soon after the signal discomfiture that had been inflicted upon them after the sack of Mr. James Cockerill's house. After a residence of about a couple of months in Aix-la-Chapelle we were comfortably installed at the Château de Bernsberg—a country-house belonging to Mr. James, about four miles from the city.

I soon saw all that was to be seen at Aix, the city of Charlemagne, who is reported to have built the Cathedral, and to be buried in it; I drank the foul-smelling waters, the supposed remedial effects of which in gout and rheumatism, and many other diseases, first raised the town into importance, and still brought visitors to it from every part of Europe; and mingled in a very juvenile, but, as I thought, manly way, in all the amusements and gaieties of the place. Among the other attractions of this health-resort was the Casino, whither the invalids betook themselves, both by day and by night, to try their luck at *rouge et noir* and *roulette*. I, though not an invalid, was tempted to follow the evil example, like a foolish moth dazzled by the flaming torch that was waved over the heads of idle people by the two demons of Chance and Cupidity. I had been present at the Casino during many evenings, without being able to summon up courage to tempt fortune at the *roulette* table; but, at length bolder grown, I made up my mind to risk five francs on a square of four numbers. One of the four turned up, by which I became the winner of a louis d'or. I was amazed at my own good fortune, but had strength of mind to resist the temptation to play again during the evening, the more especially as I noticed that a policeman was honouring me with his particular attention, and was apprehensive that he might report my appearance at the gaming-tables to the Cockerill family. I played no more for a whole week, though I was in nightly attendance in the saloon, where I had made the acquaintance of a Mr. Scudamore, an old resident of Aix, the brother of the then eminent London physician, Sir Charles Scudamore. Mr. Scudamore was a constant attendant at the *rouge et noir* table, and fancied that he had discovered a kind of martingale, by persistence in playing which, he hoped that he would one day break the bank and make a fortune. *Roulette* had fewer attractions for him, though he sometimes risked a five-franc piece on a single number, and still oftener on a nest of numbers, and was occasionally, though but rarely, a winner. One night, at his request, when he was more than usually impecunious, I lent him five francs. He placed the coin upon a single number, and won thirty-six times the amount of his stake, or 180 francs.

"Your money has brought good fortune," he said, as he paid me back my five francs; "why don't you try your own luck?"

I did so, and won a small stake. Emboldened, I tried again, staking a napoleon. Once more I won. Again I tried, with a like fortunate result. "You're in the vein," said Mr. Scudamore, handing me ten francs, "play for me." I placed the ten francs on the cross of four numbers, one of which turning up, Mr. Scudamore became the winner of ninety francs. By this time the glamour and fascination of the play were in full possession of me. I became adventurous and even reckless, and won so much and so often, that the eyes of the whole company were directed upon me, and neighbours to the right and left, and in front of me, ladies as well as gentlemen, pressed their coins upon me, and solicited me to play for them. Nearly every time I risked anything, I was successful, both for myself and for those on whose behalf I put down a stake, until at last my eyes were dazzled, and my brain began to reel with the excitement of the game, and the gratified greed of seeing such piles of money before me, all my own, to have, to hold, and to enjoy. I felt myself to be a Rothschild, a Crœsus, or a Midas before his ears began to sprout as a punishment for his unwise love of gold.

Had I discontinued play when these sensations

possessed me, I should have been the possessor of at least a couple of thousand francs, all fairly won in less than an hour—a larger sum, twenty times told, than I had ever before been able to call my own. But I did not know how to let well alone, or reflect that fortune was proverbially inconstant. I continued to solicit her favours, not only once, but many times, with varying results, sometimes making slight gains, sometimes heavy losses. The ultimate result was that before midnight all my piled-up gold and silver had been swept back into the yawning gulf into which the croupier consigned it.

All the night long I tossed about in my bed, unable to close an eye, engaged in the useless task of heaping maledictions upon my own head for the folly of which I had been guilty;—not in playing, but in not retaining my winnings.

The gens-d'armes on duty in the saloon had been observers of all the proceedings of the night, and had duly informed Mr. James Cockerill of the play, the winnings, and the subsequent losses, of the young man who, they had been informed, was in his employ and that of his father. Immediately breakfast was over, he requested me to step into his private room. He was most kind and fatherly. He did not blame me, he said, for trying my fortune at *roulette,* he himself had often done so, though not at so early an age as mine; but he warned me of the danger of allowing a love of play to take possession of me, or of permitting it to grow upon me unchecked. No good, he said, ever came of it; and he quoted the lines of Burns in reference to another folly, or crime, into which young men, in the hot blood of their youth and inexperience, were often betrayed:—

> I waive the greatness of the sin,
> The hazard of concealing,
> But oh! it hardens a' within,
> And petrifies the feeling.

The affectionate exhortation sank so deep into my mind, and the paternal kindness so unexpectedly displayed by a gay man of the world, a man of pleasure, as he notoriously was, so took my heart by storm, that, with tearful eyes, I made a vow to him that I would never again risk a frank at *roulette*, or any other game of chance. That vow I have religiously kept, and have never, from that early day to this, been tempted to break it.

While at Aix-la-Chapelle, and still taking an interest in the progress of the revolution at Brussels, I wrote some verses on the inauguration of Prince Leopold of Saxe Coburg as the first King of the Belgians, and sent it to my father. I was favourable to the revolution; he was opposed to it, for political as well as for personal reasons, having a great regard for the Prince of Orange, with whom he was personally acquainted. He sent me the following letter in reply, which I quote, to show that, in my love of literature, I did not run counter to his feelings or prejudices in addicting myself to its pursuit, or by indulging myself in the idle habit of rhyming.

83 Montague de la Cour,
15th September 1831.

MY DEAREST CHARLES,

I received your letter containing the stanzas upon the *inoculation* of Leopold. Without flattery, allow me to assure you that they are much admired, even by better connoisseurs than myself. A copy of them (elegantly ornamented with flags and other devices) is in the hands of Mr. Taylor, who has promised to place it under the royal eye! You may well suppose that I care but little as to the fulfilment of such a promise. We are all down in the mouth here, not even excepting Royalty itself, *et bouder semble être l'ordre du jour*. *Hélas! la pauvre blouse!* How art thou fallen!! The *ci-devant* civic guard, hitherto the terror of the Nassaus, are now termed by the *refined* part of the population, "*la garde chie-vite*, or *la garde sauve qui peut!*" You have heard, perhaps, of the large *haystack* of moustachios left by these Trojans at Louvain, etc.? The Government, it appears, intends purchasing the lot to stuff mattrasses for the various hospitals.

His Majesty goes regularly to Laeken to dine, sup, and (perhaps) to sleep. He does not appear to enjoy as great a share of spirits as myself.

Write soon, and believe me to be,
Yours affectionately,
GEO. MACKAY.

I remained in Aix-la-Chapelle and the Château de Bernsberg for nearly a year and a half, occupying my abundant leisure with literature, especially with poetry and the study of German, until the rapidly-declining health of Mr. Cockerill, accompanied by the total cessation of all the interest he was once accustomed to take in private and public affairs, rendered my situation in his household a complete sinecure. This state of affairs did not reconcile itself to my sense of independence or of personal dignity, and, seeing no prospect of any change for the better in the condition of Mr. Cockerill, I took a holiday in Brussels towards the end of the year 1831, that I might take counsel with my father. His opinion was strong that I should cultivate the Cockerill connection, and, on the death of the elder gentleman—of which there was unfortunately a speedy prospect, as his health continued rapidly failing—that I should endeavour to procure mercantile employment in the great engineering establishment at Seraing. My own opinion was equally strong, if not stronger, that I should return to London, to carve out for myself, if possible, a literary career, to which all my tastes and sympathies so irresistibly impelled me.

I endeavoured to strengthen the arguments which I used, by the fact within my personal knowledge, that Mr. John Cockerill, the head of the establishment of Seraing, was in depressed spirits with regard to the future prospects of that

CHILDHOOD AND YOUTH. 41

important concern; that the disturbed state of the whole continent had acted very prejudicially to his interests; that he was reducing the strength of his commercial staff, and that, not being a skilled mechanic, it was only on that staff I could expect employment; that, moreover, the King of Holland, a sleeping partner in the concern, had withdrawn, or had given notice of the withdrawal of, his capital as a shareholder; and that, all these things considered, London and not Seraing would afford the most favourable field for my industry and my ambition, and for the exercise of such abilities as I might possess. My father became, very reluctantly and slowly, a convert to my opinions, and finally agreed, with many misgivings, as to the wisdom of my determination, and resolved to accompany me to London in the spring of 1832.

In the meantime I returned to Aix-la-Chapelle, and, failing anything to do in the interest of Mr. William Cockerill, made myself useful to Mr. James by acting as tutor to his young family of boys and girls, grounding them as well as I could in the English language, in arithmetic, and the rudiments of mathematics. Though my time passed pleasantly enough—what with the slight duties I had to perform, and the heavier duties I imposed upon myself in the gratification of my literary tastes, both in prose and verse, and in the amusements and distractions of which Aix-la-Chapelle was not by any means deficient—the winter of 1831–32 appeared preternaturally long. I was impatient to be a man, though only eighteen. In my foolish fancy I qualified myself for the coveted advancement by losing my heart, or thinking that I lost it, to more than one fair damsel in the town, to whom I indited—as is the custom, and doubtless always will be, among precocious and fanciful youths — love-sonnets, indulging the while in imaginary transports, and equally imaginary woes and despairs. "But thereof came in the end"— nothing! and I escaped from Aix-la-Chapelle with a few bruises on my affections, but happily without a serious wound, and reached Brussels at the close of the year 1831.

Return to London.

It was early in May, 1832, that my father and I took our places in the diligence from Brussels to Ostend, to embark for Dover. Our arrival in England did not impress either of us very favourably with our countrymen, at least with those of Dover, or with the excellence of the arrangements of the authorities of that town for the comfort and convenience of travellers from the Continent. Owing to the state of the tide, the steamer was unable to discharge her passengers at the wharf which did duty for the pier that has since been erected, and boats put off from the shore, into which all the passengers entered as a matter of course. We expected that the charge for the service would not be more than one shilling per head; but, when half-way between the vessel and the land, the rowers ceased to row, and a demand was made of five shillings each for about a dozen yards of transit. Most of the passengers remonstrated loudly, and some violently, while two or three of the most irascible went so far as to threaten to throw the extortionate boatmen into the sea, and take possession of the boat. Ultimately, however, after much useless expenditure of breath and indignation, we all had to pay; not, however, without vehemently threatening the boatmen with the police and the magistracy, at which the hardened and impudent scoundrels but laughed, knowing, as they did full well, that no redress was obtainable, without the delay of probably several days in Dover, and considerable expense, as well as trouble and annoyance.

Nor was this the whole amount of the extortion to which we were subjected. The boatmen, instead of causing the boats to be pulled to the shore, so that passengers could step to land from the bows, came to a stoppage about two yards from *terra firma*, to give their confederates on shore the opportunity of placing planks, so that the passengers could land dry-shod. For these planks a charge of one and sixpence was made on each passenger, supplemented by another charge of one shilling for every article of luggage and baggage, great or small, that was seized by these harpies. No redress was possible, except at a cost that was not worth incurring, and the vengeance vowed by the indignant travellers was utterly wasted.

Among the earliest acquaintances which I made in London, through the medium of Messrs. Stewart and Barron, of 26, Parliament Street—who had acted for my father for many years, during his residence in Brussels, as his agents for the receipt and the transmission of his military half-pay—was that of Mr. William Brewer Roberts, connected with the then well-known publishing firm of Fisher, Son and Jackson, of Newgate Street, the proprietors of *Fisher's Drawing-room Scrap-Book*. This favourite annual was edited by the popular poetess, Miss Letitia Elizabeth Landon, better known as L. E. L. Mr. Roberts had a large connection among watercolour artists, and acted as an intermediary between them and the booksellers for the sale of their copyrights, for engraving in the annuals and other illustrated periodicals.

Among other artists with whom he had social or commercial relations were Mr. George Cattermole, Mr. Samuel Prout, Mr. De Windt, Mr. Coxe, Mr. J. D. Harding, Mr. Charles Bentley, and Mr. E. H. Bailey, the sculptor. By this gentleman I was introduced to Mr. Benjamin Lumley, a young solicitor, residing in Quality Court, Chancery Lane, acting at that time as legal adviser to Monsieur Laporte, the lessee of the Royal Italian Opera. Mr. Lumley, a few years afterwards, on the bankruptcy of M. Laporte, became the successor of that gentleman, and carried on, with great personal credit and more or less pecuniary success, the affairs of that establishment. I read Italian with Mr. Lumley, and grounded him in the grammar of that language, which I had studied both at Brussels and Aix-la-Chapelle, and in which I had become so proficient as to be able to converse with facility.

I also made the acquaintance, about the same time, of a young man named Henry Russell, a friend of Mr. Lumley, and, like him, of Hebrew parentage, though not of faith. Mr. Russell had been known in his boyhood for his musical accomplishments, and especially for his brilliant playing on the pianoforte. He had also made a successful *début* as a vocalist at one of the transpontine theatres, and was considered by his family and friends as a musical prodigy. He was my senior by three or four years, and had made himself a growing reputation in the musical profession by the composition and publication of some songs and ballads, of which he had found the poetry in the works of Lord Byron, and older authors. He aspired to write an oratorio, or an English opera, if he could but procure a libretto. He learned by some means or other that I had written a few ballads, and applied to me, in the hope that the much-needed libretto might be forthcoming from my pen. In this hope he was disappointed; but I fell in with his desires so far that I showed him some of the songs I had written, which he took away with him.

Two days afterwards, he asked me to accompany him to Walker's music warehouse, in Soho Square, where he played over and sang to me two of my songs to which he had composed the melodies. After I had expressed my pleasure at hearing them, he asked my permission to publish them. This I gave him, nothing loth, but highly flattered, and never thought of asking for payment. One of them, a very inferior composition, entitled, "Some love to roam o'er the dark sea-foam," happened to tickle the taste of the town, and became extremely popular. It was to be heard for many months on all the barrel-organs, that then, as now, infested the streets of the metropolis. The other—which, as a poem, was infinitely superior, in my estimation—attracted no notice, and, in fact, fell still-born. The publisher ultimately cleared about two hundred pounds by "Some love to roam." Mr. Russell, I believe, received a guinea for the music, and I received nothing but a barren "Thank you" from the composer, though not even as much as that from the publisher—unless a couple of copies of the song might have been considered an equivalent for the thanks which he did not render. I allowed Mr. Russell to compose music to, and the publisher to publish, two or three other songs, on the same unremunerative terms; but none of them achieved the popularity of the first, though, in my opinion, and in that of everybody among my friends who had either taste or judgment, they were all infinitely more worthy of it.

Mr. Russell also composed the music to a set of six sacred melodies that I wrote, which were published at the expense of my friend, Mr. Roberts, by the bookselling firm of Fisher, Son & Co. The speculation was not successful, excepting so far as it made me favourably known to a publishing house with which in after years I became profitably connected. Mr. Russell, however, found the partnership of his music with my verse to answer his purpose, inasmuch as he was not only a composer but a vocalist by profession, and was extremely popular as a singer.

After two or three years I lost sight of Mr. Russell, who had left England, with a newly-married wife, for a professional tour in the United States. He was one of the first, if not the very first, who ventured on that new and almost unknown field of English dramatic enterprise, which has since been so largely cultivated, not only by English, Scotch, and Irish, but by other European vocalists. The voyage at that time was made in sailing ships, and was long, tedious, and expensive; and the Transatlantic press was only partially developed, and was unable to afford the foreign adventurers who tried their fortune in America the immense publicity which is at their command in the present day, so that the difficulties to be encountered were more numerous and the chances of success were fewer than they have subsequently become. On Mr. Russell's return to England, with cash in his pockets, he renewed his connection with me, as I shall have occasion to record hereafter.

CHAPTER II.

THE "MORNING CHRONICLE" AND THE NEWSPAPER PRESS HALF A CENTURY AGO.

It was in the year 1834, two years after I had been knocking about in London, a mere floating straw on the great river of literature, that I succeeded in obtaining a firm hold on journalism as a profession. My first anchorage was on the *Sun*, a Liberal evening paper, the proprietor of which was Mr. Munro Young, a warm-hearted and able man, whose memory I shall always cherish with affection and respect. My second anchorage, after a year, was on the *Morning Chronicle*, the leading Whig and Liberal journal of the metropolis, the commercial and literary rival of the *Times*, with which it was running a neck-and-neck race for power, popularity, and influence.

The present generation has but vague and imperfect ideas of the impediments to success which in that early day beset the career of journalism.

Governments obliged to tolerate newspapers, and compelled to a large extent to be indebted to them for support, feared rather than loved them, and did their best, or worst, to render their establishment difficult, their existence disagreeable, and their prosperity precarious. The tax-gatherer laid his heavy hand upon them *ab ovo*, by an excise duty of three-halfpence per pound on the raw material, levied at the paper mill. The next burthen placed upon them was a stamp duty of fourpence on every copy printed; and the last was a tax of three shillings and sixpence for every commercial announcement, whether long or short, important or unimportant, which was made in their columns. A landed estate for sale, a house or lodgings to be let, a servant wanting a place, or a master wanting a servant, Warren's blacking for the feet, Rowland's Macassar Oil for the head, or a quack pill for the stomach, warranted to have been habitually taken during his whole life by Methuselah, had severally to contribute three and sixpence on each advertisement to the greedy gullet of the Chancellor of the Exchequer.

The price of the daily papers, whether morning or evening, was sevenpence, though they were not half or even a quarter of the size of the *Standard* and *Daily Telegraph* now published at a penny. The consequence was that comparatively few persons bought them, but were contented to hire them;

and thus every paper, when it had served its turn and gone through several hands in London, was sent by post to a new set of customers in the country. The space at the command of the editors being limited, as well as the capital at the command of the proprietors, the weary nuisance of unnecessary comments upon public affairs in the shape of leading articles, was kept perforce within moderate bounds; and it was rare that the *Chronicle* or *Times* indulged in more than one or at most two leading articles on the principal topics of the day. These articles were mostly political and seldom social, and never expatiated on any minor events recorded elsewhere. The comic leading article was undreamed of. The death of an elephant, a cow with a wooden leg, a mouse caught by the tail in an oyster-shell, were facts that, if recorded at all, were recorded in a paragraph, and not made the texts, as they are in this drearily comic age, for the overflow of editorial balderdash in a column or more of pumped-up attempts at fine writing.

The principal editor wrote the leading articles himself, being unprovided with any editorial staff to assist him. It is true that he often received, and was glad to welcome, the aid of volunteers in political life, who desired either to attack or support the policy of an administration. Many of the most eminent party leaders in those days contributed, *sub rosa*, to the columns of the daily press. Among others that might be mentioned were George Canning, Sir James Mackintosh, and Lord Brougham.

I remember once, when assistant sub-editor of the *Morning Chronicle*, that I waited on the Duke of Sussex at the Hyde Park Hotel, where he was resident, for a few days, with the proof of a leading article which he had either written or dictated. The Duke was an earnest and consistent Whig, and had fallen into disfavour with his royal father, and with George IV. I do not at this distance of time remember the subject of the royal article, except that it was in support of some Liberal measure, and that the style was crude and involved. I remember well that the proof was a rough one and contained several grammatical as well as literal errors that required correction. I also remember that the Duke detected the errors very readily, but that he was not able to correct them, *secundum artem*, and that he had ultimately to ask me to show him how to make such technical marks as would be understood in the printing office.

All the London journals at the time were particularly careful to exclude from their reports of the law proceedings the shameless evidence that it is but too often necessary to produce in courts of justice. They generally dismissed it unreported, with the curt statement that it was "unfit for publication." Even those scandalous journals the *Age* and *Satirist* were decent in their language, though filthy in innuendo and suggestion and prolific in foul libels. These latter were quite as often punished by the horsewhips or cudgels of the slandered persons as by the slower and more uncertain process of the law.

Mr. Murdo Young of the *Sun*, under whom I was happy to serve when only in my twentieth year, was a sound Whig, with a leaning more or less towards Radicalism, a ready writer, a poet of considerable reputation, and an able and very enterprising man of business. He was much pleased with two articles I submitted on my first introduction to him. The one was on the literary controversy that had been raging for some years in Paris on the merits and demerits of the rival schools of Classicism and Romanticism; the other on the leading prophet of the Romanticist faith, Victor Hugo, with a review of the works by which he was then favourably known, *Le Dernier Jour d'un Condamné, Notre Dame de Paris*, and his stirring poems *Les Orientales*, the latter all but unknown in England. The articles were published in the *Sun*, and paid for handsomely. Mr. Young expressed at the same time his wish to be useful to me in case any vacancy should occur in the literary staff of his journal. He was as good as his word, and speedily found or made an opportunity to appoint me to the post of junior or assistant editor, under Mr. Deacon, author of a novel called the

Bashful Irishman, and Mr. Collins, who afterwards and for many years edited the *Hull Advertizer*.

I was principally employed in writing notices on foreign literature, of which I knew something, and on foreign politics, of which my residence on the Continent had given me a somewhat more familiar knowledge than was possessed by my two older colleagues. In this employment I remained for about a twelvemonth, publishing in the meanwhile a small volume of songs and poems, which fortunately attracted, through the intervention of my friend Mr. Roberts, the notice of Mr. Dubois, a contributor to the *Morning Chronicle*, and through Mr. Dubois and Mr. Robert MacWilliam, a Middlesex magistrate, the still more important notice of Mr. John Black, the editor of that powerful journal. The *Chronicle* had for some years been in a failing condition under the proprietorship of Mr. William Clement of the *Observer* and *Bell's Life in London*, a mere tradesman, without literary training or political knowledge. He had long been anxious to disembarrass himself of the *Chronicle*, which his mismanagement had well-nigh ruined; and, about six or eight months before I was appointed by Mr. Black to a subordinate position—such as befitted my youth and inexperience, but offering, nevertheless, a fair field for my ambition—it had been purchased, for seventeen thousand pounds, by Mr. John Easthope, a flourishing stock-broker,

Mr. Simon MacGillivray, a retired Mexican and Canadian merchant, and Mr. James Duncan, a London publisher in Paternoster Row. These gentlemen had found Mr. Black in possession of the editorship, and retained him in it; and had set themselves, by a judicious and liberal expenditure, to improve the paper and extend its influence in all its departments. They appointed an Irish barrister, Mr. Michael Joseph Quin, author of *A Voyage Down the Danube*, to be Foreign Editor; Mr. Eyre Evans Crowe, author of a History of France, to be their Paris Correspondent; Mr. George Hogarth, of Edinburgh, a friend and intimate of Sir Walter Scott, and a musical amateur and violoncello player of some celebrity in the society of the Scottish capital, to be Sub-editor; and engaged a numerous staff of the best Parliamentary reporters in London, with the view of making the *Chronicle* the channel of the fullest and most correct reports of the proceedings in both Houses of the Legislature. Among the reporters so engaged were Mr. John Payne Collier, the afterwards celebrated Shakespearean editor and commentator; Mr. Charles Dickens, then only partially known to fame as "Boz," but soon afterwards to shine forth brilliantly as the most popular novelist of the age; William Hazlitt, son of the famous critic and essayist of a previous generation, and now one of the Registrars in Bankruptcy; James Harfield, the secretary of Jeremy Bentham; Mr. William Bernard McCabe, and other able men of less note.

My immediate duty was to assist Mr. Hogarth in the sub-editorship, to which, after his transference to the theatrical and musical department, for which he was better fitted, Mr. Collier succeeded for a short time. The latter gentleman was finally displaced under somewhat mysterious circumstances, which I was never thoroughly able to understand, to make way for Mr. Thomas Fraser, who was about ten years my senior, the son of the Laird of Eskadale, in Ross-shire, to which estate he succeeded at his father's death, and afterwards disposed of to the then Lord Lovat for a considerable sum. Mr. Fraser had formerly been connected with the *Scotsman*, and, in his capacity of reporter for that journal, had attended the memorable dinner when Sir Walter Scott had, for the first time, publicly avowed the authorship of the Waverley novels.

Mr. Fraser did not long retain the sub-editorship, having been transferred to Paris as permanent agent and correspondent of the *Chronicle*. He is the same gentleman who is celebrated in Thackeray's well-known "Ballad of Bouillabaisse," under the name of "Laughing Tom." Mr. Thackeray was himself a candidate for the sub-editorship of the *Chronicle*. His friends thought I was too young for the post, and his chances for the position, for that and other reasons, seemed to be greatly superior to mine.

But I had two advantages over him: first, I was in possession; and, secondly, I had the support and influence of Mr. Black, that never failed or slackened, and that of his friend and countryman, Mr. MacGillivray, who was an enthusiastic Highlander, and took a fancy to me because I also was of Highland blood and extraction.

But what, as I afterwards learned, had been greatly instrumental in securing me the victory over Mr. Thackeray was the publication in the *Morning Chronicle* of a little political squib which I had contributed to its columns. It was *apropos* of the coy reluctance to accept office, if it were offered to him, recently expressed in the House of Commons by Sir Robert Peel. It was highly to the taste of my friends MacGillivray and Black, and approved, on their verdict, by Messrs. Easthope and Duncan —who had but few literary tastes, and scarcely any appreciation of literature. It ran as follows:—

> Beauty, when maiden, on the brink
>   Of the ripe age of thirty-two,
> Cries, "Aid me, Virtue, lest I sink,
>   When teasing lovers come to woo.
> Should they plant kisses on my cheek,
>   And speak me fair, and sue me long,
> I fear I should be very weak,
>   And the temptation very strong."
>
> And so says coy Sir Robert Peel,
>   When dreams of Office charm his sight;

"Guard me," he cries, "in coat of steel
　Against that siren of delight!
Oh! Virtue, aid me when I speak.
　Should Place, the charmer, woo me long,
I feel I should be very weak,
　And the temptation very strong."

Old women both! You flaunt in vain;
　In vain expose your fading charms,
And broadly hint your wish to gain
　Husband and Office to your arms.
Resign yourselves, and live at ease;
　Bear your lone lot with patience meet,
For young men now are hard to please,
　And nations difficult to cheat.

Mr. Thackeray was often a paid contributor to the *Chronicle*, especially on subjects connected with the Fine Arts, but never succeeded in establishing a permanent connection with it.

Two incidents connected with the *Morning Chronicle*, during my tenure of the sub-editorship, have firmly fixed themselves in my memory. The one was the reported death of Lord Brougham by a carriage accident, in the North of England, when in company with his friend, Mr. John Temple Leader—who either was at the time, or had previously been—the representative in Parliament of the city of Westminster. The news was so minute and particular in the details which were given of the fatal catastrophe, that it received general credence; and the conductors of the *Morning Chronicle* went so far, in the manifestation of their sorrow for what they considered a public calamity, as to put the whole page which contained the particulars of the event, and the reflections of the editor and conductors upon it, into mourning, such as English newspapers are only accustomed to use in announcing the death of the Sovereign or a member of the Royal Family. The press generally—though not all so eulogistic of the character of the supposed defunct—agreed in recognition of his many noble qualities, and of the great place he held in contemporary politics and history. But, in two or three days, indignation, more or less fervid, gave place to the admiration which had been extorted, when it was found that the whole narrative of the fatal accident was a falsification, and that the supposed victim—even if he had been thrown from his carriage, which was doubtful—was alive and unhurt, and ready to resume the part he had so long played as the stormy petrel of politics. Mr. Black, who had been more enthusiastic than his contemporaries in laudation of the great virtue of the "departed," was louder than any in the expression of his disgust, and did not hesitate to express his belief —which was also that of the Clubs, and of Society in general—that Lord Brougham himself was the concocter and author of the hoax. Mr. Black, who had been familiar in his earlier days with the literary gossip of Edinburgh, remembered that, in

1825, John Gibson Lockhart had caused to be inserted, as a practical joke, in the *Edinburgh Weekly Journal*, with which he was at the time connected, a report of the death of his friend, John Wilson, the well-known "Christopher North" of *Blackwood's Magazine*. The report was accompanied by a highly eulogistic memoir and review of the Professor's literary character and genius. Mr. Black maintained that Lord Brougham had taken the idea of the mystification from his remembrance of this frolic of Lockhart's, and that he desired, in the excess of his morbid vanity, to know what good, if any, posterity would say of him. Doubtless his lordship was gratified for the time, as his contemporaries were all more or less friendly, and found more good than evil to report of him, when they thought that, after "life's fitful fever," he was finally at rest. But the *Chronicle*, and the other leading journals, had their revenge in after years, and Lord Brougham became, whenever his perversities and eccentricities afforded an opportunity for newspaper or party attack, "one of the best abused men in the country."*

---

* "So little reliance is placed upon his (Brougham's) words that everybody laughs at his denials, and hardly anybody has a shadow of doubt that he was himself at the bottom of it. He has taken the trouble to write to all sorts of peoples, old friends and new, to exonerate himself from the charge; but never was trouble more thrown away.

The next incident which I remember was the visit of Marshal Soult to London, when Mr. Easthope, the principal proprietor of the *Chronicle*, received a hasty message from the Admiral in command of the fleet in the Thames, stating that the Marshal, on his departure for France, had consented to lunch with him on board of H.M.'s warship *Howe*, stationed opposite Sheerness, and suggesting that a gentleman from the office should be sent down immediately, to give an account of the proceedings. There was no time to be lost when the notification arrived, and, as I happened to be in the office, I was requested to start immediately, though it was the business of a reporter, not of a sub-editor, and do the best I could in the sudden emergency. I was nothing loth, made no preparation, and no difficulties; and by a liberal expenditure of money for the hire of the means of locomotion on land and water, just managed to arrive in sight of the *Howe* as the French steamer, conveying the Marshal to his own country, was within a quarter of a mile's distance. This was intensely provoking, but, on boarding the *Howe*, I was hospitably received

D'Orsay says that he carefully compared the supposed letter of Shafto with one of Brougham's to himself, and that they were evidently written by the same hand. The paper, with all its marks, was the same, together with other minute resemblances, leaving no doubt of the fact."—*Greville's Memoirs: Journal of the Reign of Queen Victoria.*

by the Admiral, who, while regretting the inevitable lateness of my arrival, due mainly to the shortness of the notice which he had given, made, like a wise man, the best of the circumstances, and invited me to lunch, which was set on the table, at which several of the officers were still seated. He afterwards supplied me with such particulars as he could command of the toasts that had been given, and the speeches that had been made. An adequate report of the speeches of the Admiral and the Marshal, both full of friendly sentiments and hopes for the permanent alliance of France and Great Britain, as necessary to the happiness and prosperity of both nations, and to the peace of Europe, duly appeared in the *Morning Chronicle*.

Among the able men employed as reporters at this time by the *Chronicle* was one whom, for the purposes of this narrative, I shall call "Hooper." He was expeditious, correct, thoroughly conscientious and trustworthy in his profession; but in all matters relating to himself and to his intimacy with the great men whom he knew, or fancied he knew, he was incorrigibly addicted to boasting, exaggerating, romancing, and inventing. So well was he known in literary society for this peccadillo, and so famous had some of his exaggerations of his own importance become, that Hooper's last escapades were famous in half of the Clubs of London—so famous, that Theodore Hook introduced him in one of his novels as Jack Brag.

It happened one day, at the usual afternoon meeting of the proprietors and editors of the *Chronicle*, that Mr. Charles Buller, the well-known Liberal Member of Parliament, and one of the leading-article writers, who was present, accidentally mentioned "Jack Brag," and said how much he would like to see him. I had seen Mr. Hooper in the reporter's room a few minutes previously, and mentioned the fact to Mr. Black. Mr. Black, remembering that he had himself sent for Mr. Hooper to receive his instructions before proceeding to Lewes, in Sussex, to report the speeches of the Liberal candidate, and, if possible, to aid the cause by the local and other knowledge which he possessed of the town, directed that he should be shown in accordingly, that he might receive his instructions *vivâ voce*. Hooper, true to his character, and innocently unsuspicious of any *arrière pensée* on the part of Mr. Black or any of the company, replied: "I shall start immediately; but it will be of little use, except to report the speeches. You should have sent me earlier, if you expect me to be of any service in the election. *I* know well how to manage an election, in any doubtful and close contest like that of Lewes. Mr. Canning taught me how to win an election!"

Mr. Charles Buller, much amused, though discreetly showing no sign of surprise, said, without meaning any imputation on his veracity: "You must have been very intimate with Mr. Canning, if he took you into his confidence, Mr. Hooper. You cannot have been much more than fourteen or fifteen years of age when Mr. Canning died."

"Yes!" replied Hooper, without hesitation or a blush, "that is true; but then, you see, I was a very precocious boy!"

Another all but forgotten incident of my early days at the *Morning Chronicle* was vividly recalled to my memory in 1876, by an accidental meeting at the foot of Boxhill, Surrey, with a gentleman, who remembered me after an interval of forty years.

An action had been brought against the *Morning Chronicle* in 1836, by Mr. Powell, a gentleman once engaged in the sub-editorial department, for wrongful dismissal. I was summoned as a witness by the proprietors, to depose to the fact that the plaintiff was dismissed for frequent intoxication in business hours, which rendered him unable to perform his duties in a satisfactory manner. I was submitted to a very severe cross-examination by Mr. Earle, the plaintiff's counsel, who was afterwards raised to the Bench, which he adorned for many years. Mr. Earle persisted in asking me what was the "occasion" of the dismissal, and the constant iteration of the question puzzled me to know whether the counsel meant, by the word "occasion," the *time* or *date* at which the dismissal took place, or the cause of the dismissal. I believe I was nettled at the manner in which the questions were put, with the evident design, as I thought, of making me contradict myself, and I replied in a manner that amused the judge, and amused the counsel, by asking Mr. Earle to define what meaning he attached to the word " occasion." " If you mean," I said, " the date at which the dismissal took place, I have already declared, more than once, that I do not exactly remember; if you mean 'cause,' I have already said, and again repeat, that it was intoxication." Mr. Earle, in his summing-up the case for the plaintiff, alluded pointedly to my evidence, which he denounced as that of an " arrogant and presumptuous boy." I was at the time a young man of two-and-twenty, and took silent revenge in my own mind, by reflecting that barristers were too often reprehensibly insolent to the unfortunate victims submitted to their untender mercies in the witness-box.

Acacia Grove, Dulwich,
15.5.76.

DEAR DR. MACKAY,

How strange was our meeting on Saturday, after an interval of forty years; and no less strange that I should have recognised you. It was in the year 1836, that, going into court upon some other business, I saw you being baited in the witness-box, and wondered at hearing you were "sub-editor," you looked *so* young. I had not seen you since then, and you have not yet lost your boyish features. Since then we have both been climbing different hills, you of literature, and I of law. We parted in a law court, and met again, accidentally, in a lovely Surrey lane. There are few left (who were known to me) forming the assemblage at that trial: Easthope, Duncan, MacGillivray, Black, the Judge, and all the counsel are gone, all the Jury—all gone, perhaps, but you and me.

I never go into that part of Surrey without lounging about where you met me. I was in what is now called the coffee-room, at the "Hare and Hounds," before I was "breeched," in fact, when I was in petticoats, and lunched there on Saturday! There is a melancholy pleasure in these revisits, like the lake described by Moore in his "Epicurean," in the Land of Roses, whose waters were half sweet, half bitter.

Believe me, with pleasing recollections of having met you again, and of our place of meeting,

Yours truly,
W. WALLER.

When I joined the *Morning Chronicle* in 1835, the *Morning Chronicle* had been in existence for seventy-five years. It appears, according to a deed signed on the 23rd of October 1760, that the original proprietors of the *Morning Chronicle* amounted in number to twenty. Their names, and, as far as known, their businesses and professions, were as follow:—

  William Kenrick.
  R. Highway.
  William Griffin (bookseller).

John Nicod.
T. Evans (bookseller).
Samuel Webb (pattern-drawer).
Louis Lenoir (silversmith).
John Richards.
David Richards.
J. Spilsbury (bookseller).
George Kearsly.
J. Fletcher.
James Robson (bookseller).
W. Woodfall (printer).
Peter Elmsly (bookseller).
Peter Crawford.
John Murray (bookseller).
James Bowles (stationer).
Henry Barford (upholsterer).
James Christie (auctioneer).

This information, though of no public, and but slight literary, importance, may be of interest to many living persons if they chance to be the descendants of any of the enterprising pioneers of the daily press in London, and as such I here reproduce it.

CHAPTER III.

THE EGLINTON TOURNAMENT.—ASCENT OF GOATFELL, IN ARRAN.

My principal object in visiting Scotland in the autumn of 1839 was to be present at the famous Tournament arranged by the Earl of Eglinton, at the instigation, it was said, of a fair, accomplished, and romantic young lady, whose wishes were his law. My second object was to enjoy a month's holiday, and take a needful rest from the engrossing night-work of the *Morning Chronicle.*

I had only received leave of absence from my duties for a month, on condition that I should describe the Tournament, which was to extend over three days. I should, of course, have preferred the holiday without its accompanying task; but, equally as a matter of course, and of wise philosophy, I made the best of a bad bargain. And a bad bargain it proved to be—not from any lack of pomp and magnificence in the Tournament, and of good-will to all concerned on the part of Lord Eglinton, but from the persistent malevolence of the clouds, that poured down the rain literally in torrents, by night and by day, during nearly the whole of the time allotted for the grand mediæval revival. Great crowds were naturally attracted to the immediate neighbourhood, and the small town and port of Ardrossan, which owed whatever importance and prosperity it enjoyed to the immediate predecessor of Lord Eglinton in the title and estate, was crammed full of visitors, seeking in vain for accommodation. I was thought to be fortunate when I secured a miserable room in a small cottage, at a princely price, whence I had to turn out in the morning in search of a breakfast, which money was not always able to secure, and which, when secured, was not always palatable, or inclusive of either tea, coffee, eggs, or butter. "Though victuals and drink were the chief of my diet," as the nursery rhyme has it, the victuals that fell to my lot at Ardrossan were oat-cake, and the drink, milk; but both were in abundance, and retailed to me at a by no means exorbitant price. The walk from Ardrossan to the grounds of Eglinton Castle would have been pleasant but for the rain, and the walk was compulsory in the absence of other means of locomotion.

Of all the great or fashionable personages present at the Tournament, I remember, at this distance of time, the names, in addition to that of Lord Eglinton himself, of Lord Worcester (the present Duke of Beaufort), the Marquis of Londonderry, Prince Louis Napoleon Buonaparte (afterwards Napoleon III.), and last, but by no means least, Lady Seymour (afterwards Duchess of Somerset), who graced the proceedings as " Queen of Beauty." This title was due to her personal charms, though possibly conferred upon her in the first instance on account of her exalted rank and social position, but would have been equally appropriate to her if she had been the beggar-maid who married King Cophetua.

Among all the gallant company who took parts more or less conspicuous in the festivities and performances of the three days, the Marquis of Londonderry stands out most prominently in my memory. Clad in complete steel, with casque and nodding plume on his head, mounted on an unexceptionable steed, that bore his burden bravely, the Marquis, as far as looks went, might have posed to an artist as a veritable re-incarnation of a *preux chevalier*, or knight of the olden time. But *horresco referens!* The rain beat so heavily upon him that his knightly nature could not endure it, and, to shield himself and his finery from the pitiless downpour, he hoisted a large umbrella over his head, and brought the fifteenth and the nineteenth centuries into inharmonious and ludicrous juxtaposition, and forced the Queen of Beauty herself, and all who beheld the show, into irreverent but natural laughter. The Marquis himself, however, saw nothing to laugh at, but rode unmoved, suggesting, in all except his rubicund and by no means rueful countenance, Don Quixote rather than Amadis de Gaul, or a Knight of King Arthur's Round Table.

On the first day of the Tournament, before the correspondents of the London morning journals had despatched, or even written, their accounts of the performances which they had come so far to witness, a little misunderstanding arose, which threatened to deprive the London public—and, indeed, the whole community—of all except the baldest and most meagre record of the mock prowess of the doughty knights, and the influence rained upon them by the Dulcineas and Queens of Beauty assembled to do them honour. The correspondents were informed by Lord Eglinton's butler, steward, or major-domo, that refreshments were provided for them in the servants' hall.

"Perhaps," said Dr. Richardson, the representative of the *Times*, "the servants will be asked to sit down with us!"

The other correspondents of the *Morning Chronicle*, the *Morning Post*, the *Morning Herald*, and the *Morning Advertizer* (then irreverently called the "Tap-Tub"), followed suit in denunciation of what was considered a gross affront to their personal dignity, and to the Press generally. I ventured to hint that possibly Lord Eglinton himself was unaware of the want of politeness displayed towards the gentlemen of the Press, who claimed to be gentlemen by as good a warrant as his own, and that an effort should be made to bring under his personal notice the fact that we could not accept of the questionable hospitality that had been offered to us.

It was agreed *nem. con.* that the attempt should be made, and that, if it failed of success, or if his Lordship, being duly informed, refused to interfere with the arrangements of his major-domo, we should refuse to partake of any refreshment whatever at his expense, or to give any account whatever of the proceedings, except the simple statement in one sentence that the Tournament had taken place! without mentioning the name of anyone who had taken part in it, or giving the slightest description of it.

The threat proved sufficient. After the lapse of a considerable time—which was probably occupied in the endeavour to receive his Lordship's instructions on the weighty question, and an interview with him, either in the Lady's Bower, the banqueting-hall, or the tented field—the correspondents were waited upon by Lord Eglinton's secretary, deputed by him for the purpose, who expressed his

Lordship's regrets that he could not personally attend to explain his sorrow at what had occurred, and to repudiate all share in the want of courtesy of which one of his upper servants had been guilty, without his knowledge or authority, and to say that he would have been glad to invite us to his own table, had the space in the improvised banqueting-hall or pavilion allowed. He added that proper arrangements would be made for our comfort that day, and every succeeding day that the Tournament lasted, and that we should, in all respects, be treated as if we were his honoured guests. This was satisfactory. The promise was duly kept: the board was bountifully spread; the servants were attentive and deferential; but the chief butler, or major-domo—if such were his title—was discreetly absent. Full accounts of the tiltings, the mock heroics, the knightly paraphernalia, and the whole proceedings of the day were duly despatched to the London papers, and as duly published. In none of the accounts that I afterwards saw was the description omitted of the brave Marquis of Londonderry, in his panoply of steel, his spear in one hand and his umbrella, held over his head, in the other.

Utterly weary of the Tournament and its frivolous and scarcely picturesque unrealities, I was delighted on the fourth day to look up at a blue sky, scarcely speckled by a cloud, and to know that a little steamer was to start at 10 o'clock from Ardrossan to Brodick, in the island of Arran, glimpses of which, and the beautiful mountain called Goatfell, I had obtained in the rare and short intervals of fair weather which had prevailed during my stay in Ayrshire. I resolved forthwith that I would ascend Goatfell, or the Hill of the Wind, otherwise Ben Gaoth.

I prefer the Gaelic name to the corrupt Teutonic one, which has perverted the Gaelic *gaoth*, "wind," to the English "goat," and enjoy the grand and stern realities of Nature in preference to the shams of the Tournament. It was the first time in my life that I had had the opportunity of seeing, much less of climbing, a real mountain, a veritable Highland Ben, and worthy of the name. The passage across the estuary of the Clyde is but fifteen miles; and, after a short stay at the little cottage that nestles in the shadow of Brodick Castle—the residence of the Dukes of Hamilton —I inquired of the landlady of the inn the way to the mountain from whence the ascent was most easy. She looked at me with evident surprise, as if she thought I was demented; and, on my questioning her whether she herself had never been to the top of the Ben, she answered very emphatically, "No; never!" She added that she had no desire to "fash hersel', or wear out her shoon in ony sic feckless undertaking!"

ASCENT OF GOATFELL.

"Does nobody who comes to Brodick," said I, "ever think of climbing the mountain?"

"Oo, aye," she replied; "a wheen Glasgow or Edinbro' lads, and London bodies, who dinna ken what better to do wi' themsels."

Seeing there was no other help to be got from the landlady, I borrowed a stout walking-stick from the hall, and started alone. Thanks to the directions given to me by a labouring man whom I met on the way, I managed to reach an open space at the foot of the Ben, whence the ascent was plainly visible. The way, however, was hard and rugged; a steep climb often led to a deep morass, from which return was imperative; or as often to a crag, which might be flanked but could not be scaled. There were other difficulties and impediments new to an inexperienced mountaineer, but familiar and of no great account in the estimation of all who have learned to ascend mountain peaks, and to thread the mazes of the upward way with patient feet, and eyes that know how to measure distances and to see clearly before them. Every step was both a labour and a joy, and when I at last reached the summit, after a battle with gravitation that lasted three hours, or more, I was as proud of the achievement as any military chieftain might be after his first dearly-bought victory. I have never forgotten the delightful sensations which I experienced when I stood on the top, and beheld all Arran, and a great part of the Scottish mainland, and a wide expanse of sea, stretched beneath my feet. Since that early time, when life was new, I have ascended many Scottish and English mountains: Goatfell thrice, Ben Lomond thrice, Ben Nevis twice, Ben MacDui, the highest of the Grampians, once, Skiddaw twice, Helvellyn once, the Langdale Pikes once, and been sorely tempted to try Mont Blanc, the monarch of mountains, himself. I was forced by circumstances to relinquish the last great achievement, and to content myself with his very formidable spur or shoulder, the *Tête noire*, which I ascended from Chamouni. For forty years I have never looked upon a mountain, in my own or any other land, without a strong, and often an irresistible, desire to climb it; and never on any occasion, in storm or sunshine, or driving mist, felt unrewarded for the effort I made, in the great and sometimes unspeakable delight it afforded me.

> O wild sublimities!
> None can imagine you but those who 've seen;
> And none can understand man's littleness,
> Who has not gazed from some dread altitude
> Upon the world, a thousand fathoms down,
> O'er precipice of perpendicular rock,
> Which but to look at makes the brain to reel,
> And fills it with insane desire for wings,
> To imitate the eagle far below
> And free itself of earth. And here I 've stood,

Awe-stricken and delighted, great yet small;
Great that my soul might dare aspire to God,
To Whom the mountains and the universe
Are but as sands on the eternal shore.

My remembrances of the Eglinton Tournament remain blurred and indistinct, and scarcely worth recalling, while those of my first ascent to the peak of the sublime Goatfell remain clear and delightful.

A Holiday in Edinburgh.

AFTER leaving Eglinton Castle, I proceeded to Edinburgh. The dearly-beloved country was new to me when I thus revisited it in my young manhood. My mind was fully stored with the incidents of its history, its poetry, and its romance, and the beauty and grandeur of its scenery were enhanced and sublimated in my sight by the legendary lore with which my memory was imbued and my imagination fully laden. The first sight of Edinburgh, one of the most picturesquely beautiful cities of Europe, or, indeed, of the world, surpassed all I had dreamed of it in my youthful enthusiasm. Every step that I took in the old town and the new, especially in the old, evoked reminiscences either of the great and good who had once trodden its pavements, or of the greatly wicked whose deeds of guilty ambition had contributed to the eventful and tragic history of the turbulent Middle Ages.

I was well provided with letters of introduction to the literary notabilities of the venerable city; but I scarcely needed them, inasmuch as I was already acquainted with Mr. Robert Chambers of the great publishing firm of W. and R. Chambers. These gentlemen were the earliest pioneers of popular literature in Scotland, and their well-known *Edinburgh Journal* had been long engaged in the task of educating the youth of that generation in a knowledge and love of letters and of science. Mr. Robert Chambers was the literary partner of the firm, and an author of high and well-deserved repute.

On the second morning after my arrival, I found myself engaged to breakfast at the hospitable board of that gentleman, preparatory to spending the day in a ramble through the historical and legendary portions of the city. The guests, besides myself, were the venerable George Thomson, the well-known correspondent of Robert Burns, and Hugh Miller, author of *The Old Red Sandstone*, a famous geologist, who had raised himself from the humble position of a journeyman stonemason to be the equal and the associate of the principal scientific and literary notabilities of the time.

George Thomson, born in 1759, the same year as Robert Burns, possibly a year or two earlier or later, had, at the time I met him, attained the venerable age of eighty. He was a hale old gentleman, known by name and reputation, to every reader of the immortal poems of the Ayrshire bard, as the projector and editor of the famous collection of the national melodies of Scotland, to which Burns contributed many of his best songs. He was also known to a smaller circle as the grandfather of Miss Hogarth, who, a few years previously to the time at which I met him, married Charles Dickens, the author of the *Pickwick Papers*, the forerunner of a score or more of equally popular and infinitely better novels.

The worthy gentleman had a grievance, on which he had doubtless expatiated to my two companions at the breakfast table, his fellow citizens, and familiar friends, and which, I was told, he took all proper occasions to discuss with every new literary acquaintance with whom he might be brought into the contact of conversation. Of course I did not escape all allusions to a subject which had lain near his heart for nearly half a century.

Burns and Thomson were in constant correspondence for four years, from September 1792 to June 1796, and between them both had investigated, with most interesting results, the history and genesis of the old songs and pathetic music for which Scotland was then, and is now, famous. Burns, in his last fatal illness, only nine days before the close of his career, imagined, it appears erroneously, that a ruthless creditor was threatening him with legal process, for the recovery of a debt of five pounds, and, in his distress of mind, wrote to George Thomson, for whom he had done so much, without fee or reward, to advance him that small sum. "After all my boasted independance," wrote the dying man, "curst necessity compels me to implore you for five pounds. A cruel wretch of a haberdasher, to whom I owe an account, taking it into his head that I am dying, has commenced a process, and will infallibly put me into a jail. Do, for God's sake, send me that sum by return of post. Forgive me this earnestness, but the horrors of a jail have made me half distracted. I do not ask this gratuitously, for, upon returning health, I hereby promise and engage to furnish you with five pounds' worth of the neatest song genius you have seen." Thomson replied immediately to the urgent, but modest and touching appeal to his generosity, or, rather, to his sense of justice, and told the poet that he had often thought of offering him a pecuniary recompense for the work he had done, but was afraid lest he should hurt his proud spirit, as manifested in a previous letter on this very subject. In enclosing the five pounds as requested, he added that it was "*the very sum he had proposed sending*, and wished that he were Chancellor of the Exchequer, if only for one day, for the poet's sake."

The passage, "the very sum he had proposed sending," brought down upon the head of poor George Thomson all the vials of the critical wrath of a succession of editors and commentators, who all united in accusing him of meanness and ingratitude, in hinting, though inadvertently, that he valued at exactly five pounds the priceless assistance that the poet had rendered him. "Nothing," said Mr. Thomson to me, "was further from my intention. In the first letter which I wrote to him in 1792, introducing myself and explaining the objects of my proposed work, I offered to pay him any reasonable price that he chose to demand for his assistance. He indignantly rejected the offer, as all the world knows, stating that in the 'honest enthusiasm with which he embarked in the undertaking, he considered that any talk of money, wages, feè, hire, &c., would be downright prostitution of his soul.' Nearly a year afterwards, when I ventured to send him what he called a 'pecuniary parcel,' which he accepted, 'lest its refusal should savour of affectation,' he swore that on the least repetition of any such 'traffic,' he would indignantly spurn the by-past transaction, and from that moment drop all intercourse with, and become an entire stranger to me. What was I to do? I knew his proud and sensitive nature. I wanted to keep on the most friendly terms with him. I desired, above all things, a continuance of his invaluable assistance to my work, and dreaded to offend him. I did not know that he was on his death-bed, neither did he know it himself; for, had I known it, I would have hurried from Edinburgh to his side, to be of what comfort I could to him, both pecuniarily and otherwise. I might further urge, on my own behalf, that with every desire to be liberal or even generous, I was a poor man at the time. I published the Melodies at my own risk, and the book was not successful until after the death of the poet whose genius had enriched it. But these considerations had in reality no influence on my mind or actions, and, had Burns asked me for five times five pounds, I would have procured it for him, at any inconvenience to myself, even if I had had to pawn my watch to procure the money. I own that, by the light of after occurrences, the phrase the 'precise sum,' which I used in my letter, was awkward and unfortunate, and I have never ceased to regret that I used it."

To my mind this explanation was satisfactory, and I said so, with hearty emphasis, to the evident pleasure of Mr. Thomson. I had not thought much on the subject before, and was gratified to find that my hastily-formed opinion had been shared long previously by Mr. Hugh Miller and by Mr. Robert Chambers, and that the latter had already given in print the weight of his authority and critical judgment to this effect.

There was at this time in Edinburgh a small association of kindred spirits, lovers of literature and song, who met once or twice a week at each other's houses in the evening, and who called themselves the "Egg and Toddy Club." The members were strictly forbidden to incur any expenses for convivial gatherings, beyond a frugal supper of eggs, oatcake, and fresh butter, moistened by temperate libations of whisky and hot water, which the Scotch call "Toddy."

The next meeting was appointed to be held at the house of Mr. Thomson, and I had the honour of an invitation. I went accordingly, spent a pleasant evening, and made the acquaintance of several agreeable persons, and speedily discovered that the members were not only lovers of poetry, but most of them aspirants to poetic fame, and authors of books of poems in the Scottish language. The dialect of the Scottish lowlands lends itself more easily than English does to the exigencies of rhyme and rhythm and poetical expression, in consequence of the great number of affectionate diminutives which it employs, and of its copious vocabulary, which not only includes every word in the English, but many hundreds, if not thousands, of expressive and forcible words that have become obsolete in the English of the South, and of London more especially, and which still retain their literary and colloquial beauty in the North. I was not surprised to find so many poets (perhaps poetasters) in the "Egg and Toddy Club," not professional authors, but gentlemen engaged, for the most part, in business, or in the exercise of the legal and medical professions. I knew, as has been said elsewhere (*The Book of Scottish Songs*), "that not only the scholar in his study and the professed rhymers and authors, but the tradesman behind his counter, the weaver at the mill, the ploughman in the field, and the fisherman in his boat, had written and composed songs, and that even tramps and vagrants, from the days of Allan Ramsay and Burns to our own, had been the authors of no contemptible compositions, and emendations of old songs and ballads. These bards, many of them nameless, made no pretence to be refined, yet amid their modest snatches were often to be found the happiest thoughts expressed in the happiest phraseology." Three of the gentlemen present on the occasion achieved eminence in literature. Mr. Henry Glassford Bell, Sheriff of Lanarkshire, author of a life of Mary Queen of Scots, and several lyrical poems of great beauty; Mr. Alexander Smart, a printer, author of *Rambling Rhymes*; and Mr. William Anderson, author of *Landscape Lyrics*, and of a Biographical Dictionary of eminent Scotsmen.

After breakfast, Mr. Robert Chambers volunteered to act as my guide in a ramble through the city of Edinburgh. On his part, Mr. Hugh Miller undertook to escort me, on the morrow, to Arthur's seat and Salisbury Crags, and explain, as we went, the geology of the mountain. Nothing more agreeable could have happened than both of these arrangements. Mr. Chambers was familiar with every stone in the pavement of the old city, and with all the history, tradition, romance, and poetry of every nook and corner of it; and Hugh Miller, though a learned geologist, was not a hard and dry man of mere science, but a poet, who brought to the study of scientific facts a richly-stored mind and a fertile imagination.

As the record of the scenes and conversations of a single day, passed in the streets of Edinburgh with Mr. Robert Chambers, would fill an interesting volume, it would be useless to attempt in this place, even an epitome of the subject. Mr. Chambers himself has well performed the task in his excellent *Traditions of Edinburgh*, a work that has gone through several editions, with ever increasing favour. Suffice it to say that in the walk from the Castle to Holyrood, down the long, steep street that assumes the several names of the Cowgate, the High Street, and the Cannongate, scarcely a house or the narrow entry of a "wynd" or "close" was passed, of which Mr. Chambers had not something to say of historical, antiquarian, legendary, or literary interest. Squalid for the most part in their accessories, grimy and ill-favoured and ill-odorous, teeming with life in its vulgarest and most forbidding aspects; this great historical thoroughfare, seen in the adorning light of memory which Mr. Chambers threw over it like an aureole, became picturesque as the portrait of a ragged beggar when painted by a great artist, who turns the very squalor of his model into grace and beauty, on the canvas.

The conversation of Hugh Miller, though agreeable and instructive, was not equal in charm to that of Robert Chambers. The mind of Hugh Miller was so wedded to the study of geology as to leave him but little inclination to diverge into the wider fields of history, philosophy, romance, and poetry, where he might have roamed to his own advantage, and that of the world, had time allowed and preoccupation not prevented. The no-wise related subjects of geology and the politics of the Free Church of Scotland occupied him fully; geology for the love he bore it, and Free Church politics for the discussion and dissemination of which he had become dependent for the daily bread of himself and his household. The clerical and other supporters of the movement which ended in the disruption of the venerable Church of Scotland and the establishment of the Free Church, differing from its parent in no point of doctrine, but solely on the question of patronage and the appointment of clergymen by any other than the congregations to whose spiritual instruction and comfort they were to administer, came to the conclusion, while yet the controversy was in progress, that they required a newspaper to support their views before the public. The result was the establishment of the *Witness*, a weekly and afterwards bi-weekly journal, published in Edinburgh. The next want of the party was that of an editor, and, fortunately, as it appeared at the time, for Hugh Miller, the choice of the shareholders fell upon him. He had acquired a great reputation for sound sense and discretion, and the possession of a literary style of unusual force and elegance; and he gladly accepted the appointment, which secured him not only bread, but the certainty of a rise in the social scale, and a chance of fortune. He entered upon the duties of the post with zeal and ability, never admitting to himself, nor allowing the world to suspect, that the task was an uncongenial one, at which he chafed, but which he could not abandon, under the heavy penalty of a too possible penury. Little, and that little precarious and uncertain, was to be earned by the literature of geology; much, comparatively, was to be earned, and that, whether much or little, was certain, by the able advocacy of Free Church principles; so he wisely, as it appeared at the time, stuck to his newspaper. But " thereof came in the end despondency and madness." But of the tragic ending of a seemingly bright and promising career there appeared at this time neither trace nor presentiment; and when, in pursuance of our previous agreement at the breakfast table, he acted as my guide, geological and poetical, to the picturesque heights of Salisbury Crags and the summit of Arthur's Seat, he was in the enjoyment of robust health, and full of spirit and animation. Dressed in a suit of "hodden grey," with a geological hammer in his hand, he skipped rather than walked up the hill, or it might well be called the mountain-side, from St. Anthony's Well to the summit, discoursing as we went

     Of mica-schist,
The old red sandstone and the great fire mist,
Of nebulæ—exploded—and the birth,
Myriads of ages past, of a young earth,
Still new and fresh, though venerably old,
And of the wondrous tale in "Cosmos" told.

The geological lessons, which I learned on that day from the lips of one so pre-eminently qualified to teach them, I have either forgotten or allowed to mingle in the stream of my general knowledge of the subject. But the recollection of his conversation on the natural beauties of the noble panorama of land and sea, that spreads before the eyes of the delighted visitor who stands on the summit of "Arthur's Seat," remains as vivid as ever. The scene is one which, once beheld, is never likely to be forgotten. To the east is the Firth of Forth, with the Isle of May, and the Bass Rock, and beyond them the great German Ocean; while along the shore stretch the villages or towns of Musselburgh, Preston Pans, North Berwick, with the conical hill of Berwick Law, Dunbar, the castled crag of Tantallon, and the plains of Lammer Muir, all renowned in poetry and romance, as well as in history. In front, to the north, is the low-lying country, sometimes called by the Edinburgh people the "Kingdom" of Fife, every square mile of which is of historical interest. To the west is the narrowing river, flowing from beyond the picturesque rock and city of Stirling, almost as romantic in situation and in history as Edinburgh itself, while still further to the north-west are the entrances to the Highlands, dominated by the noble hills of Perthshire, and the magnificent range of the Grampians. Among the most conspicuous of these hills is Ben Ledi, or the Mount of God, more perfectly the Mount with God, a memorable hill in pre-Christian and pre-historic times, sacred to the great annual festival of the Scottish Druids, where every year, on the first of May, the Druidical priests, in their three orders of judges, bards, and prophets, followed by the multitude, marched to the top of the hill, and kindled the holy fire, direct from the rays of the sun. The broad pathway from the base of the hill, commencing near Callander, to the summit, is still plainly traceable by the grass that grows all the way on the soil, trodden into comparatively fertile earth, more than two thousand years ago, by the feet of the annual multitudes that wore down the rough and rocky way, into the smoothness and pulverisation which permitted the growth of the all-pervading grass. Mr. Miller was not particularly acquainted with Druidical history—who is? but the fact of this annual procession on the morn of Beltain, or the fire of Baal, or the sun, was familiar to him.

It was not till many years after this visit to Arthur's Seat with this eminent philosopher and amiable man, that the world heard of his lamentable death by his own hand. Wide-spread sorrow was felt—far beyond the boundaries of Edinburgh —at the sad catastrophe; and among the mourners, none mourned more sincerely than the writer of these slight remembrances.

CHAPTER IV.

A CHARGE OF PLAGIARISM.

On the death, in 1839, of the ill-fated and maligned Lady Flora Hastings, Lady of Honour in attendance upon the Queen, a copy of a juvenile poem written by me in 1834, entitled the "Enquiry," was found in her own handwriting among the papers in her private desk. The poem appeared originally, with my name as the author, in the *Sun* evening newspaper, then edited by my highly-esteemed friend Mr. Murdo Young, and was afterwards included in a collection of my early poems, published two or three years later. The lamented lady had literary tastes and poetical pretensions; and her friends and relatives, not knowing my name, at that time almost wholly unknown or but very partially known to the public, came to the conclusion that, being found in her own handwriting, the poem was her own composition. It was re-published after her death, and when the melancholy circumstances of her history — mortally smitten as she was by foul calumny, and by the venomous shafts of idle tongues—were fresh in the public mind, with her name appended as the author, in several newspapers and literary journals, more than one of which, on its reappearance in a volume published for me by Mr. Richard Bentley, accused me of having stolen it from her. I vindicated myself, as I could well do, from the accusation. But accusations and calumnies run faster than, and obtain readier and wider credence than, refutations, and my claim to my own composition failed to reach the ears of all who had been taught to believe that the poem was Lady Flora's.

The charge of plagiarism would not have been a very heinous one, if only an idea, a line, or a phrase had been implicated, but was serious indeed when applied to a poem of four stanzas of ten lines each, word for word, couplet for couplet, stanza for stanza.

Notwithstanding my demolition of the baseless accusation which had been brought against me, from ignorance rather than from malice in the first instance, the lines still appear occasionally with Lady Flora's name appended to them in the so-called "Poet's Corners" of English and American journals. They are also to be found occasionally in obscure books of poetical extracts, issued by irresponsible and catch-penny publishers, who manufacture books with paste and scissors, without literary knowledge or judgment.

Another poem of a later date, entitled "A Defiance to Time," which appeared in the "Poet's Corner" of a Yorkshire newspaper, had been found in the handwriting of a poor old man who had recently died in the workhouse. The manuscript was submitted to the Chaplain on the supposition that it was the pauper's own, as he had signed it with the addendum, "These are exactly my sentiments." The reverend gentleman had either written or caused to be written to the local journal a communication making "honourable mention" of the "remarkable poetical talent" displayed by the poor man, and suggesting that something should be done for the relief of the helpless family he had left behind him. The letter and poem attracted the notice of Mr. Leitch Ritchie, the acting editor or sub-editor of *Chambers' Edinburgh Journal*, who, not knowing it to be mine, copied it into that popular and influential publication, with some more highly eulogistic remarks on the merits of the poem and the genius of the supposed author, than had been indulged in by the Workhouse Chaplain.

I wrote to Mr. Robert Chambers, directing his attention to the page in my published volume, where the poem had originally appeared. He, of course, saw the error into which his sub-editor and the Chaplain of the workhouse had both been led. Mr. Chambers informed me without delay that, as far as *Chambers' Journal* was concerned, the mistake should be rectified and acknowledged. He kept his word, no doubt through the agency of the sub-editor who had committed the error; but, as is natural to detected culprits, the *amende* was made to the real author in a somewhat niggardly and grudging spirit.

"Omniscient editors"—popes in their own little hierarchy—do not like to be convicted of fallibility any more than other popes do, and his sub-editor went as far as his literary pride would allow him to go in acknowledgment of the mistake he had inadvertently made. The supposed pauper's poem had been inserted with a flourish of trumpets in a prominent page, as befitted its estimated value as a literary curiosity. The real author's name was inserted, with a bald and curt apology, in an obscure corner in small type, about a month afterwards, when the poem and the pauper were alike forgotten.

Accusations of plagiarism are easily made, often maliciously, but still oftener ignorantly or thoughtlessly, by critical parrots who repeat what they have heard from others, without taking the trouble to investigate for themselves. And even in cases where the charge seems to be fully proved, the accused author may be wholly innocent of any design of larcenous misappropriation, and the idea or phrase alleged to have been stolen may be of such little intrinsic value as to render it not worth the while of any writer of the smallest intellectual worth or reputation to steal it. To accuse a really great author, who has proved his greatness by works of acknowledged genius and originality, of appropriating the thoughts of others in their own words, knowing that he has done so, is like accusing a Vander Bilt or a Rothschild, having millions at command, of stealing half-a-crown from a chance wayfarer against whom he has rubbed shoulders in the street. The people who indulge so freely in these accusations forget, as Coleridge finely says, in one of his prefaces, "that there are such things as fountains in the human mind, and imagine that every stream which they see flowing comes from a perforation made in some other man's tank."

Another explanation of the involuntary repetitions of other people's thoughts, which seem to the envious or ill-natured to resolve themselves into plagiarisms, may be found in the fact that many thoughtful men, whose minds are eminently receptive, but whose memories are not retentive in an equal degree, are liable, in the hurry and fervour of composition, when the "divine afflatus" is strong upon them, to accept the ideas as well as the phraseology that comes at their call, as born of the moment, and as spontaneous as the lilt of the skylark, singing in the sunshine on the edge of the cloud. The little bird inherits its song, but does not borrow it from, its tuneful predecessors that sang hundreds or thousands of years ago.

There are plagiarisms—which I prefer to call borrowings—which so far from being reprehensible are praiseworthy. Robert Burns found two old songs in Allan Ramsay's Collection, that had floated on the popular breath for a century or centuries before he was born, entitled "Old Lang Syne" and "A man's a man for a' that, and twice as meikle as a' that." The idea of each found favour with the newer and better bard; but the execution of both seemed utterly unworthy of the sentiment. He appropriated the titles and the ideas to his own use, without acknowledgment of the sources from which he borrowed, as, indeed, he had no necessity for doing. The results were the two immortal songs of "Auld Lang Syne" and "A man's a man for a' that"—as superior to the originals as a bright new guinea to a damaged farthing, and sufficient of themselves to enshrine the name of Robert Burns in the hearts of the people and of all lovers of true poetry, if he had written nothing else.

There are plagiarisms, either voluntary or involuntary, which merit no toleration, even though no moral blame be attributed to the plagiarist. It has been well said of some of these offenders against the amenities and the proprieties of literature that they may not unjustly be compared to gipsies who steal children, and disfigure them, and stain their faces to conceal the theft. One of the most glaring of these offences—perhaps, however, they are only accidents—which the history of English literature supplies was that afforded by the fine poet, my excellent friend Thomas Campbell, in his often-quoted line—

> Like angel visits, *few* and far between.

Campbell borrowed this, perhaps unconsciously, from a previous poet, Blair, the author of "The Grave," who wrote—

> Its visits,
> Like those of angels, *short* and far between.

Blair himself seems to have taken the idea from John Norris, commonly called the Platonic Philosopher, who flourished between the years 1657 and 1711 who wrote in a poem "To the Memory of his Niece"—

> Angels, as 'tis but seldom they appear,
> So neither do they make long stay;
> They do but visit, and away!

Campbell's verse is somewhat pleonastic, for visits that are "far between" are necessarily *few*. Visits that are "far between" may be of long duration, and their brevity may add a regret to that occasioned by their rarity. But owing to the parrot-like repetition of common-place expressions by the half-educated and wholly thoughtless portions of the public, the corrupt version has taken its place in the popular mind, and the correct and far more beautiful version is unregarded and unquoted, even if it be not utterly unknown.

But the accusation of plagiarism in this case against Campbell lies lightly upon his reputation as a poet and a man, inasmuch as it may be pleaded on his behalf that the borrowing or stealing was done unconsciously; and that if he had known that the much-admired phrase was not really his own, he would not have employed it.

The same excuse of unconsciousness cannot be pleaded on behalf of those who, knowing better, wilfully accuse that eminent, and in many respects great, poet of stealing, not alone a line or a phrase, but a whole poem from another author, and palming it off upon the public as his own. The over-zealous and injudicious friends of an Irish gentleman named George Nugent Reynolds, obstinately—and, I think, malignantly—assert, for what they are eager to consider patriotic reasons, and in vindication of the so-called honour of their country, that Mr. Reynolds, a very mediocre versifier, was the author of the beautiful poem "The Exile of Erin," and that Campbell did not write a line of it. The only foundation for the claim set up for Reynolds —not by himself, however, but by his foolish friends, who were doubtless prepared to assert in like manner that the sceptre of the British monarchy was made of an Irish shillelagh, stolen from an Irish bog-trotter—was that a copy of the poem was found after his death among Mr. Reynolds's papers, in his own handwriting, with his name at the foot of it. A cat is proverbially said to have nine lives; an eminent falsehood, literary, political, or historical, has at least a thousand, and, though slain nine hundred and ninety times, still manages to survive. But truth prevails in the long run; and even if it do not, there is this consolation to be found in the longevity of the falsehood, that the lapse of time renders it impotent and innoxious.

Work and Recreation at the "Morning Chronicle."

During the nine years that I was chained to the desk at the *Morning Chronicle* office, a willing slave to the toil by which I earned my daily bread, I managed to find or to make time for other literary work, which might or might not provide me with butter for my bread, or put money in my purse, but which I loved for its own sake, independent of pecuniary rewards. I published in the interval three volumes of Poems, *The Hope of the World, The Salamandrine, or Love and Immortality*, and the *Legends of the Isles*, for all of which I received much praise from many critics and condemnatory disparagement from a few, unaccompanied, however, by either gold or silver from publishers or the public. I also published four works in prose—a *History of London*, in one volume, for which I received £50; *Longbeard, Lord of London, or the Revolt of the Saxons*, an historical romance in three volumes, for which I received a preliminary payment of £40, and the promise of one half of the ultimate profits, which remained a promise never destined to fulfilment; *Memoirs of Extraordinary Popular Delusions, and the Madness of Crowds*, in three volumes, for which Mr. Richard Bentley paid me £300; and *The Thames and its Tributaries*, for which he paid me £200. I also contributed to *Bentley's Miscellany*, *Chambers' Edinburgh Journal*, *The New Quarterly Review*, and other periodicals, leading a busy and, on the whole, a prosperous and happy life. I also tried my hand at dramatic composition, and wrote two plays, which I submitted to Mr. Frederick Yates, of the Adelphi Theatre, but from whom I never succeeded in getting a decision or an opinion, or even a return of the manuscripts after my patience had become exhausted. Mr. Charles E. Horn, the popular composer of " Cherry Ripe " and other well-known favourites of the musical public of the day, was so favourably impressed with the capabilities of the *Salamandrine* —founded upon the Rosicrucian fancy of a fire spirit, in the shape of a beautiful woman, like the Undine of La Motte Fouqué, and, like her, unendowed with a soul, which she could only hope to attain through the true love of a man—that he applied to me for permission to convert it into a fairy opera. As I gave my consent willingly, he asked me to undertake the task myself, and to write half-a-dozen songs, to be sung by the hero and heroine, informing me at the same time that he had already composed a few melodies to some of the descriptive passages, and inviting me to come to his rooms in Great Russell Street, where he would play them over to me. I accepted the invitation, was hospitably received, and very much pleased with the beauty of the music with which my verses had inspired the famous composer. Mr. Horn, however, did not live to complete the opera; and I have never since been able to learn what became of the unfinished work.

Annually during the last five years of my connection with the *Morning Chronicle* I took a holiday of a month in Scotland, partly in Edinburgh, among friends and relatives, and partly in the Hebrides and the Highlands of Argyllshire, Inverness-shire, and Ross-shire. My ascent of Goatfell in Arran, in 1839, and the keen pleasure and delight with which it had filled my mind, had inspired me with what I may truly call a passionate love for moorland scenery. To breathe the pure, invigorating air of the hills, to clamber over the rugged mountain and up and around the beetling crags, to the very topmost summits of the hoary Bens, was both physical and mental joy. I could quite understand the animal pleasure of the angler, the grouse-shooter, and the deer-stalker, during a month's relaxation from business or politics, amid the magnificent solitudes of glen and mountain to which their "sport" impelled them; but I had as great, or even greater physical delight than theirs, and a mental satisfaction besides in reflecting that the infliction of pain and death to the meanest living creature—unless it were a gnat or a gad-fly—was neither a necessity nor an amusement to me. I found more true pleasure in tracing a Highland burn upwards, from the glen where it flowed into the river to its upland source far upon the heathery hill-side, on the very shoulder of the mountain, than I could possibly have found in stalking the deer.

The literary outcome of these annual recreations and wanderings, and their effects upon my mind, were the series of Ballads entitled, *Legends of the Isles* and *Highland Gatherings*, first published in 1845. "Wherever I went, I could not but remember," as Samuel Rogers, in the introduction to his *Italy*, said, in imitation of Samuel Johnson, in the introduction to his *Tour in the Hebrides* with Boswell; nor "could I sleep over any ground that had been dignified by wisdom, bravery, or virtue." Almost every mile of the Highlands, every stream, every lake, is rich in historical or traditionary lore, and sanctified by poetry and song.

The mountain-tops and the water-falls were my favourite haunts, sometimes alone and sometimes in the congenial company of my dear and accomplished friends, Patrick Park, the sculptor, and Alexander Mackay, author of a book of travels in the United States, entitled, *The Western World*. We three climbed together, not only Goatfell, but Ben Lomond and Ben Nevis, each of them twice or thrice, each time with new pleasure and profit; and once, Skiddaw and the Langdale Pikes, in

Westmoreland, on our way to Scotland, returning each time to London to our several avocations "like giants refreshed."

In Edinburgh I made the acquaintance of a blind cousin, John Mackay, of Rockfield, who claimed to be a lineal descendant of the famous General Hugh Mackay, of Scoury, who commanded the forces of King William III. at the battle of Killicrankie, where the gallant Viscount Dundee—better known as Claverhouse—lost his life, and his equally gallant opponent lost the battle. Mr. Mackay had, before the great affliction of blindness came upon him, written the life of his celebrated ancestor, and I agreed to see through the press a new and cheaper edition, and otherwise give such service as I was able to afford in the revision and completion of the work. On my first personal introduction to him, he passed his hands over my head, brow, and face, which having done, he paid me a very great compliment—at least, I thought so—when he said: "Cousin Charles, I am very glad indeed to *see* you. You remind me of my dear old friend, Sir Walter Scott; not only in your head and face, but in the tones of your voice."

In the preface to the new edition of his Life of the General—which had been for eight years a labour of love to him, although commenced in blindness, in his seventy-second year, and carried on amid difficulties that might have well proved insurmountable to a man of less mental energy—he stated that, in consequence of the pressure of age and infirmities, he had applied for assistance in the task of the original work to the Rev. Dr. McCrie, so advantageously known to the public by his learned historical and biographical researches, and to Mr. Thomas Thompson, the Deputy Keeper of the Records, but that both, though highly approving of the object, had reluctantly declined their aid in consequence of the multiplicity of their other avocations. He added that, under the circumstances, and deeply impressed with the imperfections of a first edition, issued under such all but overwhelming difficulties, he had applied, "for the preparation of a second, to his friend and relative, Charles Mackay, who frankly and kindly undertook to carry through this object, and, in thus becoming eyes and a staff to a blind and aged relative, would, he trusted, add another laurel to those which his talents and genius had already won."

Mr. John Mackay had not the satisfaction of living until the issue of the new edition, but died in 1841, while the last sheet was in the press, in the eightieth year of his age, followed to the grave by the regrets of all the prominent members of Edinburgh society, and of the people to whom the venerable form and placid, intellectual face of the sage and philosopher had for many years been a familiar object in the streets.* Mr. Mackay was intended by his family, in his early manhood, for a public career in India, from which, however, he was debarred by the calamity of blindness which afflicted him in his twenty-ninth year. The influence that would have been exerted for him was

---

* I sent an early copy of the *Life of General Mackay* to the then Duke of Sutherland. The Duke acknowledged its receipt by the following letter:—

"Lilleshall, Aug. 7th, 1841.

"SIR,—I am very much obliged to you for the *Life of General Mackay*, a work which cannot fail to be interesting to me. I first became acquainted with Mr. J. Mackay of Rockfield when I was very young, and it gave me much satisfaction to have occasion to make a communication to him, regarding one of his family in whom he took much interest, and which I heard gave him pleasure, not very long before his death. The Mackays in former times evinced military ardour equal to that of any of the Clans; and my conviction of the same spirit still existing and animating them, when proper occasions require it, has occasioned my very lately desiring a copy of the *Duke of Wellington's Dispatches* to be sent as my present to a Library which has been established at Tongue for the use of the district. The place of Scoury is very interesting, surrounded with magnificent scenery, and with improvements carried on, such as the nature of the country allows; but poverty represses necessarily, and chills the genial current, where exist the many disadvantages which, I fear, must be a condition of existence in a remote, bare corner of the land with an uncertain climate.

"I am, Sir, very truly yours,
"SUTHERLAND."

afterwards employed in favour of his nephew, Mr. James Matheson, afterwards a partner in the well-known house of Jardine, Matheson and Company. Mr. Matheson returned home in 1842 with a large fortune, and became Member of Parliament for Ashburton, and afterwards for Ross-shire, in the Liberal interest, and purchased from Mrs. Stewart Mackenzie, of Seaforth, as I have stated in a previous page, the large island of the Lewes. Here he was monarch of all he surveyed; acted the part of a benevolent despot in the interests of the long-neglected people, and spent large sums in public improvements, to the advantage of the whole island and, in a minor degree, to his own. He received a baronetcy—not so much for his political services and wealth as for the beneficial use he made of it, more especially in alleviating to a large extent the famine that afflicted the Lewes and other islands of the Hebrides in the doleful years of 1848 and 1849.

The widow of John Mackay of Rockfield was a great pillar of the Free Church of Scotland, and contributed largely of her means to support the movement. The disruption, under the leadership of Dr. Chalmers, known to his foes as the Pope of Scotland, created a vast amount of unfriendly and indeed unchristian feeling in all classes of society, especially among the "free" seceders from the Established Church, not on a point of faith and doctrine, but entirely on a point of discipline and patronage, or of ultra-democracy in Church affairs; and Mrs. Mackay was conspicuous for her zeal, her liberality, and, it must be added, her intolerance in support of the cause, on which, in default of any claims on her domestic affections, she had set her whole heart. She quarrelled with all her former friends, acquaintances, and gossips who remained faithful in their allegiance to the old Church of her fathers, declined to shake hands with them, or to know them, and proved her zeal not only in this negative fashion, but in the positive fashion of subscribing five hundred pounds at a time, sometimes publicly with her name, and still more often by anonymous gifts, of whom none knew the donor but her favourite ministers. One of her principal favourites, guides, and teachers was the Rev. Dr. Candlish, whom she invited me to meet at her house to partake of tea. I accepted the invitation, and found from eight to a dozen persons, of whom the majority were women, assembled to meet the eminent preacher, who requested us all to kneel while he asked a blessing. We all knelt accordingly. After remaining in this reverential position for five minutes, that seemed to me to be half-an-hour, I put my hand unobserved into my waistcoat pocket and drew out my watch. The "blessing," or rather the "sermon" continued for another five minutes without the slightest symptoms of coming to an end. Keeping the watch in my hand, and taking furtive glances at it every now and then, I timed the length of the Reverend Doctor's unconscionable grace at exactly twenty-one minutes, nor more nor less, and arose with aching knees and a ruffled spirit, to partake of the Bohea and the cake that were provided. I resolved, as the result of this wearisome experience, to accept no further hospitalities in Edinburgh from any hostess or host whatever, unless I ascertained beforehand that Dr. Candlish was not to be among the guests, fearing that if grace before tea demanded twenty-one minutes from that portentous divine, grace before dinner might in his estimation require an hour at the least.

The first circulating library ever established within the British dominions was established in Edinburgh early in the eighteenth century by a Scotsman, who was originally a barber and a wigmaker, afterwards a poet and a bookseller. His name was Allan Ramsay—written large in the History of Scottish literature. The successor to Allan Ramsay, towards the close of the century, after one, perhaps two removes, I am not certain which, was Mr. Alexander Mackay, publisher of the *Scots' Magazine*, a monthly publication of some influence and authority in its day, who, during one of my early visits to Edinburgh, claimed cousinship with me and sought my acquaintance. He had long retired from business, and bought a small estate that once belonged to Mary Queen of Scots. He was known to the world as Alexander Mackay, Esq., of Blackcastle, and to his immediate neighbours, according to the Scottish custom, as "Blackcastle," just as Mr. Gladstone's father, who possessed the estate of "Fasque," was known and addressed as Fasque. "Blackcastle" lived in good style in George's Square in the old town of Edinburgh, in the next house to that in which Sir Walter Scott was born. His daughter-in-law kept house for him in his widowhood, and with her husband did the honours of his hospitable establishment. The old gentleman had the hearthstone of Allan Ramsay's house removed from Allan's shop in the High Street, near St. Giles's Cathedral, and placed in his drawing-room in George's Square, where it still remains and is likely to remain, treasured by the new generation of the Mackays that have since arisen, to keep up the old traditions both of Blackcastle and of Allan Ramsay.

My connection with the *Morning Chronicle* lasted a little more than nine years, from the spring of 1835 to the autumn of 1844. I left London with the good wishes of all my colleagues and the proprietors of the paper, and was entertained at a farewell dinner at Blackwall under the presidency of my old and eminent political and legal friend Mr. Joseph Parkes, the wire-puller and Nestor of the Reform party.

CHAPTER V.

OLD LONDON LIFE AND MANNERS.

I CAN remember when there were neither cabs nor omnibuses in London, and when the worn-out, shabby, discarded, and disused carriages of the nobility and the wealthy, with the coronets and armorial bearings uneffaced upon the panels, did duty in the streets, drawn each by two horses, driven by elderly coachmen called "Jarvies." I can remember the sensation created when cabs were first introduced. In those early days they were always called *cabriolets*, and the word "cab" was considered vulgar in the extreme. A caricature appeared in the shop windows, of a gentleman directing a villainous-looking "cabbie" to drive him to the Old Bailey, and cabbie asking him, with a look of well-feigned astonishment, "Where is the Old Bailey, your honour? I never heard of such a place!" I also remember the watermen that plied in their wherries on the Thames. They were all dressed in uniforms peculiar to the companies to which they were severally affiliated, and wore pewter and sometimes silver badges on their breasts in sign of their calling. They jealously excluded from the privilege of rowing for hire upon the river all persons not duly authorised by the rules and usages of the fraternity. Their livery was a relic of the olden times, when the great English nobles had their palatial mansions on the banks of the Thames from the City to Westminster, the last of which (Northumberland House) was only recently demolished; and when each noble retained his own watermen in his own liveries to row him on the river, for business or pleasure; to visit, perhaps, the Globe Theatre on Bankside, to see a play written by "the ingenious Mr. Shakspeare." These men were proud of their vocation, maintained a strict monopoly or trades union, and managed, in the absence of competition —steam vessels on the river above London Bridge being non-existent, and possibly unimagined—to earn a comfortable subsistence.

Charles Dibdin celebrated a member of the fraternity in the once popular song "Tom Tug."

> Then farewell, my trim-built wherry,
> Oars and coat and badge, farewell.
> Never more at Chelsea ferry
> Shall your Thomas take a spell.

He also commemorated another who plied lower down the as yet unpolluted river, in a song often sung by John Braham, and still sung, I believe, by Mr. Sims Reeves.

> And did you not hear of a jolly young waterman
> Who at Blackfriars Bridge used for to ply?
> * * * * * *
> What sights of fine folks he rowed in his wherry.
> 'Twas cleaned out so nice, and so painted without;
> He was always first oar when the fine city ladies
> In a party to Ranelagh went or Vauxhall.

I remember once being rowed, when a child of eight or nine, down the river from Wapping to Woolwich, and of being struck with the sight of the rotting corpses of the pirates hanging in chains, as a warning to evil-doers, on the river bank, either on the Greenwich or the Blackwall side, I forget which; and on another occasion of seeing no less than five men hanging in front of Newgate, for forgery, for horse-stealing, for sheep-stealing, for burglary, or shop-lifting, or other offences far short of the crime of murder.

I remember old London Bridge, and the commencement as well as the opening of the new, the old Houses of Parliament and the old Royal Exchange, to the musical chimes of which I have often listened, and that rung out in its tower, when the building perished by fire, the mournfully appropriate Scottish melody "There's nae luck about the house." I also remember the old Royal Mews that stood on the site of the present trumpery

National Gallery, with its too suggestive pepperboxes; when there was no such place as Trafalgar Square, the Nelson monument, the fountains, or the Lions; when the palatial clubs of Pall Mall, Carlton House Terrace, the York steps into St. James's Park, and the Duke of York's column were non-existent; when the Haymarket justified its name by its business, and when the roadway in the early morning was blocked up by heavily-laden wains of sweet-smelling hay, and the public-houses in the street drove a thriving trade, for early purl and other drinks, among the buyers and sellers of the provender.

I remember when the servants and the women of the labouring classes wore pattens instead of the clogs that afterwards came into fashion, when they paddled in the rain or braved the mire of the crossings—contrivances better than the clogs that superseded them, but neither so serviceable as, but possibly more graceful than, the wooden shoes of the Continent. In those days lucifer matches had not been invented, and the only mode of procuring a light, unless borrowed from a light previously burning, was by the aid of flint, steel, and tinder-box. On the first introduction of the new system —quite a godsend to the growing multitude of pipe and cigar smokers—a small phial filled with acid was carried in the waistcoat pocket, into which the match was dipped to produce the light. The rapid increase of smoking consequent upon the facilities afforded by Congreve matches, as they were first called, gradually led to the abandonment of the practice of snuff-taking, except among the male and female lovers of tobacco who were too old to desist from a habit which had become their second nature.

I remember the poor, decrepid old men who were employed as watchmen in the London streets, who were familiarly called Charlies, and whose duty it was to perambulate the principal thoroughfares, to call out the hours and the half-hours, with such information as to the state of the weather as it pleased them to afford ; and who were armed with rattles to give the alarm when necessary in case of sudden attack, either from thieves bent on serious business, or from "swells" and blackguards bent on frolic and roystering mischief. I remember the popular opposition excited by the "New Police," established under the auspices of the late Sir Robert Peel, then Mr. Peel. The unpopularity of this effective and excellent force was great, and very slow in subsiding.

In those days it was a favourite amusement of young and middle-aged scapegraces of the towns, or "bloods" or "young bloods" as they were often designated, to carry off poor old watchmen in their sentry-boxes, and pitch them, box and all, into the nearest puddle. A story sometimes told was of one of the semi-intoxicated "Charlies," who, seeing the reflection of the moon in a pool of water, after a heavy shower, called out "Half-past two in the morning, and more moons than usual." The "new police" soon put a stop to the escapades of the aristocratic snobs, who indulged in their gambols at the expense of these poor, decrepid old fellows. And it was high time!

The "new police" were popularly called "Bobbies," as they often are to this day, in the idea that the name of "Bobbies" was derived from Sir Robert Peel, the founder of the force. But this is an error. *Boban* simply means a boy, or a big boy, in the ancient language of our British ancestors, still spoken in Scotland and Ireland, employed as a word of affection and familiarity. The German *Bube* and the vernacular *booby* are of the same derivation. The epithet "Peelers," still applied to the force by the vulgar, is, of course, derived from the name of the great statesman.

Newspapers in those days were small and dear, as I have already recorded in a previous page of this volume, and were remarkable for the decent reticence with which they were conducted. The world was not then more moral or society better behaved than at the present time, but the newspapers were far more reticent and decent, and their editors always refused to give publicity to the filthy details of adultery cases which are now too often divulged in all their hideousness.

Theological opinion was by no means free. Richard Carlile, a bookseller and publisher in Fleet Street, and the "Rev." Richard Taylor, commonly called the Devil's Chaplain, printed and promulgated attacks upon the Bible and the Christian religion, that brought them within the clutches of the law and subjected them to fine and imprisonment. The opinions they then expressed, to the scandal of the authorities, and a large proportion of the public, are now published with impunity, and scarcely excite either animadversion or notice. I remember being taken to visit Carlile in Giltspur Street Prison, long since pulled down, where he was confined for the expression of views on the Pentateuch that Bishop Colenso and other high ecclesiastical dignitaries, in a later day, might have adopted without reprobation, and even with assent and approval.

In my boyhood and early youth I remember to have paid several visits to Bartholomew, or "Bartlemy," Fair—that venerable nuisance which has long since been happily abolished. I also have been taken to Greenwich Fair—a nuisance even worse than Bartholomew Fair—and to Horn Fair, at Charlton, then a rural village between Greenwich and Woolwich. Any more frightful and vulgar saturnalias than the two first-mentioned it is difficult to imagine. If the palm for vulgar vice and rampant blackguardism can be awarded to one above the other, to Greenwich Fair it ought to be given. Anyone who remembers, as I do, the scenes enacted annually at these licensed places of popular unreason, and who remembers at the same time the saying of the ancient French writer, that the English as a people amused themselves *moult tristement*, or very sadly, might feel inclined to substitute another more appropriate adjective than "sad"; for the popular amusements of these fairs were not sad, in the ordinary meaning of the word, but uproariously and vulgarly disgusting and immoral. The morality of the English people may possibly not have greatly improved in the substance; but the form of immorality, and its outside show, have certainly changed vastly for the better. Immorality is no longer nude, but decorously draped. It is no longer aggressively public on the highways, but discreetly private in the byways. So far the change has been a clear gain to society.

Among the physical eye-sores of London which have been happily removed, I perfectly remember Field Lane—infamous with the reminiscences of Jonathan Wild, his contemporaries and successors. It stood at the bottom of the valley, since spanned by the handsome Holborn viaduct, and exposed to the view of every pedestrian who chose to look up it, as he passed from the corner of Hatton Garden to the church of St. Sepulchre and the prison of Newgate, long rows of stolen pocket-handkerchiefs

—" wipes " or " fogles " as they are called in the thieves' vernacular—all dangling publicly for sale at low prices to such hardy adventurers and reckless wayfarers as were rash enough to pass through on their way to Clerkenwell. It skirted the Fleet Ditch, which, in the days of Pope, as that poet records in the *Dunciad*,

> With disemboguing streams
> Poured the large tribute of dead dogs to Thames,

at Blackfriars Bridge; but which, long before my time, had been covered over. I remember it, however, when I was a boy, wholly uncovered in that portion of its course further to the north towards Pentonville, black, fetid, and disgusting, and laden visibly with the similar tribute of dead dogs, and the half-solid, half-liquid contents of the cesspools.

I also remember the famous " Rookery " of St. Giles, which was partially removed when New Oxford Street was cut through it, and its foul denizens dispersed to new quarters, which they soon did their best—or their worst—to make as unsavoury as the old. Co-eval with Field Lane and the Rookery was Monmouth Street, a name of such evil omen that it .was deemed expedient to change it to Dudley Street. The shopkeepers who did business on the level of the pavement dealt in cast-off garments of all kinds, from court-dresses to liveries, from worn-out ball-room fripperies to the veriest beggar clouts; while those in the cellars beneath, thickly inhabited as bee-hives, dealt in old shoes and boots, which they renovated in a poor and ineffective fashion, making them to the sight, though not to the touch, almost as good as new.

I was sometimes taken by my father to one of these miserable cellars, where dwelt a worthy old cobbler, engaged in the common business of the street, and often watched him, with curious eyes, as he sat with his lap-stone in lap, hammer in hand, plying his avocation, to observe, if I could, some of the mysteries of the craft. The old fellow, whose name was Crompton, claimed to be a brother of the famous Samuel Crompton, of Bolton-le-Moors, in Lancashire, the inventor of the spinning-jenny, by means of which the first Sir Robert Peel and many other Lancashire manufacturers had made large fortunes, though he himself had been but scantily rewarded. The cobbler, in his day of youth and strength, had served as a sailor on the *Hydra*, commanded by Admiral Sir Francis Laforey, on board of which my father was a midshipman. Crompton had rendered some service to my father on ship-board, or, in some manner or other unknown to me, had acquired his favour and regard. The poor fellow had been wounded in the leg, in some naval engagement—I forget which—and was a thoroughly good seaman. He had, however, the misfortune to incur the displeasure of Sir Francis Laforey, the hardest and sternest of all possible disciplinarians, who had gained for the *Hydra* the distinction in the naval service of being a "hell afloat." Sir Francis had ordered him to be flogged for some minor offence—or for no offence at all—a sentence which was duly inflicted, and entered in the ship's books. When Crompton retired from the service at the peace, he applied for admission to Greenwich Hospital; but the rules of that institution closed its hospitable doors against every seaman who had incurred the penalty of a flogging, either rightfully or wrongfully. My father always held that Crompton had been unjustly punished; and when the poor fellow took to shoe-mending as his only resource against beggary, my father never lost sight of him, but continued to befriend him, and occasionally visited him in his underground cellar in Monmouth Street, leaving such little benefactions as he could afford to bestow upon him. And it was in this manner I made the old sailor's, and new cobbler's, acquaintance, and that of his buxom wife.

The latter did her part to increase the earnings —I will not say of the household but of the cellar-hold—by selling common crockery in the streets, or exchanging her pots and pans, her cups and saucers, milk-jugs and tea-pots, for old boots and shoes of men or women for her husband to vamp and repair, and make a profit of. The Monmouth Street cellars were closed as human habitations when the street took its new name of Dudley. It is now in course of demolition for the construction of the new and greatly-needed thoroughfare which, piercing through the sordid, squalid, and malodorous district of the Seven Dials, will connect the filthy centre of London with the cleaner and more wholesome North.

I remember when Vauxhall Gardens provided the principal musical and out-of-door recreations for the Londoners, which of late years have been afforded by what vulgar people, high and low, persist in calling the "Fisheries," the "Healtheries," the "Inventories," and, more odious word than all, the "Colinderies." During the last years of the protracted and, in the main, the prosperous existence of Vauxhall Gardens, I was introduced by the Rev. Dr. Richardson—then all-powerful in literary and non-political matters in the editorial department of the *Times*—to Simpson, the Master of the Ceremonies at Vauxhall. Dr. Richardson was the first to proclaim to the world the merits and peculiarities of that eccentric personage, and to make him famous, through the columns of the *Times*, not alone to all contemporary London, but to secure him a place in the minor social annals of his age.

On this occasion I was also introduced to a person of minor, but still of great, importance in the Gardens, a man who had acquired a high reputation for his skill in carving cooked hams into the thinnest of all possible slices—so thin, that it was popularly said of him that he could cover a whole acre with the slices of one moderately-sized Yorkshire ham. Engaged in this operation, he suddenly caught sight of a man who was clambering over the wall to evade payment for the refreshments of which he had partaken, and, without ceasing in his work of carving, called out to another waiter: "Look sharp, Joe! there's a lobster and two glasses of brandy and water climbing over the wall!" The man was stopped, found to be wholly impecunious, and given into custody, to appear next morning before Sir Richard Birnie at Bow Street.

Before the comparatively recent opening of the Zoological Gardens in the Regent's Park, there was a menagerie in the Tower of London, and another at Exeter Change, in the Strand. The first was of royal origin, and was an appendage to the pomp and paraphernalia of the Kings of England for many centuries. The second was a private speculation, established as a part of the attractions of a once popular bazaar, that stood on the site of the present Exeter Hall, built on the demolition of the old "Change," or Exchange, for the widening and improvement of the Strand. The lions in the Tower, though long ago removed to the Regent's Park, hold their place in popular tradition, and are believed by many credulous and ignorant people to be still maintained by the Crown, as irremovable as the Armoury, the Beef-eaters, or the White Tower itself.

When the *Illustrated London News* was established, in 1842, M. Guys, a very clever French artist, was invited from Paris by Messrs. Ingram, Cooke and Little, the original proprietors of that journal, to assist in the pictorial department, which he was abundantly well qualified to do. I have often heard of a practical joke played off upon him by one of the trio, who deputed him to go to the Tower and make a sketch of the washing of the lions, which was represented to him as an annual ceremony, performed with much pomp and elaboration. The unsuspecting M. Guys proceeded on his mission, and on the following day presented himself at the office with a beautiful sketch of the ceremony, with all its stately accessories, in which the Beef-eaters, in their quaint, picturesque, mediæval attire, figured very prominently. The sketch, which was exceedingly well done, had doubtless as much claim to exactitude and truth to actual fact as many hundreds of much-admired pictures by great artists that exist in the National Galleries of London, Paris, and other cities, and in the halls of the noble and wealthy in every country in Europe. The conductors of the *Illustrated London News* had their little joke, and the artist had his, with the additional advantage, if the old French saying be true, that *rira bien qui rira le dernier*, of making the joke tell against its perpetrators, and being well paid for his time and ingenuity.

The great elephant in Exeter Change, belonging to a Mr. Cross, and purchased by him for 900 guineas, went mad in the year 1826, and it was found necessary to shoot it. The slaying of the infuriated beast—who was known to all London by his name of " Chunee "—was a matter of extreme difficulty and danger, and created a great sensation in London. It was the talk of the town for weeks, and, according to tradition, its dead body, as it lay in its cage for two or three days afterwards, was visited by thousands of people, whose payments for admission went far towards making up to the proprietor the loss incurred by his sacrifice of the animal. This statement, however, is not confirmed in the long and interesting account of the whole circumstances, which appears in Vol. II. of Hone's *Every-Day Book*, in which the writer states that the body was dissected with the least possible delay, and was *not* exhibited to the public.

I never bought a lottery-ticket, or took the slightest interest in any lottery or raffle whatever, but I perfectly remember to have seen London placarded with lottery advertisements—to have had announcements of forthcoming lotteries, with prizes varying from £1 to £30,000, thrust into my hands by shabby touts and other agents of the lottery offices as I passed along the streets. I also remember, when I was at school, to have heard that lotteries were finally abolished in England, and hearing the celebrated Edward Irving, in the pulpit of his chapel in Hatton Garden, expressing his gratitude to Almighty God for the great blessing thus conferred upon the nation, and upon the cause of public morality.

CHAPTER VI.

MUSICAL EPIDEMICS IN LONDON.

THE Londoners, of all classes, in the early days of my adolescence and young manhood, were quite as fond of music as they are now, though music-halls were non-existent. Vauxhall Gardens supplied their place, to a great extent. At this favourite resort of pleasure-seekers, every popular vocalist, male and female, was, at one time or other, engaged during its long enjoyment of public favour. There were two or three other minor establishments, such as White Conduit House, where instrumental and vocal music was provided in the fine summer weather, when out-of-door recreation was possible. But for the greater part of the year the middle classes, the tradesmen, the clerks, and others, resorted for amusement, at the close of the day, to drink, and smoke, and gossip at their favourite public-houses. Great numbers of publicans held "harmonic meetings" in their parlours, when songs were sung, sometimes by the guests and sometimes by professional singers engaged for the purpose. Sometimes, but not very generally, these parlours were provided with a pianoforte, but only in such establishments (and they were in a decided minority) as admitted ladies to the mysteries.

Among places of this kind which I particularly remember, were the *Coal Hole* in the Strand, and a well-frequented public-house in St. Martin's Lane, kept by Ben Caunt, the noted pugilist. There were many others in the purlieus of Leicester and Soho Squares, and other populous parts of London. Many of these were frequented by persons of a rank and position in life who, in the present day, would not think of showing themselves in such places, even if they existed. There were then no palatial club-houses, to offer superior accommodation and more eligible company; so that the upper strata of the trading and professional and middle-classes, who did not always choose to pass their idle evenings at home, put up perforce with the best substitutes that offered, and found them in taverns and respectable public-houses.

The harmonic meeting not only patronised the favourite airs of the newest opera, Italian or English—and English Opera was then alive—

though partially moribund—but the old English songs which Incledon, Braham, Mrs. Jordan, Mrs. Waylett, and Madame Vestris had rendered popular. The consequence was that to a greater extent than in the present day—when all the best known tunes are monopolised by the organ-grinders, who are among the greatest, if not the very greatest, plagues of London life—the people, in the evident and most ordinary acceptation of the term, did their best, or their worst, to show their love of music, and express their gaiety, or possibly their vacancy of mind, by shouting in the streets the songs of the day.

This class of men and boys had always some favourite song or tune, which reigned in undisputed possession of the popular ear, which haunted alike the aristocratic square and the plebeian alley, was whistled by butcher and errand boys, shouted by costermongers, howled by beggars, sniffled in parlours and tap-rooms, sung by "dandies" at evening parties, ground by pestiferous organs and hurdy-gurdies, until it became, by constant iteration in all places and at all times, the terror of the studious, the disgust of the cultivated and refined, and nothing less than a public calamity and nuisance.

The first of these favourites to which I am able to assign a date was "Cherry ripe, ripe I cry," a pleasant melody by Charles E. Horn, a musical composer of some celebrity in his day. The next was "The Sea, the Sea, the open Sea!" neither a bad song nor a bad tune, which reigned, I think, in the year 1833, or thereabouts. Prior to that time, I have a vague recollection that the town had been haunted by a succession of other favourites; but how long they severally reigned, or in what order they followed each other, I cannot recall. Among the number were "The Soldier's Tear," which, for its allotted period, was a heavy affliction; "I've been roaming where the meadow dew is sweet," which was a milder kind of nuisance; "I'd be a Butterfly," which was, perhaps, the most ridiculous and provoking of them all, when sung by some portly costermonger of anterior and posterior rotundity sufficient to come up to the popular idea of an alderman; "Meet me by Moonlight alone," which was very lackadaisical and absurd; and a very pathetic ditty, that took captive the hearts of the young ladies of that day (who, whatever their present ages may be, have, in all probability, sons and daughters older than they were then), and which was entitled, "Oh, no! we never mention him," and which ran—

> His name was never heard,
> My lips are now forbid to speak
> That once familiar word.

This sorrowful composition must have reigned for a twelvemonth at least, till it was dethroned either by "All round my hat I wear a green willow," or "Shades of evening, close not o'er us," I am not certain which, for I cannot speak of any of them in their due chronological order, but only by guess-work. But all these, whatever was their sequence as respects each other, were superseded, extinguished, thrown into oblivion, and rendered *rococo*, stale, and unfashionable by "The Sea, the Sea, the open Sea!" the lustiest musical nuisance that ever took possession of the town, and that swept everything else before it with remorseless and irresistible tyranny. The parodies that were made upon it must have been numerous enough to fill a volume; and the copies of it sold must have been quite a fortune to Barry Cornwall, the author, and the Chevalier Neukomm, the composer, unless they were foolish enough (which I have no doubt they were) to sell the copyright to a musical publisher, in which case they got all the honour, glory, and success, and he the solid pudding. The song threatened to be as eternal and as unchanging as its mighty subject; but, luckily, the world is a world of change. Trees cannot be always in blossom or in fruit, roses must fade, and tunes that are continually dinned into our ears, in season and out of season, must end by forfeiting our favour. So "The Sea, the Sea!"

was consigned to neglect, and "Some love to roam o'er the dark sea foam," a composition to which I plead guilty, reigned in its stead; and everybody—speaking in a musical sense—went chasing the deer over the mountain and through the forest, and singing a chorus of "Oho! and Oho!" in celebration of the joys of a life in the woods. This song carried on the musical war until 1835 or 1836, when it, too, yielded to the inevitable, and died of its own excess to make room for "Kate Kearney," who dwelt by the lakes of Killarney, and to "Jenny Jones," who dwelt in Llangollen, two rival fair ones, who greatly wearied the ears of the town by the iteration of their charms through all sorts of voices and instruments. But Saxon and Celtic music was growing effete. A great but not beneficial change was at hand. A dark shadow of impending calamity hung over the musical and the unmusical world; and the nigger mania broke out with a virulence that has never since wholly subsided.

The infection was brought from America, inoculated into the blood of Englishmen by an operator of the name of Rice, who blackened his face and dressed himself like a negro—I suppose from the cotton, the sugar, or rice plantations—and sang a very silly, if not utterly stupid song, which he called "Jim Crow," and of which the burden, repeated at the end of every stanza, accompanied by a grotesque dance, was—

> Turn about and wheel about,
> And do just so;
> Turn about and wheel about,
> And jump Jim Crow.

Nothing like it was ever before seen or known in England. To use a common phrase, "it took like wildfire." The famous dancing mania of the Middle Ages cannot have been a worse epidemic that this was; and the small beggar-boys of the streets—some of whom, it is to be hoped, are by this time well-to-do citizens at the Antipodes—drove a flourishing trade by imitating the fashionable comedian of the Adelphi, and "jumping Jim Crow" in the public thoroughfares by day and by night. It became an indescribable nuisance. Many must have been the sermons, the poems, the plays, the leading articles, the forensic arguments, and the mathematical calculations that it spoiled by its horrible iteration under the windows of studious men! But, worst phase of all in its unhappy history, its popularity was so great that it became the first of a series, which has lasted—with an occasional oasis of something better—until the present day, to disgust and plague the real lovers of music, and put them out of humour with the divine art that can be perverted to such monstrous purposes. The thing must have been in vigorous existence from 1836 to 1841, when two or three competitors of a similar kind, but somewhat better in quality, began to struggle for and obtain a hearing. These were "Old Dan Tucker," who was always told to get out of the way because he was too late for supper; "Buffalo Gals," who were entreated to come out and dance by the light of the moon; and "Sailing down the River on the Ohio"—all of which were sung to excellent but not very original melodies, with the composition of which niggers had as little to do as they have with the government of Kamtschatka.

People who would have been sorry to associate with negroes, acted (musically) as if they themselves had been negroes of the woolliest and blackest kind; and nothing was to be heard but their vulgar jargon, until Mr. Henry Russell, popular vocalist and composer, managed to stem the tide of niggerism in some small degree by introducing "The Ivy Green" and "I'm afloat, I'm afloat, on the dark rolling tide." These had a very considerable run, and all but extinguished the black minstrels for a short period.

But a greater triumph for anti-niggerism was at hand. Mr. Russell set to music a poem never intended for a song, which was entitled, "There's a good time coming, boys," sang it at his "Entertainments" in every part of the country, and hit upon the excellent idea of inducing the overflowing audiences, who had paid their money to hear *him*, contribute to their own amusement by joining in the chorus:

> There's a good time coming, boys;
>   Wait a little longer.

The phrase and the tune took the public fancy, and drove every other musical pest out of the streets. Nothing was to be heard for many months but that eternal refrain, the guilt of which still lies heavily on my conscience. It invaded the theatres, the concert-rooms, the music-halls, and the public-houses; was parodied in all the pantomimes of the succeeding Christmas; and was actually taken into the service of religion, and sung every Sunday at the celebrated George Dawson's chapel in Birmingham, with the single alteration of the word "boys" into "yet":—

> There's a good time coming yet,
>   A good time coming;
> We may not live to see the day,
> But earth shall glisten in the ray
>   Of the good time coming.

It had a long reign and a weary one; and though I am informed, on the excellent authority of its author, that it did not put a farthing into his pocket, it put many hundreds of pounds into the pockets of the vocalist and composer, and of the fortunate publishers. It sold, in various editions, upwards of four hundred thousand copies.

By perpetual iteration the phrase at last degenerated into slang, and was gradually dying out, when another song from the same source, entitled, "Cheer, boys, cheer"—a far better song, with an immeasurably better tune—was brought into popularity by the same means, and sent travelling over the length and breadth of the land, until it became almost as ubiquitous as the atmosphere. When our gallant soldiers embarked for the Crimea, the bands struck up that tune, to inspire them with hope and courage, as they left their native land. It shared with "Annie Laurie" the privilege of being the favourite of the camp during the long siege of Sebastopol; and, at a later period, the ruffian Nana Sahib found it of good effect in encouraging the revolted sepoys to the attack or the defence, and actually ordered the band to strike up the air while he martyred the unhappy English women in the well at Cawnpore. Since that melancholy incident was recorded, I have never cared to think of my composition with any pleasure, though it was rather the music than the poetry that found favour with the ruthless wretches who committed the murders. The tune still does duty at Liverpool and other ports on the departure of emigrant vessels to the United States and the Colonies, and seems likely to survive. Its London popularity lasted for about three years, when two competitors for public favour appeared almost simultaneously, the one a very silly song indeed, called, "Pop goes the Weasel" —how a weasel could go "Pop!" was, and is, a mystery—and a very lugubriously funny ballad, called "The Ratcatcher's Daughter." Both of these were insufferably vulgar, but none the less suitable on that account for the favour of the unmusical but music-loving multitude, that cares nothing for wit, or sense, or feeling in a song, but is carried away (by the ears) by any flowing melody repeated often enough in public places to become familiar. These lasted on the barrel-organs till 1854 or 1855, when they were dethroned by " Old Dog Tray" and " Willie, we have missed you," good tunes in their way, but strikingly deficient in originality, and founded upon Scotch airs, well enough known to the grandfathers and grandmothers of the present generation, but not quite so well known to the fast men of to-day.

About this period a song called "My Name it is Sam Hall!" fascinated the town by its singular blending of the tragic and the comic, and the dramatic manner in which it was sung nightly to admiring audiences, that, as time wore on, and its fame extended, included some of the highest members of the aristocracy, in addition to the ordinary middle-class frequenters of what were known as "Night Houses"—of which "Evans's," conducted by "Paddy Green," was the best known, and by far the most respectable.

For a time, Mr. Sims Reeves, by singing frequently the song entitled "Who shall be fairest?" introduced it to very considerable popularity; but the song was of two refined a character to be entirely acceptable to the admirers of the "Ratcatcher's Daughter" and the great London multitude. And although it reached the organ-grinders, and became, to that extent, more or less of a street nuisance, its fame was ultimately confined to the drawing-room.

Shortly afterwards, the nigger melodies broke out again with redoubled fury, and stormed the town, to the sore annoyance of everybody who had his bread to earn in London by the exercise of his intellect, unless, perchance, he had chambers in the Temple, where no organ-grinder or street-singer is allowed to enter. I make no objection to the "music of the million," for music, whether for the hundred or the million, is the soother and refiner of mankind, and a beneficent agent of the highest civilisation. If instrumental music were alone employed to attract customers for the beer, the alcohol, and the tobacco that are the main supports of the music-halls, those establishments (leaving out of consideration the question of temperance or intemperance) would be comparatively harmless. Music in itself and by itself is of necessity pure. " Songs without words," or songs of which the melody is played upon a wind or a stringed instrument, without any aid from the voice, are always more or less beautiful. Every tune gives some degree of pleasure, and no tune or melody can of itself, without association with human speech, convey to the mind any ideas that are not innocent. Music can express joy, hope, love, tenderness, sorrow, martial ardour, and deep religious feeling; or, by a discordant note, it may possibly express fear or anger. But music cannot convey the idea of indecency, spite, malice, jealousy, hatred, falsehood, revenge, or any of the mean and wicked passions. All music, in fact, is sacred.

It is only when vulgar, silly, or indecent writers of verse associate tunes to their compositions that music becomes linked in the mind with unworthy ideas. Music, in the case last mentioned, is in the pitiable plight of a Venus Aphrodite dressed, against her will, in the dirty rags of a street virago. And this is the offence committed by the music-halls that infest our cities in the present day, and form so many academies or colleges where nothing is taught or learned but bad manners and low vulgarities, with a superadded flavour of vice. Time was when English lyrists wrote songs that were alike acceptable to the rich and poor, to the educated and uneducated—songs that inculcated the noblest sentiments of honour, virtue, patriotism, love, and friendship, and that, if they ministered to mirth, did so without offence to delicacy or reason. But if the world is to judge by the popular lyrics of the music-halls of the present day, the meanest and most prosaic doggerel has superseded poetry.

The immense leap that has been made from the high standard of our fathers and grandfathers to the very low standard of the year 1886, may be measured by the distance which separates such a magnificent song as " Ye Mariners of England," by Thomas Campbell, from the ignoble drivel that now finds favour with the multitude :—

> We don't want to fight,
> But, by Jingo! if we do,
> We 've got the ships, we 've got the men,
> We 've got the money too.

The patriotic songs do not monopolise the applause of the music-halls. If anyone will look through the advertising pages of the London journals, and note the titles of the comic songs especially written for the entertainment of the frequenters of these places, he will have reason to believe that these songs, mostly written in the coarsest vernacular, appeal to the fancy, if they have any fancy, or to the understanding, if they have any understanding, of the least educated of the classes that supply the community with shop-boys, housemaids, scullions, costermongers, and other useful but not refined people. He will also find, that if these song-writers want to be more than usually comic, or, as they call it, funny, they go a grade lower, and borrow their language, their illustrations, and their imagery from thieves and beggars, as well as from the wholly illiterate vulgar. As examples of the first class may be cited : " There's Somebody minding the Shop," " We're about to have a Baby," " He knew how to do it " (announced by the publisher as having had a *terrific* success), " Take this Sausage to my Mother," " It's nice," " They all do it," " He always comes Home to Tea," " Oh, place a Mustard Plaister on my Chest," " Tiddly Wink the Barber," " When the pigs begin to fly," " The Girl in the Eelskin Dress," " The Chickaleery Cove," " Champagne Charlie," and other abominations which there is no necessity to mention. To apply any weaker epithet than " execrable " to compositions like these would be too merciful to their vast demerits. The songs and ballads of previous generations stirred the blood to patriotic or tender emotions. The songs of the music-halls, if they stir up anything, stir up the bile and provoke nausea.

And even when these inferior songs of the million are morally unobjectionable, they are too often contemptible in a literary sense for the ignorant misuse of the beautiful and copious English language which their writers display. One of the least offensive of these effusions is entitled "When the hay is in the mow." If this were good English, why should it not be followed by such companion compositions as "When the corn is in the reap," "When the sheep are in the shear," or even "When the cows are in the milk"?

It was said by the French poet, Auguste Barbier, who wrote in 1830, and who wrote too little, when speaking of the profligate Parisian song-writers of that and a previous time—

> Ils ne savent donc pas, ces vulgaires rimeurs,
> Quelle force ont les arts pour démolir les mœurs.

The same may be said of the "vulgar rhymers" of London, who are doing their best, with the aid of the music halls, to "demolish the manners" of a large section of the people.

CHAPTER VII.

THE SCOTT MONUMENT AT EDINBURGH.

In the memoirs of my excellent friend, Mr. Adam Black, twice Lord Provost of Edinburgh, and for many years member of Parliament for the city, which were published in 1885, and edited by Dr. Alexander Nicholson, it is stated, in reference to the monument to the memory of Sir Walter Scott, erected in Princes Street in 1846, which forms one of the most beautiful ornaments of a beautiful city, that a committee had been formed many years previously, " had raised large subscriptions, which were not sufficient to complete the monument; *and that a second committee was formed, consisting of tradesmen, who succeeded in raising among this one class a sufficient sum for the purpose.*"

This is an unpardonable mis-statement. It imputes to the tradesmen of Edinburgh a liberality which, if they had indulged in, would have been highly creditable to their appreciation of the literary genius of their illustrious fellow-citizen, and would have been a natural and in every way becoming expression of their gratitude to the man whose fame had attracted to their city so many thousands of admiring tourists and visitors from every part of the world, to pay homage at his shrine, and to spend money among them by so doing. The "tradesmen" may have possibly formed themselves into a committee, with the praiseworthy design of raising funds for the completion of the monument; but if they did so, a fact, if it were a fact, of which I have never heard until I saw it stated in Dr. Nicholson's memoir of Mr. Adam Black, they certainly failed in their object, and did little or nothing towards its fulfilment.

In the year 1844, as I have elsewhere fully recorded, with full particulars,* and documentary evidence, I was applied to by Sir Thomas Dick Lauder, Bart., to form a committee in London for the purpose of aiding the lagging and dilatory exertions of the Edinburgh people, who were either too poor, too niggardly, and too ungrateful, or who had been too inefficiently appealed to to do their duty in this respect. I succeeded in forming a London Committee, composed of some of the

* *Forty Years' Recollections of Life, Literature and Politics*, 2 vols. 8vo. Published by Messrs. Chapman and Hall, London, 1877.

highest and most influential and most liberal members of the aristocracy, together with the most eminent literary men of the time. The sum of £3,000 was needed for the completion of the shrine; and, as the greater portion of the members of the committee which I succeeded in forming had previously subscribed, and were not all inclined to subscribe a second time, except in a few instances, the subscription was not a brilliant success, and produced less than £300 of the £3,000 required. Under the circumstances, an idea, first broached by Sir Thomas Dick Lauder, and warmly taken up by me as Honorary Secretary of the Fund, was communicated to the Hon. C. A. Murray, one of the most zealous members of the London Committee, who then held a high office in Her Majesty's Household. I asked that gentleman, should he approve of the project, to use his influence at Court, to procure the patronage of the Queen and Prince Albert for a grand Waverley Ball at Willis's Rooms; a fancy ball, in which every dancer was to represent a character in the poems and romances of the illustrious author. The Prince acceded readily to the request. The ball was the great event of the fashionable London season of 1844, and was held on the 8th of July. It was, in all respects, a brilliant success, and produced a clear sum of £1,100, after payment of all expenses, or nearly four

times as much as the subscriptions of the poet's
admirers.

There was thus a deficiency still left of £1,600;
but whether, under the circumstances, the Edinburgh "tradesmen" put their shoulders to the
wheel, to raise the money, which the hotel-keepers
of the Northern Metropolis might well have spared
out of the profits which had flowed into their
coffers from the pockets of the crowd of pilgrims attracted annually to the city by Sir Walter's
fame, I never heard or knew. I only know for
certain that more than a quarter of a century
afterwards, in 1878, the monument being still
uncompleted, I was again appealed to from Edinburgh to form a London Committee to solicit
subscriptions. I formed the Committee, which,
under my guidance, as its chairman, refused to
ask for a single subscription, but took the necessary measures to secure the patronage of H.R.H.
the Prince of Wales for a second Waverley Ball,
and, if possible, his personal presence at the festival. The Committee was successful in its endeavours: the Prince consented as readily as his royal
father had previously done, but only stipulated, as
a matter of personal comfort to himself and all the
ladies and gentleman who might attend, that the
number of tickets of admission should be limited
to six hundred, so as to prevent any inconvenient
pressure of the crowd. The condition was perforce

acceded to, and the otherwise possible amount of the proceeds was confined to the handsome, but relatively moderate, sum of £600.

The city and citizens of Edinburgh do not show to advantage in their appreciation of the genius of the most illustrious man who was ever born and resided among them. They may plead that they and their fathers have been too poor to render adequate homage to the great departed, and the plea might possibly be allowed, if it were not known that they spent fifteen thousand pounds in bon-fires, illuminations, junketings, and other forms of popular rejoicing, on the occasion of the marriage of H.R.H. the Prince of Wales to the Princess of Denmark; but that they were never willing to find fifteen hundred pounds, or one half of that sum, towards the Scott monument. Even on the occasion of the celebration of the centenary of his birth in 1871, Edinburgh did nothing but institute a beggarly banquet, consisting of plumcake and inferior sherry, to all who chose to pay the price for those indigestible dainties. About twelve hundred people assembled in a large hall to listen to long speeches which were inaudible to two-thirds of them. For a Prince of Wales, £15,000! For a Prince of Literature, nothing! Such is the record of the beautiful city of Edinburgh! Auld Reekie! all smoke and no flame!

It has always been a mystery to me why Walter

Scott stands so low in the estimation of the present race of Scotsmen all over the world, and why Robert Burns, a greatly inferior genius, stands so high. Is it because the majority of the Scotch people are so ultra-democratic that they cannot forgive Scott for being an aristocrat; and that they almost worship Burns because he was born and nurtured and died in poverty, because he was an ultra-plebeian, earning his scanty and precarious bread by the sweat of his brow? Or do the multitude, in all countries, love their heroes all the more because of their conspicuous human frailties, and have nothing but cold respect for the great men who are only virtuous and respectable? The popularity of King David among the Jews, and Charles II. among the English, may be accounted for on this principle.

> Passez, passez, monarques debonnaires,
> Le peuple perdra votre nom!

as Auguste Barbier sings in his beautiful *Iambes*. Perhaps Sir Walter Scott might have taken a deeper root in the hearts of his countrymen, if he had been less exemplary than he was in all the relations of life; and if he had had failings that leaned more or less to virtue's side, like those of Robert Burns. But, as the French poet already quoted sang in 1831,—

> La popularité est la grande impudique,

and its secrets are inscrutable.

Inverness and Ross-shire.

In the year 1844 my cousin, Mr. James Matheson, being then member for the small English borough of Ashburton, aspired to represent the county of Ross. The principal Liberal newspaper in the Highlands at this time was the *Inverness Courier*, edited by my excellent and accomplished friend, Mr. Robert Carruthers, who endeavoured to steer a middle course between the Conservatives and the Liberals, with a more or less decided leaning to the Liberals. His faint-hearted policy had the usual result of displeasing both sides.

> In moderation placing all his glory,
> The Tories called him Whig, the Whigs a Tory.

Mr. Matheson, in common with many other members of the Liberal Party in Ross-shire, being discontented with the often lukewarm and always uncertain support of this *Courier*, determined to establish a journal of more decided opinions, to be published at Dingwall; and applied to me, to know if I would undertake the editorship. The invitation reached me about the time when I usually took my annual holiday in the Highlands, so that I had the opportunity, of which I availed myself, of making personal investigations before I finally decided. The change from busy London, the world's metropolis, the centre of English literature, politics, and society, to a remote town, or rather village, in the wilds of Ross-shire, was too great and momentous in its probable effects upon my future career to be rashly undertaken, however agreeable and advantageous it might at first sight appear. It, therefore, behoved me, as the Scotch say, to "gang cannie," or, as the English would say, to "walk warily." Among the gentlemen more particularly interested in the project, in addition to Mr. Matheson, were Sir George Mackenzie, of Coul, Baronet, Mr. Mackenzie, of Muirton, and Mr. Hugh Innes Cameron, of Dingwall, all leading Liberals in Ross-shire, who had undertaken to raise the money for the purpose, and with each of whom it was advisable, if not absolutely necessary, that I should confer.

On leaving London for my holiday, I proceeded to Edinburgh, where I learned that Sir George Mackenzie was in *villegiatura*, at North Berwick, a bathing-place at the foot of Berwick Law, on the coast of the Firth of Forth, about twenty miles distant.

As no time was to be lost, I endeavoured to secure a place in the stage coach then run by Croll and Co., from their office in Princes Street, opposite the Register Office, the only public conveyance available, and learned, to my great disappointment, that every place, outside and inside, was bespoken for three days; and that there were at least half-a-dozen persons, besides myself, who were applicants for any chance vacancy that might occur in the interval. I thought of walking this distance, passing through Portobello, Mussulburgh, Preston Pans, and a pleasant country within sight of the sea for the whole distance; but, on second thoughts, and in order to save time, resolved to hire a one-horse vehicle from Mr. Croll's establishment, and drive myself to my destination. It was a dangerous thing for me to attempt: I was unskilled in the management of a horse, and had never driven a vehicle before. However, on the assurance that the horse was the most docile of animals, knew every inch of the road, and that I need give myself neither trouble nor anxiety, I was emboldened to make my first, and, during many subsequent years, my last, attempt as a charioteer. As all is well that ends well, my foolhardy venture turned out successfully, much to the surprise and amusement of Sir George Mackenzie, when he learned from my own lips how inexperienced I was. Giving me hearty and hospitable welcome, he augured well of my courage, though not of my prudence, and wished I might get back again to Edinburgh as safely as I had come.

I found Sir George an able and accomplished man, but more of a philosopher and a scientist than a politician; a sound and consistent Liberal, but not a very zealous one, for age had somewhat impaired his youthful ardour, or diverted what remained of it into quieter channels than those of party warfare. He was kind enough to suggest, in my interest, that I should not only be the Editor of a provincial journal, of which the salary would not be equal to what he was pleased to call my deserts, but that a place should be found for me which would give me rank as well as emolument in the county; though what the place was to be he did not tell me, nor did he perhaps know. He was quite willing to take a considerable share in the new journal. He thought, however, that the greatest amount of capital ought to come out of the pockets of Mr. Matheson, the millionaire, in whose political and personal interest the journal was to be established and maintained.

On the night of my visit, Sir George was far less interested in political and literary questions than in a chemical invention which he had lately completed, by which he hoped that the nuisance to careful housewives, resulting from the accidental spilling of ink on their dresses and personal finery, or on their table and other linen, would be wholly prevented. He had succeeded in manufacturing an ink, for which he had taken out a patent, which was wholly colourless, and would not stain any textile fabric on which it might be thrown, or leave the slightest mark on the fingers of the daintiest lady who wrote a love-letter with it. It was only when brought into contact with paper specially prepared to receive it that the colourless ink became black as jet and remained indelible. But whether Sir George had not taken the proper means to acquaint the public with the advantages of his delicate preparation, or, having done so, whether the public, obstinately conservative in the matter of ink, preferred the old method to the new one, or loved to see that its ink was black before it dipped its pen into the inkstand, the fact remained that the pretty invention of Sir George was a commercial failure, that the stationers did not and would not keep it in stock, and that customers never asked for it.

Having received all the information to be ob- obtained from Sir George Mackenzie with regard to the Ross-shire paper, and the probability of its steady and effective support by the Liberal party in the county, and learning that Mr. Mackenzie of Muirton and Mr. Hugh Innes Cameron were both in. Inverness, I proceeded to that town, where I had many friends, with the intention of making it my head-quarters during the remainder of my investigations, and the possible negotiations that might result. My oldest and best friend in Inverness was Mr. Carruthers, of the *Courier*, whose interests might or might not be affected by the establishment of a rival in Dingwall; but as he was sure to hear of the project from other sources, I thought it the more friendly course to tell him myself what the Liberals of Ross-shire intended, and the offers which they had made me. I found that Mr. Carruthers, as I expected he would be, was more or less annoyed at the proposal—perhaps more so than he allowed to appear—but that he treated it like a philosopher and a man of the world, and came to the sensible conclusion that, if opposition were to be met, he would meet it bravely, and that, after all, there might be room in the Highlands of Ross-shire and Inverness-shire for two Liberal journals.

I found Mr. Mackenzie and Mr. Cameron favourably, though not enthusiastically, disposed, but more inclined to depend than I thought they were justified in doing upon the support of Mr. Matheson, whose objects were non-commercial and exclusively personal and political. While I was in uncertainty—but far more inclined to accept than to reject the offer, and come to terms about the remuneration I might expect if I gave up a valuable and influential position on the *Morning Chronicle* for a precarious one on a yet unborn journal—I received, through an Edinburgh friend and relative, the late Mr. John Alexander Mackay, of Blackcastle, information that the editorship of an established Liberal paper, published twice a week in the great city of Glasgow, would be vacant in a month, and that the proprietors, admiring the principles and talent of the *Morning Chronicle*, were about to apply to the conductors of that journal to recommend one of their *alumni* for the office, if one fully competent could be found to accept it. The newspaper in question was the *Glasgow Argus*, whose editor, a Mr. Lang (who had succeeded Mr. Thornton Hunt, the son of Leigh Hunt), had so mismanaged it and impaired its usefulness by his unwise and persistent advocacy of mesmerism and animal magnetism, and his neglect of politics, as to have greatly reduced its circulation and to have injured its reputation. The prospect thus suddenly opened out was more attractive than that afforded by the Ross-shire speculation. To edit a bi-weekly newspaper, with no night-work, would be a sensible relief from the sub-editorship of a daily paper with night-work imperative during six nights. A life in a bustling, active, and growing city like Glasgow was far preferable in most respects to that of a life in a small and almost stagnant town in the remote Highlands of Scotland. And to a lover of grand scenery such as I was, Glasgow, being within an hour's journey by steam down the Clyde, from the beautiful lakes and mountains of Dumbarton and Argyllshire, offered the double advantages of pleasant society for my needs and delightful solitude for my pleasures, whenever I desired either.

On due reflection, I resolved to become a candidate for the *Glasgow Argus*; and, as the candidature might not be successful, though my prospects were highly favourable, I kept the negotiations with the Ross-shire people in abeyance, resolving at the same time to see Mr. Matheson, if opportunity allowed, and I could make it convenient to visit him in Stornoway. Meanwhile I remained in Inverness for my holiday, and visited, not for the first time, all the magnificent scenery of the environs—the falls of Kilmorack the "Dream" or "Druim" of Beauly, the lovely burn of Moniack, in the grounds of Mr. J. B. Fraser, the well-known author of the *Kuzzilbash* and other novels, the battle-field of Culloden, and Culloden House, the seat of a branch of the great clan of Forbes; Kilravock Castle, the seat of my maternal ancestors, the Roses of Kilravock, who had settled there in the thirteenth century, and who were popularly known as "Barons of Kilravock," though they were and are still untitled; and Cawdor Castle, the very ancient and picturesque abode of the Earls and former Thanes of Cawdor, of whom Macbeth, according to Shakspeare, was one. This old castle interested me exceedingly, presenting as it does, without modern change of any kind, except in the private apartments of the family, the furniture and ornamentation of a long bygone era. I was particularly interested in a white marble chimney-piece, bearing date in the year 1510, with many sculptured figures, among others that of a monkey smoking a short pipe. This, if a genuine work of the time, as it no doubt is, as the wing of the castle in which it is placed was erected that year, proves that, although Sir Walter Raleigh, as history and tradition agree in asserting, first introduced tobacco into Europe in 1585, he did not introduce the practice of smoking, which, on this testimony, must have been known, if it were not common, three-quarters of a century before. What was the weed or herb which people smoked before they became acquainted with American tobacco, is not known, and perhaps never will be.

Inverness at this time was noted for the convivial hospitality of its principal inhabitants, and the conviviality, if not the hospitality, extended to the lowest grades of the people. This trait of manner was by no means peculiar to Inverness, but was the characteristic of society in all the great towns and cities of Scotland, as I can testify from my personal experience of Edinburgh and Glasgow. The consumption of whisky, whether neat in the shape of drams, or diluted with cold water, when it is called "grog," or with hot water, mixed with sugar, when it is called toddy, was large in Inverness, as, in fact, it was in every part of Scotland, and as it continues to this day, though with somewhat abated and diminished intensity. During my stay in Inverness, I was told of a venerable old gentleman named Fraser (the clan Fraser is so numerous in this part of the Highlands, that the public mention of his name will not lift the veil from his exact identity), who for fifty years of his life, and up to the age of ninety, had daily drunk ten tumblers of hot whisky toddy. This regular and methodical old person died at last of intemperance, at the age of ninety-one or ninety-two, according to the testimony of the sober people of Inverness. Transgressing the bounds of temperance, which he had fixed for himself at ten tumblers *per diem*, he was rash enough on some joyous anniversary to indulge in eleven. The extra tumbler sealed his doom. Outraged nature exacted the penalty of his excess, and he was found dead in his bed the following morning after what sober people called his shameful debauch. The moral drawn by the temperate Invernessians from the unhappy story of poor old Fraser was that it was unwise and might be fatal to any man to overpass the limit that experience had prescribed, and to recklessly forget the fate of that proverbial pitcher that went too often to the well and got broken at last.

Another story, of a somewhat later date, with respect to whisky-drinking has been related of Inverness. The late eminent and universally respected philanthropist, the Earl of Shaftesbury, in his visit to the town, was waited upon by the worthy Provost, a distiller, who from respect for his high character, and his knowledge of the enlightened interest which he took in every social question that affected the welfare of the people, though it his duty to do the honours of the place, and escort him over the most noteworthy localities and buildings, not forgetting the Workhouse, the Prison, the Lunatic Asylum, and all the other evidences of a high civilisation. During the course of their peregrinations, they were met by one of the Provost's partners in business, who, not knowing who Lord Shaftesbury was, took the liberty of stopping the Provost and asking if he were not coming to the Distillery during the day, as a matter had arisen which required his presence. Lord Shaftesbury's quick ear caught the sound of the word " distillery," and, as soon as the interlocutor had taken his leave, asked the Provost, "Do I understand, Mr. Provost, that you are a distiller?"

"Oh yes," replied the worthy magistrate, "I am a distiller, and our firm, I may add, is noted for producing the best whisky in the Highlands, if not in all Scotland. Will your lordship not come to my office and tak a pree o't (take a taste of it) ?"

"Heaven forbid!" said his lordship, with a face of horror, "that a drop of such detestable liquor should ever pass my lips."

"Detestable liquor!" echoed the greatly surprised Provost.

"Yes!" reiterated the earnest philanthropist. "It poisons the bodies and ruins the souls of men."

The Provost, who had never heard whisky spoken of in such terms before, could not for some time find words to reply to so fierce and unexpected a denunciation, took breath at last, and remembering that Lord Shaftesbury was, or was reputed to be, an earnest teetotaler, said mildly: "I grant your Lordship that, taken in excess, whisky is bad, both for the body and the soul; but taken in moderation, it is a blessing, just as bread is, or beef, or any other gift of God to mankind. But intemperance in anything is a curse! And in truth, anyhow, I am as great a friend to temperance as your Lordship."

"Temperance!" said Lord Shaftesbury; "and what, Mr. Provost, is your idea of temperance, and what do you call a temperate man?"

"A temperate man, according to my notions, my Lord, is a douce, cannie, honest, respectable father of a family, who takes his six tumblers and an eke, every night, in the bosom of his family; but I hate intemperance!"

It should be added, for the benefit of those English-speaking people unacquainted with Scottish phraseology, that an "eke" signifies an extra glass, and that a very common appeal to a parting guest, by a convivially-minded host, is to say to him, " Tak an eke, man, tak an eke ! " passing the whisky-bottle to him at the same time ; an invitation which is by no means invariably refused.

While at Inverness, I received an intimation from the legal gentleman in charge of the negotiations regarding the *Argus*, that he would be glad to see me in Glasgow, and I took my departure next day for that city.

GLASGOW, 1844–1847.

The terms offered to me on the part of the proprietors of the *Argus* were satisfactory; not so much on pecuniary grounds, for the emoluments were not greater than those I derived from the *Morning Chronicle*, but on those of more abundant leisure, greater freedom of action, easier work, and, more especially, the non-necessity of sitting up nearly all night for six nights in the week, or even for one night, unless I were disposed to do so. So the requisite documents were soon signed, and I had nothing further to do than to return to London, take leave of my kind friend John Black, the proprietors of the *Chronicle*, and my immediate colleagues in the editorial department, and break up my small establishment in the capital, and transfer myself and my belongings from the first to the second city in the Empire.

I had not been long in Glasgow before I discovered that theology sat like an incubus upon the intellect of the citizens, high and low, or the great majority of them, and injuriously affected the interest they took either in politics or literature. Glasgow was socially a plutocracy, intellectually a theocracy. No aristocracy of rank or talent existed within it, unless in the pulpit. A powerful minority chafed, it is true, under the infliction of the sacerdotal tyranny, and of this minority I was speedily made aware that I was expected to be the mouthpiece, in as far as I could become so without touching upon ecclesiastical polemics. I had, however, a wide field in the advocacy of Liberal politics, and if the Glasgowegians of the Liberal party took more interest in sermons than in leading articles, it was my duty, while leaving the pulpit alone, to make the press as powerful as I could in the exercise of its own vocation, acting as if I thought that there was room enough for both.

At the first dinner party to which I was invited by one of the rich leading citizens, I was asked by the hostess, a very handsome and agreeable young woman, next to whom I sat, if I had heard any of the principal preachers of the city. It so happened that the only preacher I had heard was the Rev. Dr. King, not in his pulpit but on the platform, where he had delivered a speech in denunciation of the Corn Laws. I replied that I thought

Dr. King a most eloquent man, and that it was a great pleasure to listen to him. The fair face of my questioner seemed to glow with satisfaction, as she remarked quickly, unaware alike of the *suppressio vera* and the *suggestio falsi* of my Jesuitical answer, "I am *so* glad you like Dr. King! *I* sit under Dr. King!" And she forthwith invited me also to sit under him, or, in other words, to become one of his congregation, which, however, I never did.

On another occasion, at another dinner party, got up especially to introduce me to some of the leading spirits among the Liberals, the one clergyman present, noted for his more than usual enmity to the Roman Catholic Church, even in a country where all the clergy were not only professionally but personally hostile to the Pope and all Papal doctrine and pretensions, said, in a loud and dictatorial voice, over his toddy, "Thanks be to God, we have no Pope in Glasgow." Without pausing to reflect on the possible offence which I might give, I suddenly ejaculated, "No Pope! why, you have a Pope in every parish!" I had no sooner uttered the words than I thought how reckless I had been, and would have recalled them had it been possible to do so, but was restored to equanimity, if not to satisfaction with myself, by a burst of applause all round the table, and a simultaneous request from half-a-dozen gentlemen to be permitted to drink my health. I had unwittingly struck a popular chord, and scored an unexpected triumph over the clerical party, that was far too rampant in the city, the motto on whose escutcheon was: "Let Glasgow flourish, by the preaching of the Word." Since those comparatively early days, a sensible change has come over the mind of that great and prosperous city. Long before my time a beginning had been made, and its motto judiciously abbreviated. It now stands in emphatic simplicity, "Let Glasgow flourish!"

I remained in Glasgow for three years, with pleasure to myself and satisfaction to my political supporters. I might have remained for a much longer period, had not the Liberal party split up into two hostile and irreconcileable sections on the question of the representation of the city in Parliament. The split extended to the proprietors of the *Argus*, with the result, in 1847, of bringing my connection with that journal to an end, and, after a fitful existence of three months without a recognised and responsible editor, consigning the *Argus* itself to inglorious extinction.

Meanwhile, and until the final catastrophe occurred, my days, like those of Thalaba in Southey's immortal poem, "flew happily by." I took a rural villa, called Rose Cottage, at Ibrox Holme, on the road to Paisley, within two miles and a half of the city, and every Saturday, from the morning of that day to the evening of Monday, was able to shake off the dust of the city and to forget its theological and political squables and animosities, and to betake myself to the glorious mountains and lakes of the middle and southern Highlands of Dumbarton, Argyll, Renfrew, and the island of Arran.

The citizens of Glasgow, or such among them as appreciate fine scenery, are highly favoured by nature. They have easy and cheap access to some of the most beautiful spots on the globe, and, within two hours, may leave the smoky purlieus of the Broomielaw or the Salt Market, and find themselves on the unpolluted shores of the splendid estuary of the Clyde, in the Gare Loch, the Holy Loch, and the magnificent Loch Long, much finer than the better known and greatly boasted Rhine, on the lovely margin of Loch Lomond, at Tarbet, with the lordly Ben Lomond right in front of them.

In this region the villages and small towns beloved of the Glasgowegians are Helensburgh, Roseneath, Kilmun, Strone, the Kern, Dunoon, Rothesay, and, in the neighbourhood of Greenock, on the other side, Gourock, Wemyss Bay, Inverkip, Kellyburn Braes, renowned in song, Skelmorlie Castle, and Largs, within hail of the Greater and Lesser Cumraes.

My favourite resort during my residence in Glasgow was at Kilmun on the Holy Loch, where

I had, during the summer months, for my nearest neighbour, the celebrated Daniel Macnee, the portrait painter, afterwards President of the Royal Scottish Academy, one of the most amiable of men, a highly-accomplished artist, a univeral favourite in Glasgow society, and one of the best tellers of Highland stories, of which he had an inexhaustible budget, that ever set the table in a roar with innocent and exuberant mirth.

Daniel Macnee was as enthusiastic an angler as Isaak Walton himself, or as his friends and contemporaries, Professor Wilson, the renowned Christopher North of *Blackwood's Magazine*, Thomas Tod Stoddart of Kelso, the author of many angling lyrics, that seem beautiful to all anglers—and to me, who never caught a fish in my life, though I have two or three times endeavoured to do so—and Alexander Russel, for many years editor of the *Scotsman*. Macnee's favourite stream was the Eachaig, that runs from Loch Eck into the Holy Loch, a couple of miles above the village of Kilmun. Loch Eck, where large trout and gigantic salmon are often the reward of such patient and persistent piscators as Macnee, was, however, a more frequent resort than the comparatively barren waters of the shallow Eachaig; and thither I was often his companion as far as the little wayside inn at Whistlefield, on the shore of the lake. Here we could generally find abundant store of refreshments, after long walks, in the shape of crisp oaten cake, delicious fresh butter, salmon steaks, and whisky *à discretion*. The last time I visited Whistlefield in Macnee's company, the landlady told us the tragic story of a rich Glasgow merchant, who had made a large fortune in his business, and retired to enjoy it as a country gentleman. He built for himself a magnificent mansion on the shore of the lake — on the opposite side of the high road from Kilmun—that he might be out of the too facile reach of friends or acquaintances from Glasgow, who might signal for a boat to ferry them across if they desired to pay him a visit. The house was commodious, spacious, and elaborately provided with everything that wealth and luxury could desire; the grounds were varied by height and hollow, and laid out tastefully and scientifically by a professional gardener of high repute; the situation—at the foot of Ben More—was excellently chosen, and the landscape within view, extended over a placid lake seven miles in length, and the wood-crowned, picturesque highlands on the shore. Everyone who knew the proprietor of the domain envied him its possession, and the promise it afforded him of a peaceful autumn and winter after the busy spring and summer of his successful life. They did not suspect the danger that lay hidden in the calm and beautiful haven into which he had entered in the decline of his days. Appearances were all deceptive. The rich merchant had but little intellectual capacity, and that little had not been enlarged or cultivated by study and reflection. He was shrewd in his business, but had no mind beyond it. He had no stores of accumulated knowledge. He had a library; but he only looked upon his books as furniture. He admired their binding, and never opened their covers to see or study what was inside. He had purchased pictures at great price, though these were of little merit, and hung them upon his walls—furniture only, as his books were. He had no conversational powers, though he liked to be talked to by people who could amuse him; but, as few of these called upon him in his solitude —which he had purposely rendered difficult of access—he began, after a few months, to weary of his lonely grandeur. He had a wife, but no family, and his wife's society was not congenial to him, nor his to her, and the pair got on but ill together. The wife, on her part, having a busier and more cultivated mind, sought change of scene and intellectual intercourse in Glasgow, Edinburgh, or London, leaving him to his own devices. His pride would not allow him to go back to business, which he sometimes thought of doing. He had no fancy for wielding the woodman's axe—like Mr. Gladstone—or he might have amused himself and taken wholesome exercise by felling some of the large trees in his domain; but, in default of this, he tried to find recreation without taking wholesome exercise, by sitting for hours in the solitary boat on the lake, angling for salmon, with great perseverance but without skill, all the while thinking—if he thought at all—how slow the fish were in biting; or, perhaps, chewing the cud of bitter fancy—if he had any fancies to form a cud, or was able to chew it, or sense enough to appreciate the bitterness of experiencing in his own person how useless was wealth to secure happiness to a man who had no wealth in his mind.

This poor rich man gave orders one morning to the assistant gardener to get the boat ready, put the fishing-tackle on board, together with a paper of sandwiches, a flask of whisky, a large grindstone, and a coil of rope. The gardener wondered what the grindstone was wanted for, but, suspecting no evil, asked no questions, and in due time pushed the boat from the shore, with his master in it alone, as was his custom, and wished him good sport and good luck. He rowed off to the middle of the loch. In less than an hour afterwards the unhappy master of the big house cut a length of rope, inserted the end through the hole in the middle of the grindstone, affixed the rope and the stone to his body, and dropped himself from the side of the boat into the water, and sank immediately. His body was not recovered for several days, and was honoured with a grand funeral, as befitted his wealth. There are no coroner's inquests held in Scotland, or a jury would have been empanelled, and would doubtless have brought in the verdict, usual in such cases, of "Temporary insanity."

Among the few literary friends I made in Glasgow—which at that time was, and is now, far more renowned for trade and theology than for literature—was John Pringle Nichol, the Professor of Astronomy in the University. Professor Nichol was highly esteemed at the time when I first made his acquaintance, but was little known in Glasgow society, except by the select few that can appreciate or understand a man of genius when he appears among them. His genius did not exhibit itself more brightly until in after years he married an amiable lady of considerable fortune. The appreciation of his character increased immensely in consequence of that event. When a poor man, with nothing but the modest salary of his professorship, and the precarious profits of public lectures on Astronomy, to depend upon, he was not considered an authority on any subject except that of the science which he taught; but when he had become rich, he was looked up to as a shining light of politics, literature, and the social circle. No meeting for any public purpose was considered complete without him; his name was necessary to give *éclat* to any political or philanthropic movement; and his support to any cause was looked upon as a necessary prelude to its success.

Professor Nichol was of highly poetical temperament, though he never, as far as I know, indulged in the luxury of verse—unless in his youthful days, when most men of any literary genius, or even love for literature, are guilty of it, just as in the susceptible age they are guilty of falling in love—in reality or in imagination—with every beautiful girl they meet. But he looked like a poet, without knowing that he did so, and reminded me irresistibly of the published portraits of Schiller, with whom my temporary residence in Aix-la-Chapelle, and other parts of Germany, had rendered me familiar. I often spent my evenings at the Observatory, and was privileged to survey the stars through his great telescope, with the immense advantage of being instructed by him in their mysteries—the more mysterious to our finite and narrow human faculties the more they are studied.

One day, after a particularly interesting survey of the clear heavens on the preceding night, and a most interesting colloquy with the Professor on the mighty wonders of the universe, I wrote some lines, entitled, " The Earth and the Stars," which I read to him and Mr. De Quincey, the " Opium-eater," who was at the time his guest at the Observatory. I had bestowed a week's careful revision upon the composition before I ventured to read it aloud, and might have bestowed a still longer time, if I had known so competent and so severe a critic as De Quincey was to pass judgment upon it. The verses represented the Earth as appealing to the Stars to answer the mournful question, whether they also were the abodes of Sin, Suffering, and Death, and if there were no hope of a better time for the poor little planet on which men lived for their short allotted span, greedy of happiness, but never attaining or even beholding it. I represented the Stars as replying in hopeful terms to the querulous and half-despairing questioner :—

>   O mournful sister,
> Rolling calmly through the calm infinity,
>   We have rolled for myriad ages on our track,
>   Ever onward, pressing onward—never back—
> There is progress both for us and for thee!
>
>   Thou wilt make, O thou foolish little sister,
> The full cycle of thy glory in thy time ;
>   We are rolling on in ours for evermore.
>   Look not backward ; see Eternity before,
> And free thyself of Sorrow and of Crime.
>
> God, Who made thee, never meant thee, mournful sister,
> To be filled with sin and grief eternally ;
>   And the children that are born upon thy breast
>   Shall, in fulness of their destiny, be blest.
> There is progress for the Stars and for thee!

"The true philosophy of the stars," said the Professor, when I had finished reading. "The true lesson to be derived from the reverent contemplation of the universe."

"It is impossible," said Mr. De Quincey, "not to believe in Eternity. Matter and spirit are both eternal and indestructible, of whatever they may consist; but the forms which they assume and the functions which they perform are not eternal, either in appearance or in operation. That goodness is eternal we cannot but believe; but, if so, Evil—or what we ignorantly call Evil—must be eternal also. There can be no good without evil; there can be no evil without good. There can be no right unless there be a wrong; there can be no wrong unless there be a right. There can be no up unless there be a down; no light unless there be a dark; no joy without sorrow; no positive without a negative; no Yes without a *No*. There will be progress in the stars, as our friend supposes in his amiable optimism, for progress is infinite; but progress without the possibility of Evil, by which to measure, or understand, or feel, or know, or appreciate the good, would be equivalent to annihilation. It would be the Nirvana of the Eastern philosophy, which is impossible for God Himself to decree, inasmuch as He is eternal, infinite, and immutable—the great I AM for ever and ever, of which the whole universe, seen and unseen, is but a part, eternal as the whole; eternally immutable in substance or essence, but eternally mutable in manifestation."

"In other words," I said, "you believe that what men call evil may in reality be good, and agree with Pope, that 'all evil is partial and all good universal.'"

"Not exactly," replied Mr. De Quincey. "Evil is not partial, but inherent and necessary, and never to be estimated from the supreme, inconquerable, ineradicable law of the universe."

"We are getting beyond our depth," said the Professor. "I believe in progress both in this earth and in the stars, progress from good to better; and even in progress, or rather in retrogression, from bad to worse. There is no such thing in all the universe as stagnation. Even a stagnant pool is the source of life and consequently of movement, and breeds countless myriads of creatures, that enjoy and suffer, feel good and evil, and then pass away to make room for their successors. Neither on earth nor in the stars are the living creatures that inhabit them to expect or enjoy perfect happiness; but both on earth and in the stars they may attain to greater happiness than the ignorant dwellers on this paltry little globe have ever yet experienced or even dreamed of as possible. I agree with our friend who has just read us his verses, optimist as we may consider them to be; and the more I study the stars the more hopeful I become, and none the less hopeful because my mind, even in its utmost bewilderment, deems it foolish and wicked to despair."

At the time when this conversation took place Mr. De Quincey had been resident for more than a month at the Observatory, where the Professor had invited him to stay for a week. He had arrived without money, baggage, or a change of linen, and stayed, as I afterwards learned from the Professor, for at least six months. During this time he received occasional supplies of money for his contributions to *Blackwood's Magazine*, and so provided himself with such absolutely essential articles of under-clothing and over-clothing as he required, and with the loose silver in his pocket to purchase the laudanum that had become as necessary to his existence in health and comfort as food and fresh air. I did not know at the time that the "Opium-eater," as he was called, was so cruelly kind to his friends and admirers as to enact with them the part that the "Old man of the Sea" acted towards Sindbad the Sailor in the *Arabian Nights*; but that Professor Nichol was not the only person that he so highly favoured appears from the following extract from the *Life of Professor Wilson*, the great Christopher North of the *Noctes Ambrosianæ*, which was published by his daughter in 1862. She relates :—

I remember his coming to Gloucester Place one stormy night. He remained hour after hour, in vain expectation that the waters would assuage and the hurly-burly cease. There was nothing for it but that our visitor should remain all night. The Professor ordered a room to be prepared for him, and they found each other such good company that this accidental detention was prolonged, without further difficulty, for the greater part of a year. During this visit some of his eccentricities did not escape observation. For example, he rarely appeared at the family meals, preferring to dine in his own room at his own hour, not unfrequently turning night into day. His tastes were very simple, though a little troublesome, at least to the servant who prepared his repast. Coffee, boiled rice and milk, and a piece of mutton from the loin were the materials that invariably formed his diet. The cook, who had an audience with him daily, received her instructions in silent awe, quite overpowered by his manner; for, had he been addressing a duchess, he could scarcely have spoken with more deference. He would couch his request in such terms as these: " Owing to dyspepsia afflicting my system, and the possibility of any additional disarrangement of the stomach taking place, consequences incalculably distressing would arise, so much so, indeed, as to increase nervous irritation, and prevent me from attending to matters of overwhelming importance, if you do not remember to cut the mutton in a diagonal rather than in a longitudinal form." The cook, a Scotchwoman, had great reverence for Mr. De Quincey as a man of genius; but, after one of these interviews, her patience was pretty well exhausted, and she would say : " Weel, I never heard the like o' that in a' my days; the bodie has an awfu' sicht o' words. If it had been my ain maister that was wanting his dinner, he would ha' ordered a halc tablefu' wi' little mair than a waff o' his haun, and here 's a' this claver aboot a bit mutton, nae bigger than a prin. Mr. De Quinshey would mak' a gran' preacher, though I 'm thinking a hantle o' the folk wouldna ken what he was driving at."

It was during my editorship of the *Glasgow Argus* that *The Vestiges of the Natural History of Creation* was published—a very remarkable book, that preceded and was in some sense the pioneer of the still more remarkable work of Mr. Darwin, that has been more generally received as an authority and been more widely accepted by philosophers and physicists. The *Vestiges*, published anonymously in London, excited a great sensation at the time, as well as great curiosity as to the authorship. The book was successful, highly praised by some, violently abused by others, and went through no less than ten editions before it finally " blew over " and disappeared alike from public favour and animadversion. Many surmises were hazarded about the authorship, which was attributed to at least fifty different people of more or less literary and scientific celebrity. But Professor Nichol detected the writer from the very first, though every possible means were employed by the writer to keep the secret inviolate. The Professor had written to Mr. Robert Chambers, of the eminent house of W. and R. Chambers, of Edinburgh, many eloquent letters on scientific subjects, and he found more than one of them incorporated in the text of the *Vestiges*, not in spirit alone, but in form; not in substance merely, but in the very *ipsissima verbæ*, sometimes extending to a whole page of the printed book. There could thus be no mistaking the fact that Mr.

Robert Chambers was either the author of the volume, or that some third person had become either honestly or dishonestly possessed of the Professor's letters. The Professor, however, never wavered in his opinion that Mr. Robert Chambers was the author; that his brother and partner, Mr. William Chambers, was not in the secret; and that the mystery maintained on the subject was not due to whim, caprice, or modesty on the part of the writer, but to worldly prudence, and to trade considerations of the very highest importance to the commercial and social position of the writer. The Messrs. Chambers were the publishers of many educational works having a large and very profitable circulation in schools and colleges, all more or less under clerical and religious control; and the avowal of such a book as *The Vestiges*, which was unfairly but vehemently denounced in half of the pulpits of the land, as not only unorthodox, but infidel and God-denying, would have been in a high degree damaging, if not fatal, to the reputation and the monetary stability of a publishing firm that depended for much of its support on the teachers of the young. Suspicion from the first attached to Mr. Robert Chambers, and, as time wore on, fixed itself more generally upon him. To such an extent was the feeling of animosity in the clerical mind of Scotland developed on the subject, that when it was announced that Mr. Chambers, as one of the leading and most respected of the citizens of Edinburgh, would be proposed at the next municipal election for the high office of Lord Provost, to which he was known to have aspired, a clergyman publicly announced that if Mr. Chambers presented himself before the citizens with that object, he would ask him point-blank the question, " Are you or are you not the author of *The Vestiges of the Natural History of Creation?* " Mr. Chambers might have declined to answer, or he might have denied the fact, which no one had any moral or legal right to force him to confess; but, as refusal to answer would have been in the opinion of his opponents equivalent to a confession, and as denial would have been a falsehood, Mr. Chambers avoided being placed on either horn of the dilemma by forthwith resigning his pretensions to the greatest honour his fellow-citizens could confer upon him. All these circumstances tended to fix the conviction in the public mind that Mr. Robert Chambers was indubitably the author of the celebrated book that had so uncomfortably "fluttered the dovecots" of the believers in the Mosaic account of the Creation. Since that time the age has grown more tolerant of theological differences of opinion, and Mr. Darwin, in his *Origin of Species*, has done openly, without obloquy, though not without dissent, what Mr. Chambers was unable to avow for fear of social ostracism and financial calamity to himself and his unconscious and non-participating brother. It was not until after the death of Mr. Chambers, one of the greatest ornaments to and disseminators of wholesome popular literature that his country ever produced, that the secret of *The Vestiges* was avowed. By that time the book had ceased to be an authority, or even to be spoken of, and Darwin's *Origin of Species* reigned in its stead, uncontroverted but not unquestioned.

CHAPTER VIII.

THE DOUBLEDAY THEORY OF POPULATION.

When editing the *Glasgow Argus*, in 1845, I received a letter from Mr. Thomas Doubleday, of Newcastle-upon-Tyne, accompanying his book on the new Theory of Population, which he had lately promulgated. The work had not received recognition from the political economists and social philosophers of the time, but I devoted a leading article in the columns of the *Argus* to its consideration. The article gratified the author, and led him to become a frequent correspondent of the *Argus*. His theory was, that whenever any species of life, whether animal or vegetable, was threatened with extinction from inadequacy of healthful nutriment, its fecundity was for awhile increased, to guard it against the inevitable catastrophe, unless the causes of the temporary and abnormal fecundity were removed by more liberal and healthful diet.

He supported the argument by the fact that the

wives of the very poor were more prolific than those of the very rich—a fact which was within the commonest experience of all who had eyes to see, or who had the faculty of looking wisely about them, or studying the world in which they lived. He also cited instances of the same results in vegetable life—though not, to my mind, with the same cogency—though, on the opposite side of the theory, he supported it by the fact that too much oil put out the lamp, and that a too bountiful use of manure prevented instead of stimulated the growth of plants.

In my comments upon his ingenious theory, I quoted, in support of one branch of his argument, the opinion of King Louis Philippe—of which I had been informed in a letter from a well-informed and influential friend in Paris—that barrenness among the women of the upper classes in France was mainly caused by the excess in eating, if not in drinking, of both husband and wife. This opinion of the King was so well known in courtly circles that he was now and then consulted by the husbands of wedded ladies, who desired heirs to their estates, but who, after several years of wedded life, remained childless. Among the persons in high position who consulted him on the subject was the Duke de Saint Simon. The King asked him what he usually had for breakfast, for dinner, and for supper, and how long his course of living had continued. When the examination was concluded, the King said to him: "*Vous mangez trop, mon cher Duc. Envoyez-moi Madame votre épouse afin que je l'interroge* (You eat too much, my dear Duke. Send the Duchess to me that I may interrogate her also)." The Duchess waited upon him accordingly, and underwent a similar examination and cross-examination. His Majesty concluded with the warning that she ate too much, and that an absolute change of diet and a severer regimen were necessary for her health, and the accomplishment of the object of the mutual wishes of herself and her husband. The story current in Paris at the time I first became acquainted with it—and as I narrated it in the *Argus*, in my recommendation of Mr. Doubleday's treatise—was that the King prescribed for them both a much more meagre diet than they had been previously accustomed to; that he diminished the quantity of animal food and wine in which they indulged, increased the quantity of fruit and vegetables to be daily consumed at their repasts, and ordered both of them to take more frequent and more protracted exercise in the open air than the fashionable and artificial life of high society in Paris permitted them. He advised them to adhere strictly to the rules and regimen laid down for them for at least a year, when they might consult him again. The Duke and Duchess adhered to the rules rigorously for a year and a half or more, with the result—whether attributable to the King's prescription or not—that a healthy child was born to them. The wicked wits of Paris reported that, when the event was communicated to His Majesty, he rubbed his hands in great glee, saying: "*Cet enfant est à moi!* (That child is mine!)" The cynical jesters of the licentious capital did His Majesty injustice in their witticism, for in all his domestic relations the King was a model of virtue and propriety.

Mr. Doubleday was delighted with the anecdote, which was wholly new to him, and sent the King a copy of his book, which His Majesty duly acknowledged.

There may be much more in Mr. Doubleday's theory than the world is yet aware of, a truth which may go far towards explaining the as yet occult and unacknowledged causes of the decay and fall of great and powerful nations, the inordinate increase in squalor and misery of a weak and spiritless population, and the abnormal barrenness of the upper and too luxurious classes, having the leisure and the capacity for government. But the subject is too vast for discussion in these pages.

The "Whistle Binkie."

Among the other literary acquaintances with whom, as editor of the *Argus*, I was often brought into social and friendly communication, was Mr. David Robertson, of Argyll Street, an eminent publisher, who acted as the kindly and liberal Mecænas of second- and third-rate poets and song-writers, of whom Scotland, far more than England, is so prolific. Mr. Robertson, before I knew him, had published at intervals several small booklets, at a cheap price, and of a size and form convenient for the waistcoat-pocket, under the title of *Whistle Binkie*. The collection consisted of songs in the Scottish vernacular written by living authors. He did not know the origin or meaning of the word, neither did anybody else, but found it floating on the popular breath, and signifying vaguely an uninvited guest at a so-called "penny wedding" among the rural population of the lowest class, who, in return for a share in the whisky or other refreshments provided, either sang a song or played a tune on a flute or flageolet, or merely whistled, without instrumental aid, for the amusement of the company. He adopted the phrase "*faute de mieux*," as quite suggestive enough of the character and purpose of his unpretending collection, and as one to be easily understood by all who were familiar with broad Scotch.

The only explanation of the title which the publisher, or any of his contributors, could give was taken from Jamieson's Scottish Dictionary, in which it is stated that "Whistle Binkie is one who attends a penny wedding, but without paying anything, and, therefore, has no right to take any share of the entertainment—a mere spectator, who is left, as it were, to sit on a *bench* (a 'bink' or bunk) by himself, and who, if he pleases, may *whistle* for his own amusement." This derivation—on a par with too many others that pass muster with the industrious and too-easily-satisfied Dr. Jamieson—was not accepted as correct by Mr. Robertson, who excused himself for using it by saying that it was enough for him if the people understood it. I had not studied Gaelic when I was in Glasgow, as I have since done, or I might have informed him that neither "whistle," "bench" [*bink*], nor any Teutonic or English word, had anything to do with the strange phrase, but that it was derived from the Gaelic *uasal*, "gentle, kind, courteous," whence, *duine uasal* (*uasal* pronounced *wassel*), "a gentleman"; and *beannachaidh* (pronounced *bennakie*), "a blessing," and signified the blessing given to the newly-married couple by the superior or chief, of whom the humble guests at the penny wedding were the retainers or servants, and who usually graced the assembly for a short time, and shared in the hospitalities and festivities of the evening.

Most of the poetical contributors to Mr. Robertson's *Whistle Binkie* were men of the people, many of them in the humblest positions of life. Some were ploughmen, shepherds, handicraftsmen of various kinds, such as weavers, tailors, shoemakers, blacksmiths, carpenters, masons, compositors, even beggars, tramps, and strolling vagrants—all more or less imbued, or fancying themselves imbued, with the divine afflatus that inspired Allan Ramsay and Robert Burns. In aspiring to emulate or to rival their great predecessors and exemplars, many of these humble bards displayed a degree of genius that, had they been born a hundred years earlier, might have raised them into fame quite equal to that of Allan Ramsay, though not, perhaps, equal to that of Robert Burns; but that, appearing in an overcrowded age—when so many thousands of voices were crying in the streets, in every department of literature, and most obstreperously of all in that of verse-making, too often falsely called poetry—could not be heard amid the hubbub.

Among the multitude of rhymers that were benevolently welcomed to the shop of Mr. Robertson, to inscribe their names and their effusions in the pages of *Whistle Binkie*, half-a-dozen at least were worthy to be called poets—not of the highest class, indeed, but far up in the second—and who wrote songs equal to any of those bearing the great name of Robert Burns, and in some instances superior. Burns was a great poet, but he was not a great song-writer—as he probably would have been willing to confess, if he had been questioned on the subject—and owes much of his reputation to such beautiful songs as "There's nae luck aboot the house," "Auld Robin Gray," "Were na my heart light I would dee," "Oh, Nanny, wilt thou gang wi' me?" "Annie Laurie," "The land o' the leal," "My boy Tammie," and a score of others which he never wrote, but which have been, and still are, attributed to him by uninformed people, who imagine that every popular Scottish song was, and must of necessity have been, written by Robert Burns. Among the few of the brighter stars of *Whistle Binkie* that shine preeminently above the crowd that twinkle with inferior light, and with most of whom I was more or less intimately acquainted in Glasgow and Edinburgh, may be cited Alexander Rodger, James Ballantine, Alexander MacLaggan, Alexander Smart, and Robert Gilfillan.

Alexander Rodger was originally a weaver, afterwards a pawnbroker's assistant, a reporter of local news for the *Glasgow Chronicle*, and finally an assistant in the business department of the *Scottish Reformer's Gazette*, under Mr. Peter Mackenzie, a well-known personage in the newspaper circles of Glasgow.

Rodger's songs are alike remarkable for their humour and tenderness, two qualities that are more closely allied than the world is inclined to admit. His best-known effusion, " Behave yourself before folk," abounds in what in Scotland is called " paukieness," a word for which there is no exact English synonym, but which may be paraphrased as a mixture of archness, shrewdness, simplicity and good humour.

> Behave yourself before folk,
> And dinna be sae rude to me,
> As kiss me sae before folk.
> It wadna gie me meikle pain,
> Gin we were seen and heard by nane,
> To tak a kiss or grant you ane,
> But gude sake nae before folk!

The answer of the amorous lad to the remonstrance of the equally amorous lass, is even more spirited and full of humour, and has few equals in Scottish poetry. And both of them drew down, deservedly, the cordial praise of Professor Wilson in the *Noctes Ambrosianæ*. In a similar style and of equal merit is—

> Oh, mither, anybody
> But a creeshie weaver.

The serious songs of Alexander Rodger that

appear in *Whistle Binkie*, are entitled to as much commendation as the jocose ones; and the amorous passion expressed in them never degenerates, as some of the more fervid of the love-songs of Burns do, into the ultra heat of immodesty, or call a blush to the cheek of maidenly innocence or matronly purity.

James Ballantine of Edinburgh, who appears to have become extensively known to his countrymen as a poet in the pages of *Whistle Binkie*, ranks quite as high as, or even higher than, Alexander Rodger. He was originally a journeyman painter and glazier. By dint of good conduct, thrift, and high character, he was enabled in early middle life to establish himself in business on his own account. He ultimately became a prosperous citizen, and was noted for the artistic manufacture of stained-glass windows, in which he carried on a lucrative commerce. He never neglected his business to devote himself to poetry, nor allowed the care of business to dull his taste for poetry, or cool his love for it; but found time, to the last months of his useful and exemplary life, to write such simple, tender, and pure-minded lyrics, as endeared his name to his countrymen for the greater part of half a century. "Ilka blade o' grass keps its ain drap o' dew," "The trysting tree," "Rosie-cheekit apples," "The wee, wee flowers," and scores of others of equal grace and beauty, are familiar to that still numerous class in Scotland, and to that still more numerous class of people of Scottish descent in Canada, the United States, Australia, and New Zealand, who cherish a love for the old Scottish tongue, that recalls to the memory the happy days of their childhood, and whose hearts warm not only to the tartan, and the skirl of the bagpipes, but to the words and accents of the Scottish Lowlands, spoken by their mothers, their playmates, their schoolfellows, and their sweethearts, "in life's morning march when their bosoms were young."

Alexander Smart, the author of *Rambling Rhymes*, was a compositor in the printing office of the venerable but now defunct Edinburgh newspaper, the *Caledonian Mercury*, and wrote far better poetry than many men of superior education and more pretensions who have since sat in professorial chairs at the University, or in the high places of the learned professions.

But all the contributors to *Whistle Binkie*, who gathered under the sheltering wing of Mr. David Robertson, were not men of the labouring classes, although they formed the great majority of his *clientèle*. He doubtless found them to be somewhat expensive as retainers, and had to put his hand oftener in his pocket to relieve the necessities of clever "ne'er do weels" than was always convenient. Some of them, and these not among the least gifted, were as unwisely fond of the whisky-bottle as they were of the unprofitable pursuit of mediocre poetry, and became permanent pensioners on his bounty, or would have done so, unless he had from time to time closed his purse-strings, or doled out to them a scantier guerdon than they imagined themselves entitled to. So, in self-defence, and also, it must be said, to the improvement of the quality and the style, as well as to the increase of the popularity of *Whistle Binkie*, he drew upon the stores of lately deceased writers of a higher rank in life, in which there was no copyright, and upon those of still living poets who demanded and expected no remuneration.

Among the former were William Motherwell, once editor of a Glasgow newspaper, who died some years previously to my residence in that city; and among the latter George Outram, editor of the *Glasgow Herald* (brother of General James Outram of Indian fame, whose statue stands on the Thames Embankment), whose humorous legal song of the "Annuity" is still a favourite in Scotland, wherever convivial lawyers meet together; Charles Lever, the Irish novelist, and last, not least, John Gibson Lockhart, the son-in-law of Sir Walter Scott, and for many years editor of the *Quarterly Review*. Mr. Lockhart was the author of many songs not exactly to be ranked as poetry, one of which, the "Lament for Captain Paton," originally published in *Blackwood's Magazine* in 1819, when the author was scarcely known to fame, continues to flourish in immortal youth in the social circles of Scotland, especially in Glasgow and Edinburgh.

An Interesting Visit.

During my editorship of the *Argus*, and my residence at Ibrox Holme, my friend Robert Carruthers of Inverness, during a month's holiday that he took from business, made my house his home for a week on his way to London. Ibrox Holme was within a couple of miles or less from Pollockshaws; and Mr. Carruthers, having been informed that a daughter of Robert Burns was a resident of that little town, persuaded me to accompany him on a visit to one who stood in such near relationship to Scotland's most famous poet. Her name was Thomson, the wife of a poor weaver, and she had the reputation of being an honest and highly respectable woman, much esteemed by her own class of society. She was the illegitimate daughter of the "Annie" celebrated by Burns in "Corn Rigs and Barley Rigs," one of his most impassioned and popular songs :—

> I hae been blythe wi' comrades dear,
>   I hae been merry drinking,
> I hae been joyfu' gathering gear,
>   I hae been happy thinking.

> But a' the pleasures e'er I saw,
> Tho' three times doubled fairly,
> That happy night was worth them a',
> Amang the rigs o' Barley.

We found Mrs. Thomson without much difficulty, a comely woman upwards of sixty years of age (Burns's poem to her mother was written in 1782, sixty-four years previously), bearing traces of youthful beauty on her calm and interesting countenance, full of homely intelligence and matronly modesty. Her person and her little apartment were scrupulously neat and clean, and she received us without the slightest symptom of embarrassment, or any attempt to ignore the cause that had induced us to visit her. She was meekly proud of her paternity, and did not affect to conceal it, but spoke of the poet with as much admiration for his genius as she might have displayed had she not been so nearly related to him, and never mentioned her mother, feeling, no doubt, with womanly instinct, that, whatever the world might think, it was not for her to think ill of her. She had her troubles like other people, but the principal one seemed to be that her son, Robert Burns Thomson, imagined himself to be a poet, one day to become as celebrated as his grandfather. This idea which had taken possession of his mind, and which he had as yet done nothing to justify, rendered him dissatisfied and idle, unfitted for and averse from his work as a weaver, and made him a sore trouble to both of his parents. Neither he nor his father made his appearance during our visit; but Mr. Carruthers afterwards learned from a leading inhabitant of Pollockshaws, with whom he was acquainted, that the elder Mr. Thomson was well-esteemed in the town as a steady and respectable man. Though nearly forty years have elapsed since I first heard the name of Robert Burns Thomson, and was told by his mother of his high ambition, I have never learned that the seed implanted in his imagination ever germinated into leaf or blossom, much less into fruit, or that he generously forbore making any attempt to eclipse his father's genius by the superior splendour of his own. It is more probable that he remained "a mute inglorious Milton," a dumb Burns, who had no voice to cry, even in the wilderness.

ORIGIN OF THE GLASGOW ATHENÆUM.

I received, when in Glasgow, a flattering invitation from the directors of the Athenæum in Manchester to be present at a grand *soirée* to be held in that city, to meet, among other persons, Dr. Whateley, the Archbishop of Dublin, and Mr.

George Dawson, then celebrated as a lecturer, and the pastor or minister of a Unitarian Church at Birmingham. Several bishops who were invited refused to meet Mr. Dawson, and sent excuses more or less explanatory of their reasons; but Dr. Whateley, larger minded and more tolerant, had no personal objections, and was curious rather than otherwise to see and hear a person of whom so many uncharitable opinions had been expressed. I sat next to Dr. Whateley on the platform. After Mr. Dawson had delivered a set oration, rich in words but poor in ideas, the Archbishop turned to me, and remarked that his reverend brethren on the episcopal bench, had they been present, would have received no shock to their feelings by Mr. Dawson's discourse, except, perhaps, the shock of knowing that so shallow and harmless a person had so large a following in so intellectual a hive of industry as Birmingham. "But then," added Dr. Whateley, "popularity is no test of merit, or Barabbas would not have received the applauses of the crowd at the crucifixion of our Lord."

I was called upon to address the assembly after Dr. Whateley and several other notabilities had spoken; and being unprepared with a speech, and never having imagined that I would be expected to make one, I was utterly at a loss what to say. But a happy thought suddenly shot through my brain. Remembering that the great city of Glasgow, of which I was the representative on the occasion, had not such an educational institution as an Athenæum for the benefit and instruction of the multitudes of young men engaged in business during the day, I began a short address in praise of Manchester for having established, and in dispraise of the lack of public spirit in the still more populous city of Glasgow for not having established, an Athenæum, or any similar institution, for the benefit of its future citizens. My remarks were well received, and fully reported in the newspapers. On my return to Glasgow, I was waited on at the *Argus* office by a deputation of young men interested in the subject, who asked my assistance, both editorially and personally, in promoting the object in view. I cordially agreed to give it; and, as Lord Provost Lumsden's place of business was almost immediately opposite to the *Argus* office, I requested the deputation there and then to accompany me to his Lordship's sanctum, to which, being a privileged person and an intimate friend, I had access at all hours. Within less than a quarter of an hour, having "interviewed" the Lord Provost and explained to him what we wanted, we were authorised to form a provisional committee, under his chairmanship. A list of seven of the principal citizens of Glasgow, personally known to me, was forthwith drawn up. All of these when applied to gave their names unhesitatingly, some of them enthusiastically, and two or three subscribed liberally to the preliminary expenses. A Glasgow Athenæum was the speedy result of the movement thus happily commenced; and, after a lapse of more than forty years, is still in useful and, I believe, vigorous existence.

CHAPTER IX.

BREAKFASTS WITH SAMUEL ROGERS.

No. I.

I FIRST made the acquaintance of Samuel Rogers in 1840, shortly after the publication of a poem entitled " The Hope of the World," of which he had previously expressed his high appreciation and approval. He was at that time in his seventy-eighth year, fifty-two years my senior. He was hale and hearty, and in the full possession of his mental faculties, with a remarkably tenacious and well-stored memory, as befitted the man who had sung so well of its "pleasures," and which he had not only enriched by a wide range of reading, but by an equally wide intercourse with society. He had been personally acquainted with all, or nearly all, the celebrated men and women in art, in arms, in science, in politics, and in literature who had flourished since his early manhood. He was in possession of ample means, derived from his business as a London banker, the head of the firm, though he took but little part in its management. He was an excellent conversationalist; had great reputation as a wit, enhanced perhaps, as is common in the world, by the flavour of cynicism. He had, moreover, the reputation of being the ugliest man in England—some of his detractors said "in the world," but was at the same time, in spite of his alleged ugliness, one of the most agreeable men of his day. He was a great favourite with the ladies, and a devoted admirer of the sex, though he never carried his admiration to the extent of proposing marriage, but once only, when he was in his eighty-fifth year. It was then too late, if either marriage or courtship were concerned, for young ladies or old ones to look upon him with any other personal feelings but those of ridicule or pity, though literary admiration was still open to them.

He was celebrated for the intellectual breakfasts to which, since the beginning of the century, he had been in the habit of inviting at least three, at most five or six, of the celebrities, male or female, of the day. The hour of breakfast was 10; and so agreeable and fascinating was the conversation of the host, that the repast seldom ended before noon, and sometimes extended so late as 1 o'clock. He insisted that breakfast was a much more social meal than dinner; that there was less of ceremony and more of unrestrained intellectual intercourse in the morning than there could be in the evening; that the faculties were fresher, the memory clearer, the play of fancy more exuberant and spontaneous than at the later hours of the day, when mental labour, or perhaps care, had more or less dulled or cast a shade over the mind. He was a veritable " autocrat of the breakfast-table," and might have been so designated had my excellent friend Dr. Oliver Wendell Holmes lived in London at the time and been acquainted with the habits and characteristics of Mr. Rogers. Before I had ever seen him, I had formed an image in my mind in accordance with the spiteful epigrams that Lord Byron and others had written upon him, and was agreeably disappointed with the reality of his personal presence and the kindly suavity of his manners. He was certainly not handsome, and never could have been so; but just as certainly he was not ugly in the disagreeable sense of the word, while his conversation differed in the pleasantest manner from that of many among his contemporaries, from not assuming the wearisome shape of a monologue. He not only talked, but allowed others to talk. On the first occasion that I enjoyed the hospitality of Mr. Rogers at his favourite meal, the only other guests were Thomas Campbell, the author of *The Pleasures of Hope*, and Mr. Thomas Gaspey, the author of *The Lol-*

lards, *The Monks of Leadenhall*, and nearly a score of other novels. The title of Mr. Campbell's poem had been suggested by that of Mr. Rogers, published some years previously, as that in its turn had been suggested by *The Pleasures of the Imagination*, by Mark Akenside, written in the reign of Queen Anne. It was no small gratification to me to meet two such poets as *The Pleasures of Memory* and *The Pleasures of Hope* at one time, and to interchange ideas with them. I carefully noted down ere the day had passed the points of the conversation that took place. The discourse was mainly literary, and turned principally upon the merits of Pope as a poet. They were rated very highly by both of the speakers—to my mind rather too highly—for though I could not but admire the finished grace, the wit, the wisdom, and the exquisite though somewhat monotonous music of his verse, I could not but deplore the want of imagination, even while admitting the abundant fancy of the writer. Rogers admired Pope for the terse epigrammatic form which his wit and his wisdom assumed in the *Essay on Man*, in his *Essay on Criticism*, and in the *Epistles*, as well as the pungent force of his satire in the *Dunciad*; while I admired him more particularly, as I continue to do, for the beautiful rhythm and melody of his versification, and still more enthusiastically for the *Dying Christian to his Soul*, which Mr. Campbell agreed with me in considering a gem of unrivalled and unsurpassable beauty which had not its superior in any language, in any era of literature.

Mr. Gaspey was no poet, but a most pertinacious rhymer and manufacturer of facetiæ and epigrams in verse, and a punster of all but unrivalled facility and fertility, surpassing in that respect even Mr. Rogers himself, was not quite so enthusiastic in praise of Pope as Rogers and Campbell were. He took exceptions to the frequently prosaic nature of many of Pope's most admired passages, and to his more than occasional lapses into downright bathos. Among other passages which he cited, to prove that he did not take exception unjustly, was the couplet in praise of his particular friend Lord Mansfield, the celebrated Judge—

> Graced as thou art with all the power of words,
> So known, so honoured, in the House of Lords.

" Nothing," he said, " could be more ' bathetic.' "

"Bathetic!" interposed Mr. Campbell, "bathetic is a good word; like mobled queen, it is good, very good; did you invent it?"

"No," replied Mr. Gaspey; "I wish I had the honour. It is not to be found in Johnson's Dictionary; neither is bathos, which is a singular omission, considering that the word was in common use in his time."

"I think Coleridge uses *bathetic*," said Mr.

Rogers. "There was a famous parody made on Pope's lines, I forget by whom—

> 'Persuasion tips his tongue whene'er he talks,
> And he has chambers in the King's Bench Walks!'"

"The parody," I ventured to remark, "was admirable, and infinitely preferable to the thing parodied. I think, with Mr. Gaspey, that with all his beauties, Pope, though, like Homer, he sometimes nodded, nodded much more frequently than he ought to have done, if he claimed to be admitted among the real immortals. Can anything be poorer as verse, not to say poetry, than when he speaks of Hampton Court Palace as a place

> 'Where thou, great Anna, whom three realms obey,
> Dost sometimes counsel take, and sometimes tea?'"

"It is easy to find flaws in a great writer," said Mr. Rogers; "and it requires no particular sagacity, and only a more than common fund of ill-nature, to be a critic. What I take to be the main fault of Pope is that he wrote too much, and did not take time to polish and to correct."

I may here observe that Mr. Rogers was not guilty of the fault of writing too much, for he wrote very little, and that not always of the best. He was fastidious to a fault, and wrote with great difficulty, correcting and re-correcting with painful elaboration whatever he wrote, either in prose or verse, sometimes spending a week or more in the composition of a single sentence. He once showed me a note which he had written to Lord Melbourne—at that time Prime Minister—suggesting that he should grant a pension on the Civil List to the Rev. Mr. Carey, the translator of Dante. The note consisted but of a dozen lines, perhaps even less; but he assured me that it had occupied his time and care for a full fortnight, and that he hoped he had succeeded in rendering it so compact and so forcible, as well as so elegant, as to defy ingenuity to omit a word from, or add a word to it, or even to change a single word or phrase for a better one. He read it over to me as an example of what I and everyone else ought to aim at in epistolary, and, indeed, in all literary composition. I remember the concluding paragraph of this painfully-produced epistle, which was: "But perhaps your Lordship has already granted the pension. If so, I envy you!"

The conversation speedily diverged from the poetry of Pope to that of Byron, whom Mr. Rogers cited as a glaring offender in the sin of writing too much and too fast. "He died at less than half my age—only thirty-six, while I am seventy-eight; and he wrote ten times as much as I have done."

I ventured, though timidly, to remark that it was a loss to literature that Byron had not lived to write a great deal more; that his genius, so far from being exhausted, was in its fruitful maturity of power and splendour; and that many better things than any he had yet written might have been expected from his pen, had he not been cut off so prematurely. Mr. Rogers, by the expression on his face, did not seem to take my opinion very kindly; but he merely said in reply: "You are young, and consequently you incline to be enthusiastic. It is a pardonable fault in youth; but as you grow older, I think your opinion of Byron will tone down to a juster and calmer estimate of his genius."

It should be observed, in explanation of the feeling entertained by the elder to the younger poet, that, although they had once been on terms of intimacy and friendship, a coolness almost amounting to enmity had, from some cause or other never sufficiently explained, sprung up between them. Byron had dedicated to him, in 1813, his beautiful poem of " The Giaour," " in admiration of his genius, in respect for his character, and in gratitude for his friendship"; had written on a blank leaf of the *Pleasures of Memory*, and afterwards published, a short poem addressed to its author, of which the opening lines were:—

> Absent and present, still to thee,
>   My friend, what magic spells belong!
> As all can tell who share, like me,
>   In turn thy converse and thy song!

Byron had also, in the bitter but clever satire of "English Bards and Scotch Reviewers," gone out of his way to praise his friend as "melodious Rogers," and to declare that the *Pleasures of Memory* was one "of the most beautiful didactic poems in the English language." But a change had come over the spirit of his dream before the year 1818, and he had libelled even more vigorously than he had formerly extolled, not only the poetry, but, what was worse and more offensive, the personal appearance and moral character of his former friend. It must be said that nothing could be in more execrably bad taste, or more venomously spiteful, than the lines, descriptive of the countenance of Rogers, which he had written, and allowed to be circulated in manuscript among his private friends.

* * * *

Mouth which marks the envious scorner,
With a scorpion in each corner,
Turning its quick tail to sting you
In the place that most may wring you ;
Eyes of lead-like hue, and gummy ;
Carcass picked out from some mummy ;
Bowels (but they were forgotten,
Save the liver, and that's rotten !)

* * * *

Vampire, ghost, or ghoul—what is it?—
I would walk ten miles to miss it.

Rogers would indeed have been possessed of a temper approaching the angelic, if he had been able to entertain his former feelings of personal regard for a man who had been treacherous and changeable enough to write thus of him, without known cause of offence, the more especially as the injudicious admirers of Byron, after his death, in 1824, had given the lines to the world. To have been caricatured by such comparatively small fry as Theodore Hook, Horace Smith, and others of the like calibre, might have been borne with as much equanimity as that with which most people bear the stings of a mosquito; but the blow of a cudgel, wielded by such a literary giant as Lord Byron, was certain to cause a wound in a less sensitive organism than that of Samuel Rogers. Once, when I ventured to extol the fire of Lord Byron's poetry, Rogers replied: "Yes; he had fire, no doubt; but it was hell-fire!" On this occasion Mr. Campbell—who himself had written but very little, though that little was of the highest merit—agreed with Mr. Rogers that Byron was much too prolix, especially in *Don Juan*.

"But *Don Juan*," I said, "was of necessity prolix. No one can write a novel in verse, in short epigrammatic sentences. Undue condensity is fatal to the charm of any narrative, unless it be an episode in the main design—such, for instance, as the beautiful description of the two fathers and their two sons in the shipwreck so finely described in *Don Juan*."

"Which Moore," said Mr. Rogers, "declares to have been taken almost verbatim from a prose narrative in a small book entitled *The Shipwreck of the Juno*, and which in his opinion was, in its plain grandeur, if not sublimity, far superior to Byron's poetry."

"It was written," I interposed, "by my granduncle, William Mackay, the second mate of the ship, published towards the close of the last century, and read by Lord Byron when he was a school-boy."

None of the company had ever seen the book, which has long been out of print. I subjoin the passage, that the admirers of Byron may compare it with the beautiful lines in *Don Juan*, and adjudge the palm, if they please to do so, either to the poet or the sailor, as their taste or judgment may dictate.

The survivors of the wreck of the *Juno*, off the coast of Africa, had, it may be premised, taken refuge on a raft, when the story commences :—

Mr. Wade's boy, a stout and healthy lad, died early, and almost without a groan; whilst another of the same age, but of less promising appearance, held out much longer. The fate of these unfortunate boys differed also in another respect, highly deserving of notice. Their fathers were both in the fore-top when the boys were taken ill. Mr. Wade, hearing of his son's illness, answered with indifference that "he could do nothing for him," and left him to his fate. The other father, when the accounts reached him, hurried down, and, watching for a favourable moment, crawled on all-fours along the weather-gunwale to his son, who was in the mizzen rigging. By that time only three or four planks of the quarter-deck remained, just over the weather-quarter gallery, and to this spot the unhappy man led his son, making him fast to the rail to prevent his being washed away. Whenever the boy was seized with a fit of retching, the father lifted him up and wiped away the foam from his lips; and if a shower came, he made him open his mouth to receive the drops, or gently squeezed them into it from a rag. In this affecting situation both remained four or five days, till the boy expired. The unfortunate parent, as if unwilling to believe the fact, raised the body, gazed wistfully at it, and, when he could no longer entertain any doubt, watched it in silence till it was carried off by the sea; then, wrapping himself in a piece of canvas, sunk down and rose no more, though he must have lived two days longer, as we judged from the quivering of his limbs when a wave broke over him. This scene made an impression even on us, whose feelings were, in a manner, dead to the world, and almost to ourselves, and to whom the sight of misery was now become habitual.

A few days after our conversation on the subject I lent the book to Mr. Rogers, who returned it with a note expressive of his full concurrence in Moore's verdict.

A few words in reference to Mr. Gaspey, whose many novels are now completely forgotten—but which enjoyed a certain celebrity when they first appeared—may not be uninteresting. He is now principally remembered by a punning epitaph on the leg of the Marquis of Anglesey, buried at Waterloo, at which famous battle he lost it. The epigram or epitaph bristled with puns, for the making of which Mr. Gaspey was notorious. I remember but two of them, turning upon the fact that it was not only a leg but a *calf* that was buried; not only a body but a sole (*soul*).

Mr. Gaspey, who was my colleague in the editorial department of the, at that time, leading journal, the *Morning Chronicle*, often had occasion to write to me, and almost invariably mistook my Christian name. He sometimes addressed me as William, or George, or Robert, or Henry, but never by any chance as Charles. I thought the mistake was not so much the result of carelessness as of design; and to cure him of it, whichever it might be, I played the same game with him, and, instead of addressing him as Thomas—his real name—wrote to him as Benjamin, or Peter, or Alexander, and once as Obadiah. But it was all in vain. At last I addressed him as Nebuchadnezzar Gaspey, Esq. The broad hint was taken, and I became "Charles" in all the letters that he subsequently addressed to me.

Breakfasts with Samuel Rogers.
No. II.

It was always a literary treat to breakfast with Mr. Rogers. He had the happy art of knowing how to choose his " company " to introduce celebrities to celebrities, and to bring congenial people together, to keep them in good humour, and to send them away well pleased with their entertainer and with each other. To mix the company well at a small party, where you expect the conversation to flow pleasantly as well as intellectually, wisely as well as wittily, seriously as well as jocosely—the whole to form one homogeneous compound—is as difficult a task and as rarely accomplished as the confection of a salad sufficient to please the taste of an epicure. Mr. Rogers had this faculty in perfection, and had cultivated it from his youth upward with ever-increasing success. He had every advantage on his side—ample fortune, high position, brilliant reputation, and the entrance to the best society. He had a clear mind, an even temper, that nothing could seriously ruffle, and a wonderfully retentive memory, that took account of small things as well as great. His wit, which was unlaboured and spontaneous, was without the slightest taint of vulgarity, though it was not, it must be confessed, without the flavour of real or assumed cynicism.

On the occasion when I was invited to meet Lord Glenelg, Lord Robertson, Mr. Carruthers, and Mr. W. J. Fox, the conversation was mainly critical and literary. Lord Glenelg—a man who had long passed the prime of life, was a poet as well as a statesman; Mr. Robert Carruthers was the editor of the *Inverness Courier*, an acute and kindly critic, and one of the best *raconteurs* that ever enlivened society; Lord Robertson was also a poet, a quarterly reviewer, and one of the judges of the Court of Session in Edinburgh, and Mr. Fox was a member of Parliament, a writer of political articles for the *Morning Chronicle*, and a colleague of Messrs. Cobden and Bright in the then active agitation for the repeal of the Corn-Laws.

Lord Glenelg, who had recently been raised to the peerage, had been previously known in the British House of Commons as the Right Honourable Charles Grant, the member for the County of Inverness. He had some reputation as a poet, having published, in connection with his brother, Mr. Robert Grant, a collection of hymns and other sacred poems. But he was better known as a politician, and for his efforts in Parliament to modify the obnoxious Corn Laws at a time when the Anti-Corn Law League had never been heard of. Mr. Carruthers, as editor of the principal newspaper in the county, which Mr. Charles Grant had represented in Parliament, had often had occasion to write of him in his public capacity, but had never met him since his elevation to the House of Lords. He, therefore, took care, by apostrophising him constantly as "My Lord," to let his Lordship know that he was fully aware of the rank to which he had attained. He had addressed him as "My Lord," and "Your Lordship" at least a dozen times, when Mr. Rogers, who appeared to be somewhat impatient at the unnecessary reiteration of a title, to which he attached little or no importance, addressing himself to Mr. Carruthers across the table, said suddenly, but very quietly, "Don't keep My Lording him, Mr. Carruthers. He's much better than a Lord. He's a very good fellow."

Mr. Carruthers appeared somewhat confused at the rebuff, and Lord Glenelg, coming to the rescue, adroitly turned the conversation to the new poem of Thomas Campbell, entitled "The Pilgrim of Glencoe," which had very recently made its appearance.

"I have the highest respect and admiration," he said, "for the genius of him who wrote such noble poems as 'Lochiel's Warning,' 'The Battle of the Baltic,' 'Ye Mariners of England,' and 'Hohenlinden,' to say nothing of the 'Pleasures of Hope'; but I cannot help regretting that he should have written the 'Pilgrim of Glencoe.'"

"Why regret that he should have written it," said Mr. Rogers, "if it gave him pleasure? Pleasures are not so plentiful in this world. Perhaps it is to be regretted that he published it; but why should anyone regret that he wrote it?"

"Exactly so," said Mr. Carruthers. "Poets should write as the larks and the nightingales sing, because they cannot help it. But why, oh! why, should they publish when all the divine afflatus has evaporated, and the fires of imagination burn dim, if they burn at all?"

"I don't like to criticise a brother poet, who has deserved so well of his contemporaries and of posterity," interposed Mr. Rogers, "lest I should be accused of professional jealousy. So I will say nothing. Besides, I have not read the poem."

"I have no fear on that score," said Mr. Carruthers, "and, moreover, I *have* read the poem, inclined, if I could, to form a favourable judgment upon it. I never wrote a line of verse in my life, except when I was a school-boy. I can, therefore, speak my mind freely, even with regard to so good a poet as Thomas Campbell, if I catch him nodding. Even Homer nods at times, and it is not surprising that Mr. Campbell, in his old age, should do so also. Where, for instance, can any poetry be found in such couplets as those that are scattered through the pages of the 'Pilgrim of Glencoe,' in plenteous profusion, and that have dwelt in my memory ever since I read them?

> 'At last a sheep dog's bark informed his ear,
> Some human habitation might be near.'

Surely, the prosaic and the commonplace in verse were never more flagrantly exhibited! Or in this equally egregious couplet:

> 'The house, no common, sordid, shieling cot,
> Spoke inmates of a comfortable lot.'

And this is, perhaps, the most intolerable example of what Douglas Jerrold calls 'verse—and worse':

> 'And feeling interest in the veteran's lot,
> Created him a sergeant on the spot.'"

"Almost incredibly prosaic," said Lord Glenelg. "If Byron were alive now, and had to write the 'English Bards and Scotch Reviewers,' he would not, after the perusal of such lines, call upon Campbell, as he did before, to come forth and give his talents scope, or ask who should aspire, if Campbell ceased to hope, but might vary the strain, and exclaim:

> 'Desist, O Campbell! fold thy weary wing,
> Talk if thou wilt; but cease, oh! cease to sing!'"

"I saw Mr. Campbell," said Mr. Carruthers, "at his chambers in Lincoln's Inn Fields, when I called upon him, by invitation, and walked with him to the Clarence Club, in Waterloo Place, which is his favourite haunt. He told me, as we went along, a good story of himself and a worthy old Scotch lady, whom he had met on a recent visit to Ayrshire. 'I happened,' he said, 'to go into a bookseller's shop in Kilmarnock, when the bookseller, as I entered, whispered something over the counter to a portly and comely old lady, who was making a small purchase of sealing-wax and notepaper. "Lord save us!" she replied in an audible whisper. "Ye dinna mean it!" "It's true, I tell ye," said the bookseller, also in a whisper. The old lady turned toward me, and said, not without betraying a slight embarrassment: "An' sae ye 're the great Thomas Campbell, are ye? I 'm vera prood to meet ye, and did na think when I left hame in the mornin' that sic a great honor was to befa' me." I do not think that I blushed, though perhaps I ought to have done so, but I suppose I looked confused or flattered, or both. But confusion took entire possession, as the worthy old soul continued: "There 's na' a man in Ayrshire that has the great skill ye hae, Mr. Campbell, and I shall be greatly obleeged to ye, if ye will come and see my coo, before ye leave this part o' the country, an' let me know if ye can do onything for her. She 's a young beastie, and a guid beastie, and I should na like to lose her." It appears that there is an eminent veterinary surgeon, or cow doctor in the neighbouring county of Dumfries, whose name is also Thomas Campbell, and that she mistook me for this celebrated and doubtless highly respectable person!'"

"Well," said Lord Glenelg, attempting a mild joke, "if the good woman had not read the 'Pleasures of Hope,' and knew nothing of the author, she had, at all events, experienced them with regard to her cow. She had the pleasure of hoping that Mr. Campbell would restore the animal to its accustomed health."

We none of us could laugh or even smile at this attempted pleasantry. Mr. Campbell, however, could afford to be amused. He was not always so unfortunate as to be unrecognised or unhonoured by his countrymen, though an old woman here and there might never have heard of him, and I narrated to the company that, not many days previous to this conversation, I had met him in the street, on his return from Woolwich, where he had been to witness the launch of a great man-of-war. "The authorities of the Dockyard," said he, "knew that I was coming, and had given orders that, as soon as I made my appearance, preparatory to mounting the side of the great vessel, the band on board should strike up the air of 'The Campbells are Coming,' the spirited march of the Clan Campbell. Guess my surprise and pleasure to receive such a compliment. I consider it was the greatest honour I ever received in my life!" And, as he said this, his usually pallid face was suffused with a roseate glow of satisfaction, and his usually bright eyes sparkled still brighter with delight.

"We are all of us more or less vain," said Lord Robertson. "My late colleague in the Court of

Session, and who was known to all Scotland as John Clark—afterwards Lord Eldin—was displeased to be mistaken for Lord Eldon, the once celebrated Lord High Chancellor of England, a man whom he considered to be very much his inferior, and against whom, moreover, he entertained a slight grudge for having snubbed him for speaking with a Scottish accent. John Clark's Scotch was peculiarly broad and racy, and he took no pains to correct it. Pleading in the House of Lords before the Lord Chancellor, on some water bill that excited considerable interest in Edinburgh, he several times spoke of the *watter* as running in a particular direction. 'Pray, Mr. Clark,' asked Lord Eldon, interrupting him, 'is it the custom in your country to spell water with two *ts*?' 'No, my Lord,' replied John, 'but it's the custom to spell *manners* wi' twa *ns*.' Mr. Clark, after his elevation to the Bench, when he had corrected the mistake of some one who had called him Lord Eldon instead of Lord Eldin, was asked what was the difference between him and the English Lord. He replied, 'Difference! There's nae difference. It's all my eye (*i*).'"

Lord Robertson was a far more polished and accomplished man, though not so able a lawyer as Lord Eldin. He was more commonly called "Peter Robertson" than Lord Robertson (Peter is the familiar and affectionate synonym for Patrick), and was a universal favourite among the wits of

Edinburgh. At that time wits were more plentiful than they have since become in that intellectual and then convivial city. The aforesaid wits still retained their love for the old vernacular, and were not ashamed to speak in the broadest Scotch, as they have become in our day, when many young Edinburgh cockneys affect the lisp and the drawl of Londoners, and boast, as if it were a thing to be proud of, that they cannot read the poems of Robert Burns, or the romances of Walter Scott, with any degree of pleasure, on account of the difficulty they find in understanding the dialect.

In London, whither "Peter" was often summoned on legal business, he was as great a favourite in literary, legal, and social circles as he was in Edinburgh. He was particularly intimate with John Gibson Lockhart, the son-in-law of Sir Walter Scott, and for more than a quarter of a century the editor of the *Quarterly Review*. Their friendship was like that of two rollicking college students, as full of fun and mischief as it was of real regard. "Peter" had published a poem entitled "Italy," which was neither very good nor very bad, though it inclined to the shady side of mediocrity. Lockhart was asked to review or have it reviewed in the *Quarterly*. This, however, the great critic was unwilling to do. First, because if he had reviewed it conscientiously, on its merits, he might have lost his friend by his candour; or, if he had praised it up to the author's expectations, he would have done injustice to the proprietor of the powerful journal which he conducted, and to his own high reputation as a critic. He made up his mind, therefore, that the wisest course to follow would be not to notice the book at all. But he, nevertheless, wrote an article full of cleverness and mischief, a scathing review in fact, exceeding in bitterness of denunciation the famous review which Lord Brougham was supposed to have written in the *Edinburgh* on Lord Byron's juvenile poems. This article was put into type, one copy only of it was struck off, and inserted as if it were a part of the next number of the *Quarterly*, and duly forwarded to " Peter " in Edinburgh. It was said to have contained the famous epigram or epitaph on his Lordship, which is still well remembered in Edinburgh, though seldom quoted correctly. I have heard it constantly repeated, and seen it as frequently printed :

> Here lies the paper Lord and poet Peter
> Who broke the laws of God and man and meter.

" Paper lord," it should be stated, is the epithet often employed to designate the judges of the Court of Session, who are only lords by courtesy. The epigram, as originally written by Lockhart, ran thus :

> Here lies the Christian, Judge, and Poet Peter,
> Who broke the laws of God, and man, and meter.

This version is far superior in terseness to its unauthorised substitute, in alleging that the Christian broke the laws of God, the Judge the laws of man, and the Poet the laws of meter.

How long poor "Peter" was suffered to remain under the impression that this article had been published in the usual way, has not been recorded. Perhaps he suspected all along that it was a hoax on the part of his friend Lockhart, and did not vex his soul on account of it. But, if he believed, for ever so short a time, that it was genuine, his feelings must have been anything but kindly toward the merciless reviewer. If that particular number of the *Quarterly* be still in existence, and should turn up at a book auction, some enthusiastic bibliophile and collector, with more money than wit, would doubtless give a fabulous sum for it.

Lord Robertson was a very stout and portly man, as full of good humour as he was of wit. He was at the same time a most enthusiastic ultra-Scotsman, and thought Scotland to be the grandest country, and Scotsmen the bravest, noblest, and cleverest people in the world. In this respect, his prejudices were sometimes thought to be assumed, so great was the intensity of their unreasonableness. An amusing instance is still recorded in the after-dinner gossip of Edinburgh society—when the toddy has begun to circulate—of Lord Peter's reckless assertion of the superiority of his countrymen to the English, in every possible respect. It happened, during one of his periodical visits to the metropolis on legal business, after a visit to Covent Garden Theatre with a friend, that they both betook themselves for supper and refreshment to Offley's, a then noted tavern in the immediate neighbourhood. Offley's was almost as celebrated in its time as Will's and Button's coffee-houses had been in the days of Steele and Addison, as the resort of wits, authors, journalists, actors, and men about town. It was nearly the last of its class, and has long ceased to exist, having been superseded upwards of thirty years ago by the palatial clubs of Pall Mall and St. James's.

A discussion arose among the company—by whom provoked it is needless to inquire—on the many eminent Scotchmen who, from the days of King James I. till now, had come to London in search of fame and fortune, and had succeeded in acquiring both, very often defeating in the race many English competitors who had started with far superior advantages. Many and indeed most of such Scotsmen had no other aids to climb than their own stout hearts, lofty ambition, and indomitable pluck, and yet had reached the summits of worldly advancement and public usefulness. "Peter" took part warmly in the discussion, and asserted his opinions in a very dictatorial style, and was particularly truculent towards one particularly meek and logical old gentleman, who did battle for the superiority of Englishmen in some respects to Scotsmen, which Peter would by no means allow, and for their equality in point of talent with Scotsmen generally, which Peter would not concede, even for the sake of argument. Driven from point to point, from position to position, by his overbearing adversary, the gentle Englishman at last ventured to say, "At least, Sir, if you will not allow any other merit to England or to Englishmen, you will admit that England is a *larger* country than Scotland?" "No, I won't," roared Peter, in a tone of triumph. "If all our magnificent mountains, the pride and glory of our country, were squeezed down into plains as flat as Lincolnshire, Scotland would be a much larger country than England." The Englishman gave up the contest, apparently consoling himself in his discomfiture by the reflection that his opponent was pot-valiant, and that wine or whisky supplied him alike with his words and his arguments, but was unable to supply him with facts, or the logical use of them. He thought possibly that, after all, his Scottish friend would not like to be taken *au serieux*, if he were quite sober, and that his opinions after breakfast-time on the morrow would not be quite in accordance with those that were uppermost in his mind after supper.

Of the four Scotsmen who were present, Lord

Glenelg, Mr. Carruthers, Lord Robertson, and myself, the only one who spoke with the slightest accent that could possibly betray him as having learned to speak on the north of the Tweed was Lord Robertson. He was highly pleased with the judgment of Mr. Fox, when the latter happened to remark that the Scottish "language," as his Lordship spoke it, was particularly agreeable to his ears. "You are quite right," said Peter, " in calling it a language, and not, as the English call it, a mere dialect or idiom. It is, in truth, the purest old English, as English was spoken by the people, and not by the literary class, in the days of Wiclif. The ancient and satirical poem of the 'Vision of Piers Ploughman,' written in the purest English of the pre-Chaucerian era, cannot now be understood by Englishmen without the aid of a glossary, but is perfectly intelligible to a Scottish peasant."

"I must confess," said Mr. Rogers, "that 'Piers Ploughman' is nearly unintelligible to me. It is not without difficulty that I can even read Chaucer, whose writings I am far from considering the well of English undefiled which it has become the fashion to call them. I find that some knowledge of French is a great aid to the comprehension of Chaucer."

"So do I," said Mr. Fox, "The fact is that the English language, as now spoken and written, is the language of literature and of London, and that real old English, the language of 'Piers Ploughman,' of Wiclif's Bible, and the Bible of King James's translators, only remains among the common people, and in the provinces, from which it is fast disappearing."

"I think," said Lord Glenelg, "that the Bible and not Chaucer is 'the well of pure English undefiled,' and that English as now written and spoken by educated and literary people is one of the most modern languages of Europe. Shakespeare himself is becoming to a large extent obsolete, and if the men of his day could return to the world, it is very doubtful, I think, if they could thoroughly understand and appreciate the writings of Dr. Johnson or Lord Macaulay."

"The bulk of the people," said Mr. Fox, "manage to express all their wants and wishes, their hopes and fears, with less than a thousand words in the vocabulary. The English of our dictionaries contains at least fifty thousand, and is continually receiving accretions from Latin, Greek, and French. When the superfine ship-lieutenant, fresh from college, called out to a sailor, 'Extinguish the nocturnal luminary,' the sailor understood him no more than if he had spoken Hebrew or Cherokee; but when the boatswain, coming to the rescue, desired the man to 'douse the glim,' the immediate response was 'Aye! aye! Sir!' So, in like manner, when the pedantic Dr. Johnson declared that he would indulge in a 'post-prandial promenade,' he failed to make himself understood, until he had translated the affected phrase into the plain English of 'an after-dinner walk.' The heart of the English multitude is not to be touched, nor its brain convinced, by the too exclusive use of the classical and modern elements of the language."

Upon this subject all the guests of Mr. Rogers, and Mr. Rogers himself, were thoroughly agreed.

Mr. Carruthers, who resided in the little town of Inverness, sometimes called by its inhabitants the "Capital of the Highlands," was often blamed by his intimate friends for hiding his great abilities in so small a sphere, and not launching boldly forth upon the great sea of London, which they considered a more suitable arena for the exercise of his talents and the acquirement of fame and fortune by the pursuits of literature. But he was not to be persuaded. He loved quiet; he loved the grand and solemn scenery of his beautiful native country; and perhaps, if all the truth be told, he preferred to be a great man in a provincial town to being a comparatively small one in a mighty metropolis. In Inverness he shone as a star of the first magnitude. In London, though his light might have been as great, it would have failed to attract equal recognition. In addition to all these considerations, the atmosphere of great cities did not agree with his health; and the fine, free, fresh, invigorating air of the sea and the mountains was necessary to his physical well-being. This he enjoyed to the fullest extent in Inverness. The editing of the weekly journal, which supplied him with greater pecuniary results than were necessary to supply the moderate wants of himself and his household, left him abundant leisure for other and more congenial work. He soon made his mark in literature, and became noted, not only for the vigour and elegance of his style, but for his remarkable accuracy of statement, even in the minutest details of his literary and historical work.

He edited, with copious and accurate notes, an edition of Pope, and of Johnson's and Boswell's *Tour to the Hebrides*, and greatly added to the value of those interesting books by notes, descriptive and anecdotal, of all the places and persons mentioned in it. He also contributed largely to the valuable *Cyclopædia of English Literature*, edited by Messrs. Chambers of Edinburgh; besides contributing Essays and Criticisms to many popular journals and reviews published in London and Edinburgh. He was one of the most admirable story-tellers of his time, or, indeed, of any time, had a most retentive and abundantly furnished memory, and never missed the point of a joke, or overlaid it with inappropriate or unnecessary words or phrases. His fund of Scottish anecdotes, brimful of wit and humour, was apparently inexhaustible, and his stories followed each other with such rapidity as to suggest to the mind of the listener the lines of Samuel Rogers—

> Couched in the hidden chambers of the brain
> Our thoughts are linked by many a hidden chain.
> Awake but one, and lo, what myriads rise!
> Each stamps its image as the other flies.

The good things, for which Mr. Carruthers was famous, were not derived from books, but from actual intercourse with men; and, if collected, would have formed a more diverting repertory of Scottish wit and humour than has ever yet been given to the world. He was continually urged to prepare them for publication, and continually promised to undertake the work, but always postponed it until he had more leisure than he possessed at the time of promising. But that day, unfortunately, never came. If it had come, the now celebrated work of Dean Ramsay on the same subject might have been eclipsed or altogether superseded in the literary market.

His local knowledge and the fascination of his conversation were so great, that the notabilities of the literary or political world who visited Inverness usually came armed with letters of introduction to Mr. Carruthers, or made themselves known to him during their stay in the Highlands. The first time that I travelled so far north, through the magnificent chain of fresh-water lochs that are connected with each other by the Caledonian Canal, a leading citizen of Inverness, who was a fellow-passenger on the trip, seeing I was a stranger, took the pains to point out to me all the objects of interest on the way, and to name the mountains, the straths, the glens, and the waterfalls on either side. On arrival at Inverness, he directed my attention to the mountains and eminences visible from the boat when nearing the pier.

"That," said he, " is Ben Wyvis, the highest mountain in Ross-shire; that is *Tom-na-Hurich*, or 'the Hill of the Fairies'; that is Craig Phadrig, once a vitrified fort of the original Celtic inhabitants; and that "—pointing to a gentleman in the foremost rank of the spectators on the landing-place—" is Mr. Carruthers, the editor of the *Courier*."

Mr. Carruthers used to relate, with much glee, that he escorted the great Sir Robert Peel over the battle-field of Culloden, and pointed out to him the graves of the Highland warriors who had been slain in that fatal encounter. Seeing a shepherd watching his flocks, feeding on the scanty herbage of the moor, he stepped aside to inform the man of the celebrity of his companion. The information fell upon inattentive ears.

"Did you never hear of Sir Robert Peel?" inquired Mr. Carruthers.

" Never *dud* (did)," replied the shepherd.

" Is it possible you never heard of him? He was once Prime Minister of England."

" Weel!" replied the shepherd, " he seems to be a very respectable man!"

On another occasion he escorted Mr. Serjeant Talfourd and his friend, Mr. John Forster—who was also the intimate friend of Mr. Charles Dickens —over the same scene, and was fond of telling the story that the same shepherd shouted suddenly to another at a short distance on the moor, " *Ian! Ian!*" Serjeant Talfourd, who was the author of the once celebrated tragedy of *Ion*, with a bland smile of triumph and satisfaction on his face, turned to Mr. Forster, laid his hand upon his breast, and said : " Forster, this *is* fame!" He did not know that *Ian* was the Gaelic for " John," and that the man was merely calling to his distant friend by his Christian name.

Among the odd experiences of the little town in which he passed his days, Mr. Carruthers related that a gentleman who had made a large fortune in India retired to pass the evening of his days in his native town. Finding the time hang heavy on his hands, and being of an active mind, he established a newspaper, which he edited himself, and managed to incur much unpopularity by his personal attacks on prominent people. He grew tired of it, after two or three years, and discontinued it suddenly, without a word of notice or explanation. With equal suddenness he resumed its publication, without any previous notice of his intention to do so, and addressed his readers, in his first editorial: "Since the publication of our last paper, nothing of importance has occurred in the political world." Nothing had occurred of more importance than a French Revolution, the dethronement and flight of a King, and convulsions in almost every country in Europe, Great Britain excepted.

Mr. Carruthers, who had previously received the degree of Doctor of Laws, died in 1878, full of years and honours, regretted and esteemed by all the North of Scotland, and by a wide circle of friends and admirers in every part of the world where English literature is appreciated, and Scotsmen retain a fond affection for their native country, and the men whose lives and genius reflect honour upon it.

BREAKFASTS WITH SAMUEL ROGERS.
No. III.

On a subsequent occasion when I breakfasted with Mr. Rogers, the guests were the Rev. Sidney Smith, the celebrated wit and Canon of St. Paul's, Daniel O'Connell, the great Irish agitator, then in the plenitude of his political fame, Sir Augustus D'Este, the son of the Duke of Sussex, and consequently grandson of King George III., and Mr. Harrison Ainsworth, then in his early celebrity as a popular novelist.

The Rev. Sidney Smith was a particular friend and crony of Mr. Rogers, and a constant visitor at his hospitable board, to which he was attracted by a congeniality of sentiment in literature, in politics, and, it must be added, in brilliant cynicism of judgment on men, manners, and things in general. Many good stories were current in the clubs and in society of his witticisms and *bons mots*, most of which have by this time evaporated, and gone as hopelessly into empty space as the steam wreaths of the locomotive engines of the period. The reverend gentleman was certainly a wit; some people called him a wag—a very objectionable epithet to apply to anybody; so objectionable, in my estimation, that I ventured to tell Mr. Rogers, that morning, after the reverend gentleman had taken his departure (which he did rather early), that I had coined or invented a word which I thought more appropriate to the gentlemen who made it their business to provide amusement for the society which they frequented, than "wag," which had a flavour of vulgarity or coarseness about it. " Punster," I said, "is universally recognised as a permissible and legitimate word, and why not 'funster' ? A man may be the cause of 'fun' without being addicted to the weary vice of punning. Most puns," I added, "are altogether guiltless of 'fun,' and produce anything but merriment." Mr. Rogers agreed with me that 'funster' was a good word, and was pleased to say that I deserved credit for its invention, and to prophesy that it would, sooner or later, find its way into the dictionaries. The prophecy, however, has not yet been fulfilled, though more than a quarter of a century has passed over my head since its utterance.

Sir Augustus d'Este was a very quiet and accomplished gentleman, and, had the accidents of his birth been other than they were, would have been heir presumptive to the throne of Great Britain. His father, the Duke of Sussex, was the fifth of the six sons of King George III., and the senior of the Duke of Kent, whose daughter now sits upon the throne. The Duke married, without his father's consent, the Lady Augusta Murray, daughter of the Scottish Earl of Dunmore. The law only partially recognised the marriage, and held it to be invalid as far as any right of succession to the crown was involved, though in every other respect it was considered binding. The Duke of Sussex was next in succession to William IV., and, had he outlived that sovereign, would have inherited the throne, to the temporary exclusion of Queen Victoria. Sir Augustus D'Este had a sister who was known as Mademoiselle D'Este, though some people spoke of her as "Miss Guelph." But as D'Este is one of the patronymics of the royal family, to which they are as much entitled as the ancient kings of Scotland, afterwards kings of England, were to that of Stewart, it was ungracious to call the lady by any other name than that which she had a right to assume, to the exclusion of any other for which she had no fancy. At the time when I met Sir Augustus, the D'Este's were to some extent unpopular, especially among the literary class; for no fault of his, but on account of a disreputable piece of patronage on the part of the Crown, of which Mademoiselle D'Este was the beneficiary. The British Government has never been the patron or encourager of literature, art, or science; and literature more especially has been the profession which it has always seemed to consider it its duty to neglect and ignore; whether from jealousy of it, fear of it, or hatred of it, or perhaps from a combination of the three, it is difficult to say. The utmost that British royalty or the Government did for it, until a comparatively recent time, was to appoint a poet—or one who was thought by his contemporaries to be worthy of that high name—to the office of Poet Laureate, and to endow him with a pension of £150 a year, and a certain eleemosynary allowance of wine from the royal cellars. The duties, if any, exacted from the holders of the office, were not to write epic, dramatic, or lyrical poetry, or to contribute in any fashion to the literary renown of their country, but to write verses in celebration of royal births and marriages, laments for royal deaths, or any other events peculiarly affecting the occupants of the throne and their families. It happened that some patriotic member of Parliament—and the Parliament itself were wiser in this respect than the Court and the Government—had, late in the eighteenth century, procured the passing of a law by which pensions on the Civil List, to the amount of twelve hundred pounds, were to be annually granted for the support or pecuniary assistance of the professors of art, science, and literature. The amount was but small, yet, small as it was, it was not always permitted to reach the persons for whose benefit it was intended. A coachman, a cook, a barber, a butler, a dancing-master, or some other servant of royalty, was occasionally foisted upon the fund, to the extent of fifty or a hundred pounds a year, to the exclusion of the legitimate claimants; but as these grants seldom exceeded a hundred pounds to any one person, literary men, knowing remonstrance to be useless, submitted, though not always in silence, to the robbery inflicted upon their class. The Duke of Sussex, though a King's son, died poor, without leaving any adequate provision for his family; and Mademoiselle D'Este, granddaughter of George III., found herself in straitened circumstances, having royal needs but with only plebeian resources to supply them. The Ministers of the day objected to ask Parliament for a grant of money for her relief, and the royal family would not contribute towards her support out of their private resources. So they instructed the Minister to exercise his patronage in her behalf, and make her an allowance of £500 per annum out of the fund which ought to have been sacredly devoted to the objects for which it was established. This on all hands was considered to be a disgrace, and a faint storm of indignation rattled in the columns of the press. But it soon blew over, and in less than the usual nine days was no more heard of. But the next year the same game was played for Mademoiselle D'Este's benefit, and she received a second annuity of £500 from the same fund, and the professors of art, science, and literature, were left to suffer, or to die of neglect and penury, if it so pleased them, rather than that the daughter of a royal duke, and the grand-daughter of a king, should not be irregularly and nefariously provided for at the public expense. What made the matter more disgraceful was that the lady, in the meantime, had married Lord Truro, the Lord High Chancellor of England, who was in the enjoyment of the handsome salary of £15,000 per annum, three times the amount of the salary paid at that time to the President of the United States, and was consequently well able to support a wife. The English public, however, cared no more for literature than the Court or the Parliament. What was literature to the public, provided it amused them, tickled their fancy, and made them laugh? And literary men, it was thought, would do that all the same—perhaps, all the more—if they had to work harder for their daily bread, in consequence of the paucity or uncertainty of their literary rewards. The case was brought under the notice of Parliament, and some useless displeasure was manifested against the Minister who was responsible for the malversation; but nothing further came of it.

Among the members who had been eloquent in denunciation of the wrong done was Daniel O'Connell, one of the guests of the morning, who had not previously met Sir Augustus D'Este, but who was well acquainted with the personal history of his father, the Duke, the only one of the family who had made himself conspicuous by his

Liberal politics, and had thereby incurred the displeasure of his royal father, perhaps to a greater extent than he had incurred it by his marriage.

Mr. O'Connell was a fine, burly man, with a beaming face, redolent of merriment and good humour; with a roguish twinkle in his eye, a winning and musical voice, and a smile as warm as the noonday sun. He spoke with a decided Irish brogue, which was highly piquant, and not at all offensive to the most susceptible English ear, but, on the contrary, agreeable and attractive, and added flavour to and sharpened the point of the good stories which he delighted to tell. During this morning he was particularly lively, and laid himself out to please; an object in which he succeeded without monopolising the attention of the company or making himself unduly conspicuous. He was one of the finest reciters of poetry to whom it was ever my privilege to listen, and brought out the latent and inherent beauties of the poems—unsuspected, perhaps, by the poets themselves—with such fire, tenderness, and pathos as the occult sense demanded, and to which it required a genius almost equal to that of a poet to do full justice.

One of the stories he told us was that of a Mr. Moreton Dyer—such was the name, if I remember rightly, of the gentleman who had so high an opinion of all mankind, and took such an optimist view of every possible event that happened, or could possibly happen, in the world, as to find excuses and palliation, and even apologies, for the most atrocious crimes. He never was known to say an unkind word against anybody, and thought, or seemed to think, that even the Arch-fiend himself was more sinned against than sinning, was not nearly so black as he was painted, and that under more favourable circumstances, he might have become a credit, a benefit, and even an ornament, to the world of which he was at present the curse and the disgrace. The unkindest thing that he is ever reported to have said of a human being was in reference to the odious criminals Burke and Hare, who were convicted in Edinburgh of the murder of two poor Italian organ-boys, for the sake of their bodies, which they sold to the hospitals for the purpose of dissection. "What do you say, Mr. Dyer, of such fiendish crimes as were committed by these wretches?" was asked of him by a lady. "Well," he replied, "if you force me to speak out, I must say that their conduct was *rather eccentric!*"

Mr. Harrison Ainsworth, at this time in the heyday of his fame and popularity, was one of the four literary dandies of the period—all handsome men, and favourites of the ladies, as well for their personal graces as for their genius. These four were Mr. Benjamin Disraeli, Mr. Edward Lytton Bulwer, Mr. Charles Dickens, and Mr. Harrison Ainsworth.

None could deny that Mr. Ainsworth was unquestionably the best-looking man of the four—the very Antinous of literature, in the prime of his early manhood, and in the full flush of a popularity that continued unabated until a late period of his life. He was a nearer approach to Sir Walter Scott in the style and structure of his novels than any living competitor, though it must be confessed that opinions greatly differed as to the advisableness and morality of the uses to which he applied his genius. The whole town rang at this time with the story of the vulgar ruffian and highwayman, Jack Sheppard, whom he had glorified not only as one of the greatest scoundrels, but as one of the greatest heroes who ever lived. These words are sometimes held to be more or less synonymous ; but the scoundrels of history, noted for the magnitude of their crimes against humanity, are, at all events, scoundrels of a higher class than the vulgar "cracksmen," who break into the dwellings of citizens for the paltry plunder of silver spoons and the loose valuables of unprotected householders. Jack Sheppard, whom Harrison Ainsworth delighted to honour for his pluck, his energy, and his daring, became, during the happily short run of the popular favour with which the brilliant but most unwholesome novel was received, a model for the loose floating population of imperfectly or wrongly educated young men and boys, who swarm in all great cities (in London and Paris more especially), who thought his rascally achievements worthy of admiration, and, what was worse, of imitation. The story was dramatized by those inferior dramatists who cared nothing for morality, but much for money, and appeared at no less than eight licensed—and, perhaps, at a score of unlicensed—theatres, or "penny gaffs," frequented by boys and girls of the lowest class. The records of the police courts, and in due course of the prisons of the huge metropolis, told the tale of the mischievous influence of the too fascinating book.

But this influence, to use a phrase of the Rev. Sidney Smith, applied to a book of a very different kind, soon " blew over." Unluckily, however, the appetite of the author, who had tasted the sweets of a very unwholesome applause and of a very profitable notoriety, longed for a repetition of the pabulum on which he had flourished, and found it in the adventures of Dick Turpin, the notorious highwayman, and the record of his marvellous ride between London and York. This narrative fairly took the town by storm. The applause created by the comparatively tame story of Jack Sheppard was as a gentle breeze compared with the tornado created by Dick Turpin's ride, and, though Mr. Ainsworth shared with Mr. O'Connell the reputation of being the best abused man of his day, the abuse was lucrative, and put money in his pocket, without breaking any bones, either physically or morally, in the personality of the author.

Mr. Ainsworth's heroes were of a kind to attract the admiration of the multitude, as was shown not only in the case of Jack Sheppard and Richard Turpin, but of Guy Fawkes, a criminal whose very name was as dear as it was familiar to all the boys of the London streets, who annually celebrated, on the fifth of November, the culmination of his treasonable career, because it afforded them the opportunity and the license of a display of fire-works in the streets. There is not, perhaps, a boy living, or who ever will live, or ever did live, by whom the letting off of squibs or crackers and other pyrotechnics was not considered, as Keats says of beauty, " a joy for ever." Guy Fawkes, however, it must be confessed, though a name to conjure with in the days of Mr. Ainsworth, is fast becoming obsolete in our own, and not even the London street boys, for the sake of the fire-works, succeed in keeping up an interest in him. But Mr. Ainsworth succeeded, in a literary point of view, in making the most of him. But what gave the *coup-de-grace* to Guy Fawkes as a popular hero and a subject of harmless fun and caricature was the fact that the celebration of the day devoted to his memory was taken out of the hands of the young boys of the streets and monopolized by the stalwart rogues and vagabonds of a larger growth, who, by their coarse brutality and noisy demands for money of the householders in the streets through which they passed, and of the stray passengers on the pavements, rendered the day, and especially the night, hideous. The nuisance and the scandal, abhorred of all respectable people, required the strong arm of the police to abate They were abated, accordingly, in the fulness of the time appointed.

Mr. Ainsworth was the author of several slang songs that were heard from morning to night in the streets, sung, whistled or ground on barrel-organs, to the sore discomfort of all quiet, studious folk, to say nothing of unhappy invalids. Among the most noted of these effusions was one entitled, "Nix, my dolly, pals, fake away." The first stanza, supposed to be sung originally by a highwayman in one of Mr. Ainsworth's novels, ran:

> In a box of the stone jug I was born,
> Of a hempen widow the kid forlorn,
> And my old dad, as I've heard say,
> Was a famous merchant in capers gay.
> Nix, my dolly, pals, fake away!

Mr. O'Connell recited this to Mr. Ainsworth, and with great gusto; but expressed his inability to understand what was meant by "stone jug," and a "merchant in capers gay." Mr. Ainsworth explained that "stone jug" was the slang name among the thieves of London for the prison of Newgate, and that a "merchant in capers" was another slang name, well understood by all the villains of London, for a man who had been executed, for the reason that a few moments after the noose had been fixed round his neck, and that his feet had lost their support on the solid ground, he "cut capers with his heels in the empty air."

"Grimly humorous, but far-fetched," said Mr. O'Connell. "'Hempen widow' is highly expressive of one made a widow by the rope, and 'kid forlorn' is almost pathetic. 'Nix, my dolly,' I don't understand; but I think 'fake' is a word of my country."

"How so?" inquired Mr. Ainsworth.

"It is an Irish Gaelic word, common enough in Dublin, and is from *faigh*, to get, to acquire, and thence to *steal*. There are many Gaelic words in the vernacular of the London streets, introduced, I suppose, by my countrymen."

"Very likely," said Mr. Sidney Smith. "But can you tell me, Mr. O'Connell, what is the true origin and meaning of the words 'Irish bull,' as applied to the blunders sometimes made by, but often attributed wrongfully to, Irishmen?"

"I scarcely know," replied Mr. O'Connell, "unless 'bull' be from *buille*, a stroke, which is, I suspect, the real word, and would thence mean a stroke of wit, or humour, or stupidity, as the case might be."

"But whence 'Irish'?"

"'Irish,' I suspect," said Mr. O'Connell, "is either the Gaelic *aithris*, pronounced exactly like *Irish*, and which means mimicry, imitation, or repetition, or *air ais*, back or backward. Thus, bull-Irish, Irish bull, or *buille aithris*, would signify the repetition of a joke, or stroke of wit or humour, or else a backward stroke. If this be not the interpretation, I know of no other."

"I think the interpretation is very likely to be correct," remarked Mr. Rogers, "and that there are many more Gaelic words, both from Scotch and Irish sources, in common English use, than Englishmen are aware of."

And after this desultory but instructive philological discussion, which interested me exceedingly, and bore fruits in my mind at an after period of my life, the conversation ended and the party broke up.

Breakfasts with Samuel Rogers.

No. IV.

In the later summer of 1847 I accepted an invitation to breakfast with Mr. Samuel Rogers, to meet Mr. Disraeli and Sir Edward Lytton Bulwer.

Though familiar with their writings, I had not previously made the acquaintance of either. Their fame as novelists had at this time been partially eclipsed by the popularity of Mr. Dickens; but their reputation as statesmen and rising politicians was in full bloom. I was the youngest of the party, and my seniors, Mr. Disraeli and Sir Edward Bulwer, had scarcely one-half of the age of our venerable host.

Our conversation was, at first, more political than literary or general, and turned mainly upon the affairs of France, which, under the corrupt government of Louis Philippe—King of the Barricades, as he was called by some, and the Citizen King, or *Roi Épicier*, as he was irreverently called by others—were rapidly drifting towards the Revolution which he stolidly and obstinately provoked, and which broke out in full fury eight or nine months afterwards. But as these questions have long since lost their interest, and as my intention is not to revive obsolete politics, I pass over the discussions that arose upon them, animated though they were, and important as they seemed at the time.

Mr. Disraeli and Sir Edward Lytton Bulwer were both born in 1805, and were almost in the noon of their literary, and in the first morning of their political, fame. They had both, in their early manhood, aspired to be leaders of fashion, and many gibes and jokes were directed against them by the wicked wits of the time on the airs of foppery and dandyism which they gave themselves.

In the well-known literary portraits of *Fraser's Magazine*, published monthly from 1830 to 1836, and drawn by Daniel Maclise, Disraeli is represented as a very Antinous of personal beauty, and Bulwer Lytton—then known as Lytton Bulwer—as an exquisite of the first order. But at this time (1847) their youthful graces had somewhat faded, and years, and marriage, and the cares and struggles of life, had had the effect of sobering them down into the staid and steady appearance of respectable middle-aged gentlemen. Sir Edward had early in life married a beautiful Irish girl for love, or what he thought love; but "thereof had come in the end despondency and madness," and separation by mutual consent, on account of their utter incompatibility of temper. Mr. Disraeli, at a riper age, had married a widow, rich, accomplished, and comparatively young, who had made him an excellent and affectionate wife. Her fortune had enabled him to climb with easier efforts the steep hill of political power, and her sympathy cheered, encouraged, and sustained him in his struggles and triumphs.

Both of these eminent men published novels before they reached the legal age of manhood, and gave but faint promise of the excellence to which they afterwards attained. Sir Edward Bulwer, considered solely as a man of letters, was a born genius, and stood amongst the foremost in the second rank of the world's greatest men—almost worthy, in some respects, to be included among the select company of the first. Mr. Disraeli, looked upon in the same literary light, had no claim to genius which the world in his own day was willing to concede, and which it will not concede now; but he was undoubtedly a writer of great, if not of commanding talent.

Lytton Bulwer, the man of genius, was not a great statesman, though he aspired to be so; but Disraeli, the man of talent, was a statesman of the very highest order. At the time to which these reminiscences refer, neither the authorship nor the statesmanship of Mr. Disraeli was very highly thought of, except by a select few. The great Duke of Wellington, who at that time shared with Sir Robert Peel the leadership of the Conservative party, was accustomed to speak of Mr. Disraeli— whom he called "Dis*rawli*"—with ill-concealed depreciation, as an "adventurer," who sought to force his way into the ranks of a party which did not need his services, and which would have much preferred to dispense with his assistance.

Sir Edward Bulwer was scarcely looked upon as a politician at all, and, though an excellent orator, was not a favourite in Parliament. The matter of the few speeches which he made in that very critical assembly was always good, and the manner pleasing; but they bore too evidently the marks of careful preparation to be altogether acceptable to a house which always preferred, and still prefers, extemporaneous speeches to studied orations; which listens attentively to the former, and retires to the dining- or smoking-rooms in large numbers whenever any attempt is made to extort its praises or its attention by people who would, if they could, play the part of Demosthenes or Cicero. What the British House of Parliament admires and listens to is a ready debater, not a great orator; and for the chances and exigencies of debate Sir Edward Bulwer was, in a great measure, disqualified by his growing infirmity of deafness.

Mr. Disraeli, as a debater, though not as an orator, was greatly superior to Sir Edward; and, hearing every interruption, every contradiction, and every remark made by friend or opponent in the course of his speeches, was enabled to reply at the moment, and often very effectively, by a repartee, or a rejoinder, that was of the utmost value to his reputation as a speaker. This advantage being unhappily denied to Sir Edward, he addressed the House very seldom, and, if listened to by any greater audience than that of the reporters, was listened to as a duty rather than as a pleasure.

There was once a famous comic actor in London, named Liston, a great favourite of the public, especially in the once celebrated part, Paul Pry. Only to see the face of this admirable performer, even before he uttered a word, was to be excited to laughter. He was beyond all comparison the first comedian of his time, and commanded a large—report said an extravagant—salary. Yet he was dissatisfied with the public that appreciated his talent so highly, and insisted that he was utterly misunderstood. He considered himself to be, above all things, a tragedian, and having, in a farce, to repeat the line in answer to one of the characters, who asked, "What will the public say?" he always replied, "The public! The public is a hass!" always saying "a hass," instead of "an ass," to give more emphasis to his assertion and to mark his sense of its want of judgment. This story is also told of Mr. John Reeve, commonly called "Jack Reeve," who was greatly popular at a somewhat later period. Comedy and Farce laughed in his eyes, frolicked upon his lips and danced upon his tongue, and yet he considered himself to be a tragedian! The case of Sir Edward Bulwer was precisely similar. Next to Sir Walter Scott, he was the greatest novelist and romance writer of his time; but he thought himself to be a great poet, when he was only a versifier. He took pleasure and comfort in the thought that posterity would recognize his genius, as he himself understood it, however much his contemporaries might ignore or deny his claim, and, like Liston and John Reeve, considered the public " a hass " for preferring his first-rate novels to his second-rate poetry.

The surest passport to his favour—and sometimes to his friendship—was to admit his claim to be a poet of as high an order as Byron, or any other of the great masters of song. Contemporary critics were not of this opinion, and insisted that he never attained a higher grade than that of respectable mediocrity—which the Latin poet of two thousand years ago declared to be alike distasteful to gods and men. Douglas Jerrold declared of the poetasters of his age that there were three kinds of composition as distinguished from prose— namely, " Poetry," " Verse," and " Worse." He relegated Lytton Bulwer to the second of these classes, and the whole host of ladies and gentlemen who wrote with ease, and filled the " Poet's Corner " of newspapers and other periodicals, to the third.

Yet Sir Edward was a poet in his novels, as well as in his dramas, and the poetical colouring and rhythmical swing of his prose contributed greatly to the pleasure of his readers. He was one of the most successful dramatists of the fifth and sixth decades of the nineteenth century, and three of his plays still keep possession of the stage—viz., *Money*, *Richelieu*, and *The Lady of Lyons*. They still excite the ambition of rising, or of already risen and celebrated, actors to appear in them. Another of his plays, at one time even more celebrated, called *Not so Bad as We Seem*, has disappeared from the stage, without much probability of revival. It was written for the express purpose of collecting funds for the maintenance of homes for necessitous authors in their old age, for which purpose Sir Edward had given the necessary land on a portion of his estate at Knebworth. A strolling company of amateurs, composed of well-known authors, all favourites of the public, went from town to town in aid of this project, and by their personal celebrity, no less than by the benevolent purpose which they had in view, attracted large audiences wherever they went. Among the members of this "strolling company"—for such it was while it lasted—were Charles Dickens (an excellent actor, who would have made his mark on the stage had his taste or his necessities led him to adopt it as a profession); Mark Lemon, then editor of *Punch;* George Cruikshank, the greatest caricaturist of the nineteenth century; W. H. Wills, the literary partner of Mr. Dickens, and a constant contributor to *Household Words* and *All the Year Round*; Douglas Jerrold, the subtlest wit of the century; and a few others still living.

During the somewhat protracted period that this play was in course of performance in all the principal cities and towns of England, Mr. Dickens lost his aged father, and, not long afterwards, an infant child. These bereavements naturally caused a suspension for a time of his public appearances. Lady Lytton Bulwer—whose hatred of her husband extended, in the milder form of dislike to, or spite against, every person on whom he bestowed either his intimacy or his friendship—was particularly displeased with Mr. Dickens, and asserted in print, when he resumed his appearance in the dramatic company, in which his presence was a great attraction, that " he went about acting with his dead father in one pocket and his dead child in another." Lady Bulwer, no doubt, was of opinion that there was wit in this attack upon a gentleman who had given her no cause of offence; an opinion, however, in which we may be certain that there was not a single person in the world to agree with her.

She was a sore annoyance to her husband, and in the novels which she published, to the extent of one or two annually, took pleasure in drawing caricature portraits of him, under a thin disguise, which it needed no particular sharpness of intellect to penetrate, and of which the object was to hold him up to contempt and ridicule—an object, however, which, by the laws of eternal justice, invariably recoiled upon herself.

Sir Edward was prouder of being a man of letters, and one of the most distinguished authors of his time, than of being a man of high rank and an eminent statesman. I remember calling upon him soon after his appointment as Secretary of State for the Colonies, under the administration of the Earl of Derby. In the course of our conversation, I expressed my sorrow to see him in the position of a Minister of the Crown. His countenance darkened. He asked immediately, in a tone of acerbity: "Why should you be sorry? Do you not think me worthy of being a Minister of the Crown?"

"Most worthy!" I replied. "But I am sorry to see you in a position that will so greatly occupy your time and energies as to prevent you from writing any more novels!"

"Oh! is that all?" he replied, smiling. "Make your mind easy on that score. Nothing shall prevent me from writing novels but death or madness! Even madness itself might not, perhaps, prevent me!"

Mr. Disraeli, though eminent in literature, did not put his whole heart into it, as Sir Edward had done. As a way to distinction, when no other seemed open to him, he was glad and proud to be an author; but his real love was to sway the listening senate; to be a leader of parties, and a ruler of men; the organizer of great schemes of policy, and to achieve not alone an English, but a European and cosmopolitan reputation. The consequence was that his literary career—bright though it seemed in the morning of his life—was a comparative failure as he advanced in years, and that he never achieved any greater success than the very moderate one which the French, when they wish to be good-natured, designate euphemistically as a "*succès d'estime.*" As an author, he never ranked, and never will rank, among the "immortal few," but only as one of the crowd of mediocrities, not shining with any particular lustre during his own day, and destined to be extinguished in the blinding mists with which posterity covers the names and works of all who write for an age, or a portion of an age, and not "for all time."

Mr. Disraeli, during his literary and political career, made some awkward and unfortunate mistakes. It fell to his lot, as leader of the Conservative party, which was in office in 1852, when the great Duke of Wellington died, full of years and honour, to pronounce, as the spokesman of the House of Commons, the funeral oration of the illustrious warrior. He delivered a very eloquent speech, which was greatly admired by all who heard it, and almost as greatly admired by all who read it next morning, as fully reported in the columns of the daily newspapers. Unluckily, some person with a tenacious memory fancied that the great speech was not unfamiliar to his mind—that he had read it somewhere or other, years before, not only in the substance, but in the very phraseology and elegant terms of expression which Mr. Disraeli had employed. After a little search among his books, he discovered it, *verbatim et literatim*, in the funeral oration, said to have been written by M. Thiers, but, whether written by him or not, pronounced over the grave of a second-rate French general—one of the First Napoleon's self-made soldiers—Marshal Mortier, who died in 1834 or 1835, eighteen years before the Duke of Wellington. Being a political opponent of Mr. Disraeli, the lynx-eyed discoverer hastened to make the fact known by means of the *Morning Chronicle*, at that time the leading Liberal journal. The *Chronicle*, glad to damage a political opponent, printed in parallel columns Disraeli's oration over Wellington and that of Thiers over Marshal Mortier. They were identical, with only the slight differences that might result in any fair translation.

Great was the exultation of the Liberals at the disgrace that had fallen on the Tory chief. Apparently as great was the humiliation of the opposite party. Most people thought that the crushing *exposé* would not only be fatal to Mr. Disraeli's literary reputation, but highly damaging to his position as a statesman and a party leader. Elderly people at the clubs shrugged their shoulders as they commented on the unmerited fate that had befallen, in his grave, the greatest historical character of the age, in being eulogised at secondhand, by a literary charlatan, in the words originally applied to an enemy, whose very name was almost forgotten.

Nor did the humiliation of Mr. Disraeli end here. Two or three days after this painful exposure, and before the town had had time to forget it, there appeared in the *Morning Chronicle*—possibly from the same correspondent with the too-accurate and too-provoking memory—a sketch of the character of " Lord Cadurcis," extracted from Mr. Disraeli's novel of *Venetia*. " Lord Cadurcis" was intended for Lord Byron, the novelist, and not only described the poet graphically and accurately, but narrated, thinly veiled, the adventures ascribed to him during his residence in Venice. Side by side, in parallel columns, as in the previous case of the Duke of Wellington and Marshal Mortier, appeared an extract portraying the character of Lord Byron as drawn by Mr.—afterwards Lord—Macaulay, in a notice of the life and works of that great poet, in the *Edinburgh Review*, more than twelve years previously. The only difference between the two passages was that " Lord Cadurcis" in Mr. Disraeli's novel was Lord Byron in Mr. Macaulay's review. This was, in the eyes alike of the friends and foes of Mr. Disraeli, a great deal too bad, and was thought by almost everybody to be fatal to his reputation as an author and as an honest man; for no man, it was said, aspiring to the latter character, would deliberately attempt to pass off upon the world, as his own, the writings of another person. An explanation was absolutely necessary in Mr. Disraeli's own interest; and at last it came. Not from himself, however, but from a friend in his confidence, who was authorised to state in his behalf that, from his earliest manhood, he had been accustomed to transcribe from books, reviews and newspapers, any passages that particularly struck him for their eloquence or beauty, and carefully preserve them among his private papers and memoranda. He had transcribed in this manner the two incriminated extracts from Thiers and Macaulay. He had utterly forgotten the existence of either, when he accidentally, and at different times, when examining his papers, came across them, and imagined them to be his own. As such he had used them. This was a very lame explanation, and for a mere author and literary man by profession would not have been accepted. But as it came from a statesman, the hope, the prop, the main reliance of a powerful party, and as it had no bearing whatever upon political affairs, it was received with as good a grace as it was possible to put upon the matter. The offence, if such it were, was condoned, and none but sour-minded professional critics and habitual opponents of his policy thought any the worse of him.

The last time that I saw Mr. Disraeli he had become Lord Beaconsfield and Prime Minister of Great Britain. I was one of a deputation of authors who sought to aid in establishing an international copyright between Great Britain and the United States. Nothing came of the conference except the good wishes of Lord Beaconsfield. Mr. Charles Reade, a better novelist than Lord Beaconsfield, rose up to speak in support of the object of the meeting.

"Pray be seated, Mr. Reade," said his Lordship.

"I would rather stand, my Lord," replied Mr. Reade. "I can make a longer speech when standing than I can when sitting."

"I am very sorry to hear it," replied his Lordship, amid the laughter of the meeting.

At the close of the proceedings the two authors, who had never met before, shook hands.

Lord Beaconsfield's ambition was abundantly satisfied. He did not write his name very deeply or legibly on the scroll of England's literary worthies, though possibly he might have done so, had he tried with sufficient energy and perseverance; but he wrote it deeply and ineffaceably on the page of England's history. He died universally lamented, all his faults condoned or forgotten, amid the regrets alike of his political friends and political foes. The latter—if any remained at the time of his death—excused his errors in admiration of his indomitable courage, steady perseverance, and what, for want of a more elegant and expressive word, is called "pluck." And to be possessed of "pluck" goes a long way to secure the favour of Englishmen.

Breakfasts with Samuel Rogers.
No. V.

It was on a fine morning in June, in the heat of the parliamentary session of 1843, in the midst of the Anti-Corn Law agitation, that I found myself at breakfast in St. James's Place, at the table of Mr. Rogers, with Lord John Russell, Member at that time for the City of London, and Sir John Easthope, the principal proprietor of the *Morning Chronicle.*

Politics were seldom, or, perhaps, never, discussed at that hospitable board; and, if they had been, it is not likely that any acrimonious discussions or differences of opinion would have arisen, as Mr. Rogers was too experienced and discreet an Amphitryon to bring people together whose ideas on politics or theology were likely to come into collision, if either of these topics had been permissible.

Lord John Russell did not enter upon the domain of politics when he remarked, during the breakfast, that parliamentary life in England was a heavy tax upon the health and energy of men who were no longer young, and that he had been in the House of Commons until 3 o'clock that morning, and had not been able to retire to rest until nearly 4, fagged and worn-out, and had risen again at 9, in order to keep his breakfast appointment in St. James's Place. Sir John Easthope, who was also in Parliament, as member for the borough of Leicester, was in the same predicament, though he was but a private soldier in the parliamentary army, and not a great leader like Lord John, and might have gone home to bed at an earlier hour, if it had so pleased him, or if he had been able to pair off for the night with some adherent of the other side, who, like him, had valued sleep more than strict discipline.

Lord John was of opinion that the business of the legislature ought to be transacted during the daytime, a proposition to which Sir John agreed in the abstract, but to the probable operation of which rule or practice, if once instituted, he took the objection that it would prevent the attendance of the numerous men of business who had seats in the legislature, and who were too much occupied during the day, in the city or elsewhere, to find time to devote either the forenoon or the afternoon to the business of the country which, however important it might be, was, in their eyes, of less importance than their own. The argument was irrefutable; and Lord John Russell, acknowledging the full force of it, forbore to argue it any further, and closed the discussion by remarking that, if the Chartists, fifty or a hundred years hence, should carry the five points of the Charter—of which one was the payment of members—day sittings of Parliament might possibly be made the rule by members whose trade or profession it would thus become to serve their country for hire, and who might think it incumbent upon them to earn their money by daylight. Lord John Russell, as all the world knows, was a literary man as well as a statesman, though the laurels he had won in the arena of literature were not so green, or fresh, or so likely to endure as those which he had won in the more exciting arena of politics and statesmanship. He wrote a tragedy—of which the less said the better—which never achieved the triumph of an appearance on the stage, and which only remains in the form of a small volume, now very difficult to procure, and not likely to be reprinted. He also edited a life of his particular friend, Thomas Moore, which did, in its day, as much damage to the reputation of the man whom it was the author's wish to glorify, as has been done in ours to the memory of Thomas Carlyle by the similarly well-meant biography of his friend and admirer, Mr. Froude.

Lord John Russell was all his life partial to the society of literary men, and numbered Lord Byron, Sir John Hobhouse, Mr. Rogers, Mr. Hallam, Mr. Campbell, and Mr. Moore among his most intimate friends. His poetical pretensions, however, were not generally known, and were sometimes, when known, prejudicial to his influence as a statesman.

When he was a candidate for the parliamentary representation of the city of London, he was opposed in the Conservative interest by Lord John Manners, like himself the son of a duke. Lord John Manners in his early youth, when a member of what was called the "Young England" party, had written a poem, in which occurred the lines—

> Let art and science, laws and learning die,
> But leave us still our old nobility!

These lines as well as others in the poem had been very much ridiculed; and at a meeting of Lord John Russell's committee for securing his election, they were cited by a zealous friend of the Liberal cause, a leading merchant in the dry-goods trade, as a reason why no Liberal should vote for Lord John Manners.

"We don't want any poets," he said, "for the city of London."

"But Lord John Russell is a poet also," said another, "and he wrote and published a tragedy."

"Did he?" inquired the dry-goods man. "If he did, I won't vote for him!"

And he kept his word, and took no further part in the election.

In 1847, after the Repeal of the Corn Laws and the establishment of Free Trade in England — the successful accomplishment of which he did his utmost to promote in Parliament— when neither Mr. Cobden nor Mr. Bright, its more vigorous champions, had seats in that assembly, Lord John Russell took his annual holiday in the Highlands. I was at that time the editor of the *Glasgow Argus*. As his Lordship was to pass through Glasgow, on his way back to London, the Liberals of that great and enterprising city resolved, under the leadership of the then Lord Provost, Mr. James Lumsden, to invite him to a public dinner. Mr. Lumsden was the most influential proprietor of the *Argus*, and a very dear and much respected friend of mine, and consulted me daily on all the arrangements; the toasts that were to be given, the most advisable persons to select for proposing them, and even condescended to such details as the *menu* of the dinner. If truth must be told, the excellent gentleman was fussy in all that he undertook, and undertook nothing to which he was not prepared to give head and hand, heart and soul, and understood no such word as *fail*. He came to me on the morning of the day appointed for the dinner, and informed me, with great glee, that he had arranged that the band in the orchestra of the hall should, on his Lordship's entrance, strike up the air " See the Conquering Hero Comes." I could not help laughing ; for Lord John Russell was a very little man, considerably under the medium height, and did not in the least, or in any particular, come up to the popular idea of a hero ; and I frankly told Mr. Lumsden that he should reconsider the subject.

"I have thought it over till I am tired of thinking," replied the Provost. " Can you no' suggest onything yoursel' ? " The Provost always relapsed into broad Scotch when he was in thorough earnest. "I ken that ye're musical, and I should like if ye could suggest onything well-known and appropriate."

A sudden thought took possession of me, which I communicated to the Provost more as a joke than with any idea that he would take it seriously.

" Nothing could be more appropriate," I said, " than the fine old Scottish air, ' Saw ye Johnnie comin' ? ' "

"The vera thing," said the Provost, with a hearty laugh, while giving me a grip of his hand. "Dinna fash your head ony mair; the thing is settled!" and he repeated the first four lines of the ancient song—

> "Saw ye Johnnie comin'?" quo' she—
> "Saw ye Johnnie comin'?
> Wi' his blue bonnet on his head
> An' his doggie runnin'."

"Eh, mon! It'll do fine!" And, so saying, the worthy functionary took his departure, leaving on my mind the impression that he would, after all, take the suggestion as a joke, and that, at the last moment, nothing would be further from his intention than to act upon it.

I saw no more of him until the dinner hour, when, to my astonishment and no small amusement, the band struck up the brisk and lively air, "Saw ye Johnnie comin'?" as his Lordship, escorted by the Provost and other leading citizens of Glasgow, entered the hall. The air is familiar to most Scotsmen, and such a peal of laughter broke from the immense assemblage as I had never before and have not since heard. Lord John Russell looked surprised and bewildered. He evidently was unacquainted with the air and its name, and was at a loss to account for the hilarity of the meeting. Mr. Lumsden came to the rescue, bent down to his Lordship's ear, and explained the mystery. The gloom on the handsome and delicate face of the eminent statesman gave place to a smile, which was immediately superseded by a laugh as hearty as that of any of the company.

Of Sir John Easthope, one of the other guests of Mr. Rogers, who met Lord John Russell in social intercourse for the first time on that occasion, there is not much to be said. He was, as I have already stated, the principal proprietor of the *Morning Chronicle*, and a zealous, and it may be said "a thick and thin," supporter of every Liberal administration, whether under the premiership of Lord Melbourne, Lord Palmerston, or Lord John Russell. He was particularly noted for his all but slavish worship of Lord Palmerston. His devotion to that chief was ultimately rewarded by a baronetcy, a title which he hoped would, in course of time, be inherited by his only son. The hope, however, was doomed to early extinction; for his son died unmarried many years before his father. Under the management of Sir John Easthope and his two partners, Mr. Simon Macgillivray, who had made a fortune in Mexico, and Mr. James Duncan, a noted publisher of Hebrew Bibles (both Scotsmen), the circulation of the *Morning Chronicle* was raised from the low ebb of eight hundred copies a day to upwards of nine thousand. At this time, when newspapers were burdened with many heavy taxes and restrictions, as I have already recorded, their sale was very limited. A circulation of nine thousand copies *per diem* was considered enormous; and the penny press that now circulates by hundreds of thousands was undreamed of. Sir John was a very irascible, captious, and disagreeable man in all matters of business connected with the *Morning Chronicle*, and was, consequently, by no means popular with his employés, many of whom habitually spoke of him, with a grim attempt at jocosity, as " Sir John Blast-Hope." But in private and social life Sir John was the very soul of geniality and good-fellowship, and made his employés forget, in the kindly manner in which he received them at his table or elsewhere, all the rebuffs which he had made them undergo in the exercise of their vocation. I had for nine years left the *Morning Chronicle* for "fresh fields and pastures new," when I met Sir John for the last time. It was in 1853, when he had gone to Paris, to visit his old and once intimate friend, the Emperor of the French. He stayed at the Bains de Tivoli, a private hotel, where I also happened to be a guest. He invited me to his private room in the evening to take a hand at a rubber of whist. The occasion impressed itself upon my mind as affording a striking instance both of his irascibility and his geniality. My partner was Lady Wyatville, the widow of a once celebrated architect. She was then over eighty years of age, sharp, active, and intelligent, and still showed the traces of a beauty that must in her youth have been remarkable. The lady revoked, and, being accused of it, vehemently denied the fact, and treated the proofs afforded of it with haughty disdain and not very polite contradiction. Sir John lost patience with her; and, abruptly rising in his chair, said: "Madame! you are a cheat!" The lady's eyes flashed with almost preternatural fire as she also rose in her chair, and took a step or two towards Sir John, as if she would have inflicted summary punishment upon his face with her nails. Sir John, still standing, said: "Yes, Madame, I repeat it! You cheat abominably. And in the course of a long life," he added, laying his hand upon his heart, "I have invariably noticed that the handsomer a woman is, the more she cheats at cards!" The lady sat down; a smile suffused her ancient, but still beautiful face; and the apparent tigress of a minute before became as gentle as a dove.

BREAKFASTS WITH SAMUEL ROGERS.

No. VI.

Mr. Lumley was the lessee and manager of the Italian Opera, in the Haymarket; Miss Cushman was a successful tragic actress; and Barry Cornwall was the literary pseudonym of Mr. Bryan Waller Proctor, a conveyancer in lucrative practice. I was well pleased to meet these three people at Mr. Rogers's breakfast-table. The only one of the three with whom I was not previously acquainted was Mr. Proctor. He was the author of two or three poetical works, of no particular merit, but especially of a volume of English songs, which had been received with a chorus of jubilation by all the critics of the day, though it has long since passed into the limbo that is the ultimate destination of all mediocre books, especially of mediocrities in rhyme.

The conversation, at this social meal, mostly turned upon theatrical topics, in which these three persons were more or less interested, and in which the two first, especially, were wholly engrossed, the one as manager, the second as a performer.

I had known Mr. Lumley (whose real name was supposed to be Levi, the former having been assumed with the view of concealing his Jewish nationality) from my earliest manhood, and from the time when he had just completed his preliminary studies to qualify him for admission to practise as a solicitor. We had read Italian poetry together at his chambers in Quality Court, Chancery Lane, for which study he had then sufficient leisure in the intervals of his not over-plentiful or too-engrossing law business. His principal client in those early days was M. Laporte, a Frenchman, who had got into pecuniary difficulties in his management of the Italian Opera. He used to give Mr. Lumley free admissions to the stalls of the theatre for self and friend, whenever he asked for them. My very first visit to the Opera was made in Mr. Lumley's company, with one of those free tickets, Mr. Lumley little thinking at the time that he was to be the successor of his friend and client, in the onerous and responsible position of Manager. Another of his clients, to whom he introduced me at his chambers, was Mr. Robert Pearce Gillies, who had edited the *Foreign Quarterly Review*, a valuable work, to which Sir Walter Scott, Robert Southey, and the late Thomas Carlyle were constant contributors. Mr. Gillies was the younger brother of Lord Gillies, one of the judges of the Supreme Court in Edinburgh. He had fallen into serious pecuniary embarrassments, which he had brought upon himself by his chronic inability, shared with too many imaginative men who live from hand to mouth, and who consider hopes to be accomplished facts, and do not remember that two and two make four only; and his persistency in riotous living, and the display of an almost princely hospitality, which led him to give extravagant dinners, suppers, and other entertainments to the fashionable and literary society of the then brilliant metropolis of the North. These embarrassments proved, on investigation by Mr. Lumley, to be of such extent and complexity as to render extrication hopeless, except by the effacing sponge of insolvency and bankruptcy. Poor Mr. Gillies, hopeful, but helpless, after a long and painful struggle, was reduced to such woful straits as to become literally dependent for the meat and the drink of the day, on the shillings and sixpences which he begged or borrowed from his acquaintances (very few in number) and from the friends (still fewer) who had known him in better days, and whose patience he had not utterly exhausted by his Sisyphus-like appeals to their sympathy.

The last I saw of him was many years after my first introduction, when I unexpectedly caught sight of him—an old and decrepit man—sitting alone and bareheaded upon a doorstep, on a cold, wintry morning, in Camden Town, with scarcely a shoe to his foot, and with his hat in his lap, to receive the alms of the passers-by.

I could not find it in my heart to make myself known to him, or even to speak to him, lest he should be pained to recognise me; but, entering into a stationer's shop on the opposite side of the street, where I was in the habit of dealing, I deposited my alms, which I wished at the time had been greater, in the hands of the proprietor, with a request that he would drop them into the hat of the poor suppliant, so that I myself might not be visible in the transaction. Most grievous and desperate is the lot of a distressed man of letters in the mighty city of London, if he have once lost character and self-respect. Better for him would be the workhouse; better still the grave!

Mr. Lumley succeeded Mr. Laporte in 1842, and was now in the full flush of his popularity and prosperity. Even at that early time, when the Italian Opera, or Her Majesty's Theatre, as it was more commonly called, had the monopoly in London of opera and ballet, and when no whisper of rivalry or opposition had been heard, Mr. Lumley had a misgiving that the enormously extravagant salaries that were demanded, and received, by such singers as Catalani, Sontag, Grisi, Jenny Lind, Piccolomini, Frezzolini, Persiani, Malibran, and others of similar celebrity, to say nothing of the almost equally fabulous sums exacted by such vocalists of the other sex as Rubini, Mario, Tamburini, Garcia, and Lablache, and such dancers as Ellsler, the two Ceritos, and Taglioni, would, unless the prices were very greatly reduced, lead to the ruin of the Italian Opera in England. Its popularity in London was forced and factitious, even in its best days; and though, in Mr. Lumley's time, it had reached a height which it had never before attained, it is doubtful whether, even at that exceptional period, Italian Opera could have maintained itself at a remunerative point without the aid of the Ballet. Mr. Lumley, however, was both an enterprising and a generous paymaster, and managed, by the liberal support of the wealthy aristocracy, which he knew not only how to acquire and retain, and by the skilful management of the newspaper press, in which he excelled, to keep the Italian Opera from insolvency, with profit and honour to himself. His monopoly was finally invaded by the establishment of a rival Opera in Covent Garden, under the auspices of Mr. Delafield, a partner in the eminent brewing firm of Combe, Delafield, & Co., with a liberal patronage, and with command of a large capital. The struggle between the two houses was long and severe, and finally ended by the collapse of both. At the present time (1885) the Original Opera House in the Haymarket is, and has long been, vacant, and its rival at Covent Garden has been converted into a Hippodrome.

Mr. Lumley, on relinquishing his connection with the theatre, resumed the exercise of his old profession of the law.

The conversation at the breakfast-table on this particular morning, in which all the guests took a more or less animated part, turned almost entirely upon the Ballet as a necessary appendage and aid to the attractions of Italian music. Mr. Rogers and Mr. Proctor expressed themselves as no particular admirers of the Ballet, but did not view it with marked disapproval, and thought that theatrical managers were quite justified in humouring the public taste with regard to it as long as it paid. Mr. Lumley was enthusiastic in its support, maintained that it was far more popular and attractive than the Opera itself, and that Opera —such as the public expected it to be—could not be supported without the pecuniary aid so largely afforded by the admirers of the Ballet. Miss Cushman and I took the opposite side, while fully agreeing with the force of the *argumentum ad pecuniam* put forward by Mr. Lumley. Miss Cushman held that the Ballet, as exhibited on the stage of Her Majesty's Theatre, was meretricious and immodest, and that such pleasure as it afforded to anybody was animal, and not intellectual. She added that, unlike the drama, it served no moral purpose, and that on no grounds whatever was it worthy of toleration in a decorous and decent community. While I agreed in the main with the contention of Miss Cushman, I took the additional objection to the Ballet, that it was by no means entitled to be called "the poetry of motion," an epithet which enthusiastic admirers of shapely legs had often bestowed upon the saltatory art. I admitted that ordinary and non-professional dancing was often graceful in the extreme ; that the country dance, the minuet, and especially the Scottish reel, fully deserve to be called "poetry in motion," but thought that the epithet did not justly apply to the pirouettes, whirlings, and gymnastic feats of the Coryphees and *prime donne* of the Ballet. Where, I asked, was the poetry in the motions or postures of a woman, beautiful as she might be, who supported herself on the toe of her right foot, in a painfully vertical position, and raised her left leg to an equally unnatural horizontal line, more suggestive of the acrobat than of the dancer ? My inquiry elicited no response from any of the company unless it were the curt, but sympathetic comment of Miss Cushman : "Where, indeed ? " Even Mr. Lumley, the zealous upholder of the Ballet, for the satisfactory reason supplied by his banking account, refused to do battle for his favourite entertainment for its acrobatic and too angular developments. The Ballet was at that time in the height of its popularity, when Taglioni, Ellsler or Cerito, as the case might be, twirled upon her "pliant toe."

> And such a burst
> Of irrepressible, overpowering joy
> Filled all the air, it seemed as men were mad,
> And dancing were supremest bliss of earth,
> The fairest dancer, first of womankind.

When at the conclusion of the performance, the graceful Coryphee entered the carriage that waited at the door to convey her to the hotel, the impulsive multitude, as if suddenly imbued with the idea that horses were animals too ignoble to be entrusted with a burthen so precious

> Unyoked the prancing jennets from her car
> And drew her forth triumphant to her home.

But, even in these flourishing days of the Ballet, it was culminating to its fall; and for many years before the final retirement in 1858 of Mr. Lumley from the management of Her Majesty's Theatre, it gradually declined in public favour, supported principally by the antiquated dandies of the town. Mr. Lumley, in his *Reminiscences of the Opera*, published in 1864, records that the English people were " little accustomed to receive with regard the larger and superior kind of choregraphic exhibition, and awarded grudgingly the slightest meed of applause to male dancing." In these words he bore testimony, not the less real because it was not intended, to the truth of the allegation that it was not the dancing which had charms for the aristocratic frequenters of his theatre, but only the display of female grace and beauty when scantily draped.

At this time Miss Cushman's recent appearance as Romeo was the talk of the town, and had, doubtless, by the celebrity which she had acquired by her excellent impersonation of the character, obtained for her the acquaintance of Mr. Rogers, and an invitation to his table. Her sister Susan, then unmarried, supported her in the part of Juliet. It was considered daring by some, and improper by others, for a lady to assume a male character; but the general public not only had no objection to the assumption, but, on the contrary, looked upon it with favour. All other Romeos hitherto known on the stage had, without exception, looked too old for so juvenile a part, and Miss Cushman, though by no means a handsome woman, possessed a good figure. She looked exceedingly well in male apparel, and rendered full justice to the difficult part, by her undoubted genius, besides affording an agreeable and striking contrast to such elderly Romeos as Macready and Charles Kemble. She looked the part infinitely better than either, and performed it with a power, a spirit, and a tenderness which they may, perhaps, have equalled, but which they certainly did not surpass. Her success was conspicuous, but was not destined to be of such long continuance as that which she achieved as Meg Merrilies, in the dramatized version of Scott's noble romance of the *Antiquary*. To use the well-known phrase, her impersonation "fairly took the town by storm." Her "make-up," to which she devoted the utmost care and study, was in every respect admirable, and her masculine cast of features — for not even the politest, to say nothing of the warmest, admirers of her genius could assert that she was beautiful— added to the weird and almost unearthly reality of the portraiture. To this character, more than any other in her range, she was indebted for the great success which attended her in the metropolis, and in all the great cities of the Empire.

Miss Cushman was not only masculine in appearance, but was sometimes masculine in her language, and did not scruple to use the commonest and vulgarest words in the vernacular, when it pleased her to be unusually emphatic in the expression of her anger or animosity. But, notwithstanding such occasional outbursts, which were possibly more affected than real, Miss Cushman possessed a truly feminine heart, and was a great favourite with the most elegant and cultivated of her sex, and was the charm of every society into which she was admitted.

Of Barry Cornwall, or Mr. Bryan Waller Proctor, I have but slight remembrance. He was the son-in-law of the once well-known Basil Montague, a prosperous conveyancer, husband of the Mrs. Basil Montague, a leader in the literary and fashionable circles of London in the third and fourth decades of the nineteenth century. Mr. Proctor, as I have already said, aspired to be a poet, and was recognized as such by the literary coteries and some of the weekly (or weakly) critics of the time; but such reputation as he acquired has long since faded away, and he is scarcely known to the present generation, except as the father of the late Adelaide Anne Proctor. This young lady was a true poetess, who was removed prematurely from a world which her genius promised to adorn. Mr. Proctor, through the social influence of his father-in-law, was appointed to the lucrative office of a Commissioner of Lunacy, which he held during his lifetime. The last time I met him was at a dinner given by Sir Edward Bulwer Lytton, afterwards Lord Lytton, in celebration of the appointment of Mr. John Forster, the well-known friend and adviser of Charles Dickens, to a similar commissionership. Mr. Forster was an eminent man of letters, but owed his appointment chiefly, if not entirely, to the services he had rendered to the Liberal Party when editor of *The Examiner* newspaper—as colleague of and successor to the brilliant Albany Fonblanque. Mr. Forster's last work was the *Life of Charles Dickens*, published not long after the death of the illustrious novelist, which divulged, for the first time, the painful episodes of his early boyhood, which proved that novelists, as well as poets, are too often

> Cradled into poetry by wrong,
> And learn in suffering what they teach in song.

Breakfasts with Samuel Rogers.

No. VII.

It was during the unsettled times that preceded the great French Revolution of 1848—I think it was in January of that year—that one of Mr. Rogers's breakfasts was attended by Prince Louis Napoleon Buonaparte, afterwards Napoleon III., Dr. Whateley, the Protestant Archbishop of Dublin, Lord William Pitt Lennox, the son of the Duke of Richmond (who distinguished himself at the Battle of Waterloo, and died many years afterwards as Governor-General of Canada), and myself. I was previously acquainted with all these gentlemen, and had met the Prince a few days previously at the house of Mr. John MacGregor, formerly Secretary of the Board of Trade, and Member of Parliament for Glasgow. The Prince, who was then forty years of age, had long been a resident in

London, as an exile, spoke English exceedingly well, had thoroughly studied the working of the British Constitution, and had learned to respect and possibly to love the English people. He was very taciturn and undemonstrative; his dull grey eyes seemed to have little speculation in them, and to have been given to him—if such an expression may be used—to look inwards upon himself rather than outwards upon the world. They brightened up at rare intervals, when anything was said that particularly interested him. On this occasion, the talk of the breakfast-table turned a good deal upon French politics, and the probability, more or less imminent, of a revolutionary outbreak in Paris consequent upon the unwise opposition of Louis Philippe and his too obsequious minister, M. Guizot, to the question of the extension of the franchise and the reform of the French Parliament. As I had within a fortnight or three weeks of this time returned from Paris, where I had associated with some leading Liberal politicians, among others with Beranger the poet, and the Abbè de Lamennais, my opinion upon the situation was asked, I think, by Mr. Rogers, and whether I thought the agitation would subside.

"Not," I said, "unless the King yields."

"He won't yield, I think," said the Prince. "He does not understand the seriousness of the case."

I told the Prince that Beranger, who knew the temper and sympathised with the opinions of the people, had predicted the establishment of a Republic, consequent upon the downfall of the monarchy, within less than a twelvemonth. Lamennais did not give the King so long a lease of power, but foresaw revolution within six months.

The Prince remarked, "that if there were barricades in the streets of Paris, such as those by which his way to the throne was won in 1830, the King would not give orders to disperse the mob by force of arms."

"Why do you think so?" asked Mr. Rogers.

"The King is a weak man—a merciful man. He does not like bloodshed. I often think he was a fool not to have had me shot after the affair of Strasburgh. Had our cases been reversed, I know that I would have had him shot without mercy."

I thought little of the remark at the time; but in after years, when the exiled Prince became the powerful Emperor, my mind often reverted to this conversation. I thought that if King Louis Philippe had done what the Prince considered he ought to have done—and as he would have been fully justified by law, civil and military, as well as by State policy, in doing — the whole course of European history would have been changed.

Personally the Prince was highly esteemed by

all who knew him. Stern as a politician, and in pursuit of the great object of his ambition, as in the famous *coup-d'état* of 1851, by which he raised himself at a bound from the humble chair of a President to the most conspicuous imperial throne in the world—he was in private life of a singularly amiable temper. He never forgot in his prosperity the friends or even the acquaintances of his adversity; never ceased to remember any benefit that had been conferred upon him, and not only to be grateful for it, but to show his gratitude by acts of kindness and generosity, if the kindness or generosity could be of benefit to the fortunes of the persons on whom it was bestowed. When he sought the hand in marriage of a Princess of the House of Austria, and the honour was declined, for the occult and unwhispered reason that he was a *parvenu* and an upstart, and that his throne was at the mercy of a revolution [and what throne is not ?], he married, from pure love and affection, a noble lady of inferior rank, and raised her to a throne which she filled for many years with more grace and splendour than any sovereign born in the purple of royalty had ever exhibited, Queen Victoria alone excepted.

The Prince thoroughly understood the character of the French people. Napoleon I. had called the English a nation of shopkeepers. Napoleon III. knew that the French were entitled in a far greater degree than the English to that depreciatory epithet. He knew that in their hearts they did not care so much for liberty and fraternity as they did for " equality "; that what they wanted in the first place was peace, so that trade and industry might have a chance to prosper; and secondly, that France as a nation might be the predominant Power in Europe. For the first reason they required a master who would maintain order; for the second reason, they idolized the name of the first Napoleon. These two things were patent to the mind of Napoleon III., and formed the key-stone of his domestic and foreign policy.

When London, about three months after the breakfast at Mr. Rogers's, was threatened, on the 10th of April 1848, by an insurrectionary mob of Chartists, under the guidance of a crazy Irishman named Fergus O'Connor, who afterwards died in a lunatic asylum, the Prince volunteered to act as a special constable, for the preservation of the peace, in common with many thousands of respectable professional men, merchants and tradesmen. I met him in Trafalgar Square, armed with the truncheon of a policeman. On this occasion the Duke of Wellington, then Commander-in-Chief of the British army, had taken the precaution to station the military in sufficient numbers at all the chief strategical points of the metropolis, ready, though concealed from the notice of the multitude, to act on an emergency. Happily their services were not required ; the Sovereign was popular, the upper and middle classes were unanimous, a large section of the labouring classes had no sympathy with Chartism, and the display of the civic force, with bludgeons and staves only, without fire - arms of any kind, was quite sufficient to overawe the rioters. I stopped for a minute to exchange greetings with the Prince, and said I did not think, from all that I had heard, that the Chartists would resort to violence, and that their march through the streets would be orderly. The Prince was of the same opinion, and passed upon his beat among other police and special constables in front of the National Gallery.

As Lord William Lennox was of the breakfast-party, I took the opportunity to ask him a question with regard to a disputed point. I had lately visited Brussels, the city in which I had passed my school-boy days, and which was consequently endeared to my mind by many youthful associations. The mother of Lord William, the beautiful Duchess of Richmond, had given a great ball on the night preceding the battle of Waterloo in June 1815, at which Lord William, then in his sixteenth year, was present. Every lover of poetry will remember the splendid description of this ball, and of the subsequent battle, which occurs in the third Canto of Byron's *Childe Harold.* The passage is unsurpassed in any language in any time for the vigour, the picturesqueness, and the magnificence of its thought and diction; and to its relation to one of the most stupendous events in modern history:—

> There was a sound of revelry by night,
>   And Belgium's capital had gather'd then
> Her Beauty and her Chivalry, and bright
>   The lamps shone o'er fair women and brave men;
>   A thousand hearts beat happily; and when
> Music arose with its voluptuous swell,
>   Soft eyes look'd love to eyes which spake again,
> And all went merry as a marriage bell;
>   But hush! hark! a deep sound strikes like a rising knell!

It has been generally asserted and believed that the ball was given by the Duchess in the grand hall of the stately Hotel de Ville, in the Grande Place; and when in Brussels I heard the assertion repeated by many people, though denied by others. One venerable citizen, who remembered the battle well, affirmed it to have been at the Hotel de Ville, which he saw brilliantly lighted up for the occasion, and passed among the crowd of equipages that filled the Grande Place, when setting down and taking up the ladies who graced the assembly with their presence. Another equally old and trustworthy inhabitant declared that to his personal knowledge the ball was given in the *Palais d'Aes*, a large building that adjoins the Palace of the King of the Belgians, and is now used as a barrack;

while a third affirmed it to have been held in the handsome hotel formerly occupied by Sir Charles Bagot, the British Ambassador to Brussels and the Hague in 1830.

Thinking there could be no better authority than one who was present on the occasion, one, moreover, who was so nearly allied to the giver of the entertainment, I asked Lord William to decide the point. He replied at once that all three assertions were unfounded. His father the Duke took a large house in a small street, called the "Rue de la Blanchisserie" (Street of the Wash-house) abutting on the Boulevard opposite the present Botanic Gardens. The ball took place in the not extraordinarily spacious drawing-room of that mansion. He said, moreover, that the lines,

> Within the window'd niche of that high hall
> Sat Brunswick's fated chieftain,

conveyed an idea of magnitude, which the so-called "high hall" did not in reality possess.

Archbishop Whateley here said: "If we may be permitted, without breach of good manners, to speak of Waterloo in the presence of Prince Napoleon, I may remark that the correction of the very minor error just made by Lord William, though exceedingly interesting, is not of great importance. Though contradicted again and again, the report still circulates, and is still believed, that the Duke of Wellington was surprised on the eve of the battle of Waterloo by the rapid march of the Emperor, and was thus taken at a disadvantage."

"I never believed the report," said the Prince; "though I have my own views about the battle. I visited Waterloo in the winter of 1832, with what feelings you may imagine."

"The truth as regards the alleged surprise," said the Archbishop, "appears to be, as Lord Byron explained in a note to the passage in *Childe Harold*, that the Duke had received intelligence of Napoleon's march, and at first had the idea of requesting the Duchess of Richmond to countermand the ball, but, on reflection, considered it desirable that the people of Brussels should be kept in ignorance of the course of events. He therefore desired the Duchess to let the ball proceed; and gave commands to all the general officers, who had been invited, to appear at it, each taking care to quit the room at 10 o'clock, quietly, and without giving any notification, except to each of the under-officers to join their respective divisions *en route*. There is no doubt that many of the subalterns who were not in the secret were surprised at the suddenness of the order."

"I heard, when I visited the field of Waterloo less than a month ago," I said, "that many of the officers joined the march in their dancing-shoes, so little time was left for them to obey orders."

"It has been proved to the satisfaction of every competent inquirer into the facts," said Mr. Rogers, "that, as far as the Duke himself and his superior officers were concerned, there was no surprise in the matter. You know the story of the daring young lady, who, presuming on her beauty to be forgiven for her impertinence, asked the Duke point blank at an evening party whether he had not been surprised at Waterloo. 'Certainly not,' he replied; 'but I am now!'"

"A proper rebuke," said Lord William. "I hope the lady felt it."

Byron, in the beautiful stanzas to which allusion has been made, describes the wood of Soignes, improperly written Soignies, in the environs of Brussels, a portion of the great forest of Ardennes—

> And Ardennes waves above them her green leaves
> Dewy with Nature's tear-drops as they pass,
> Grieving, if aught inanimate e'er grieves,
> Over the unreturning brave.

In a note to this passage he speaks of Ardennes as famous in Boiardo's *Orlando* and immortal in Shakspeare's *As You Like It*. Whatever may have been the case with Boiardo, it is all but certain that Shakspeare's " Arden " was not the Ardennes near Brussels, but the forest of Arden in Warwickshire, near his native town of Stratford-on-Avon. He frequented this " Arden " in his youth, perhaps in chasing the wild deer of Sir Thomas Lucy;

perhaps in love-rambles with Anne Hathaway. Portions of the forest still remain, containing in a now enclosed part, the property of a private gentleman, some venerable oak-trees, one of which, as I roughly measured it with my walking-stick, is upwards of thirty feet in circumference within a yard of the ground. This tree, with several others still standing, must have been old in the days of Shakspeare; and in its shadow Shakspeare may himself have reclined in the happy days ere he went to London in search of fame and fortune. *Arden*, spelled Ardennes in French, is a purely Keltic word, meaning "the high forest," from *ard*, "high," and *airdean*, "heights." The English district is still called "Arden," and the small town of Henley, within its boundaries, is described as Henley-in-Arden to distinguish it from many other Henleys that exist in England.

Lord William Lennox married in early life the once celebrated cantatrice, Miss Paton, from whom he was divorced. He was a somewhat voluminous author of third-rate novels and a frequent contributor to the periodical press. He died in 1880, in his eighty-first year.

Dr. Whateley, Archbishop of Dublin, was the author of a very able treatise on Logic and Rhetoric, long the text-book of the schools; and also of a once famous *jeu d'esprit*, entitled *Historic Doubts Concerning Napoleon Buonaparte*, in which he proved irrefragably by false logic, likely to convince idle and unthinking readers, that no such person as Napoleon Buonaparte ever did exist or could have existed. In this clever little work he ridiculed, under the guise of seeming impartiality and critical acumen, the many attempts that had been made, especially by French writers of the school of Voltaire, to prove that Jesus Christ was a purely imaginary character, as much a *myth* as the gods of Grecian and Roman mythology. Mr. Greville, in his *Memoirs of the Courts of George III., George IV., and William IV.*, records that he met " Whateley, Archbishop of Dublin," at a dinner party, and describes him " as a very ordinary man in appearance and conversation, with something pretentious in his talk, and as telling stories without point." Nevertheless, he admitted him to be " a very able man." My opinion of the Archbishop was far more favourable. The first thing that struck me with regard to him was the clear precision of his reasoning, as befitted a man who had written with such undoubted authority on Logic and Rhetoric, and the second his rare tolerance for all conscientious differences of opinion on religious matters. Two years previously, as I have already mentioned, I had sat next to him on the platform of the inaugural meeting held by the friends of the Athenæum at Manchester in support of that institution. Several Bishops had been invited, and had signified their intention to be present; but all of them except Dr. Whateley had withdrawn as soon as it was publicly announced that Mr. George Dawson, a popular lecturer and Unitarian preacher of advanced opinions, was to address the audience. Mr. Dawson was at the time a very young man, spoke with great eloquence and power, and impressed the audience favourably, the Archbishop included.

"I think," said Dr. Whateley, turning to me at the conclusion of the speech, "that my reverend brethren would have taken no harm from being present to-night, and that more than one of them whom I could name would be all the better if they could preach with as much power and spirit as this boy has displayed in his speech."

On another occasion, when I was in Dublin in 1849, I heard that several ultra-orthodox Protestant clergymen in that city had been heard to express regret that Dr. Whateley was so lax in his religious belief. I asked in what manner, and was told in reply that he had publicly spoken of Dr. Murray, the Roman Catholic Archbishop of Dublin, then in his eighty-first year, as "a good man, a very good man"; adding the hope "that he himself might be found worthy to meet Murray in heaven."

This tolerant and large-minded prelate died in 1868 in his seventy-seventh year.

Breakfasts with Samuel Rogers.
No. VIII.

Mrs. Norton was not only one of the most beautiful women of her time, but one of the most accomplished and fascinating. Lady Blessington, though not so beautiful, was still a very attractive person, and aspired to fill in London society a position similar to that formerly occupied in Paris by the literary ladies who, on certain days every week, kept open house for all the literary, artistic, scientific, and intellectual celebrities of the day. This position she filled with much approval, and with as much success as the difference in social manners between the upper classes in London and Paris would allow. Mr. Macaulay, who had not then published his *History of England*, was known as the most potent critic and brilliant essayist in the ranks of literature, as it then flourished. He also enjoyed considerable reputation as a poet, which he did not, however, deserve; but was socially known as a brilliant conversationalist, unrivalled by any contemporary, the Rev. Sidney Smith alone excepted.

Such was the company, of which I was privileged to make one, that assembled one morning at the breakfast-table of Mr. Rogers, to partake of "the feast of reason and the flow of soul" that oftener accompany a refection of tea and coffee, brown bread and fresh butter, together with strawberries or other fruit in the morning, than in the evening as adjuncts to the fish, venison, and game, and the claret, Burgundy, and champagne, of what is thought to be the superior repast. At least, such was the opinion of Mr. Rogers; and that was the reason why he usually preferred to bring his friends together at breakfast rather than at dinner.

Every one of the company had written and published verses, or—as no doubt every one of them thought—poetry (which is often a very different thing), and the conversation turned upon poetic art as distinguished from poetic genius. There was a general agreement in the opinion that the rhymes of the English language were comparatively few, and that they had been all so frequently used as to be well-nigh worn out. Their constant repetitions, familiar to all readers and writers, were cited and dwelt upon, as were also the wild attempts of some poets, from the days of Butler, the author of *Hudibras*, to those of Byron, the author of *Don Juan*, to manufacture new and unexpected compound rhymes.

"I greatly appreciate," said Mrs. Norton, "the desperate ingenuity of Samuel Butler's rhymes in *Hudibras*—one more especially, where he says of the ranting and canting preachers of the conventicle, at the time of the Commonwealth, when England was overrun with rabid 'saints'—that the

> Pulpit drum ecclesiastic
> Was beat with fist, instead of a stick."

This, she thought, was excelled, if not in daring, most certainly in elaborate complication, by the very clever rhyme of Lord Byron,

> Tell me, ye lords of ladies intellectual,
> Now tell me truly, have they not hen-peck'd you all?

"Nothing could be better of its kind," said Mr. Macaulay. "But the aid of such rhymes is only available for the comic versifiers. The least attempt of any serious poet to indulge in such eccentricities would be fatal alike to his verses and his reputation."

"True poets, who write in English," I ventured to remark, "have no real need of rhyme. Blank verse is quite sufficient for poetry of the highest order. Some of the most magnificent passages in Shakespeare and Milton are in blank verse. Homer, Sophocles, Virgil, and Lucretius, and all the poets of classical antiquity, were ignorant of rhyme, and English poetry of the highest class would be none the poorer if rhyme were unknown."

"I grant you," said Mr. Macaulay. "But poetry of a class only inferior to the highest—the lyrical and ballad poetry in which English literature is so rich—would be deprived of its principal charm if rhyme were abolished. A song, a hymn, or a ballad, would, to my mind, lose one of its principal attractions if the ear were not tickled and the memory were not aided by the musical jingle of the rhymes."

"But still," said Lady Blessington, "you must allow that our rhymes are worn sadly threadbare by constant repetition; and that many excellent and highly poetical words, which poets would like to use, if they were available for the purpose, are without rhymes altogether. There is, for instance, no rhyme for 'silver,' though there are many for gold. Neither are there any to 'buxom,' 'lovely,' 'urgent,' 'kingdom,' 'picture,' 'portrait,' 'music,' 'noble,' 'orange,' 'herald,' and many others that I cannot now remember, or for disyllabic and trisyllabic words generally. For some other words in common use among poets and rhymers, the rhymes are exceedingly few, and, when they are employed, break upon the ear with all the monotony of a hurdy-gurdy or a barrel-organ."

"It has often struck me," said Mrs. Norton, "that English poets might, if consonances failed them—as they often do—produce very pleasing effects in their verse, by means of assonances. The old ballad-writers—partly from design, perhaps, but probably oftener from laziness—contented themselves with assonances when consonances were troublesome to find. In one of the most beautiful songs ever written—at least, I think so—the old Scotch song, 'There's nae luck about the house,' which is often erroneously attributed to Robert Burns, there is a stanza, of which the music, to my ear, is unexceptionable, in which there is an assonance which is so pleasing as entirely to atone for the imperfect rhyme:

> And shall I see his face again,
> And shall I hear him *speak?*
> I'm downright dizzy wi' the thought;
> In troth I'm like to *greet.*"

"The lines are very beautiful," said Lady Blessington.

"I think," said Mr. Macaulay, "that the old ballad-singers and ballad-writers would have been glad to have found good rhymes, had they been able to do so; but that they did not always care to take the trouble to be correct. And very often their carelessness did not signify. I remember two cases in the fine ballad of the 'Gaberlunzie Man,' to be found in *Percy's Reliques,*

> The night was cauld, the carle was *wat,*
> My daughter's shoulders he 'gan to *clap.*

where the assonance of 'wat' and 'clap' was sufficient to satisfy the ear of the author, and of the reader, too.

> 'And oh!' quoth she, 'an' I were as *white*
> As ever the snow lay on the *dike,*'

where he was as easily pleased."

"We must take these old ballads as we find them," said Mr. Rogers, "with all their roughness and imperfections; but we should be very wrong to imitate them in their defects. And, if we did, we might not, perhaps, be able to imitate them in their beauties. Either let us have perfect blank verse or perfect rhyme."

"But perfect blank verse," said Mr. Macaulay, "is not satisfactory to the English ear, unless it be decasyllabic, as it often is in Shakespeare, Milton, and other great writers. Lyrical measures, without rhymes, are extremely disappointing. They lead the reader to expect what he does not receive, and impress him involuntarily with the feeling that, after all, prose would be far preferable to verse that aspires to be verse, but is verse in name only. Take, for instance, one of the poems of Henry Kirke White, entitled, 'The Early Primrose,' in which there is a string of such stanzas as the following:

> Mild offspring of a dark and sullen sire,
> Whose modest form so delicately pure
> Was nursed in whirling storms
> And cradled in the winds.

Here the English is perfect as well as the rhythm and cadence of the verse; but the whole effect is tantalising. We long for something that eludes our grasp; and the bud of poesy falls from the stalk without having opened into the flower that was expected."

"I quite agree with you," said Mrs. Norton. "In the lyrical form of poetry, rhyme is imperative, but in the narrative form, especially when the narrative is serious, it might be dispensed with. I am heretic enough to think that the *Lay of the Last Minstrel* and the *Lady of the Lake*, beautiful as they are as they stand, are not altogether improved by the lyrical style and the dancing measure in which they are written, and that they have a tendency to pall on the ear by their monotony."

"There is one form of blank verse," said Mr. Macaulay, "a very ancient form, which, I must own, has a certain charm for my ear, although it is not in the decasyllabic metre. I mean that in which the excellent old poem of *Piers Ploughman* is written. Have you, Mr. Rogers, a copy of *Piers Ploughman* in your library? No doubt you have; and I should be obliged if you could let me have a sight of it."

Mr. Rogers rang the bell, and his valet, Payne, his constant attendant, who acted as his librarian, answered the summons. The book was brought immediately, and Mr. Macaulay, preparatory to turning over the leaves, fixed his attention on the very first page.

"Here, at the opening of the poem," he said,

"I find a specimen of the verse to which I wish to direct attention:

> In a *s*omer *s*eason,
> When *s*oft was the *s*unne,
> I *s*hoop me into *s*hroudès.

A little further on I find another specimen:

> Unholy of *w*erkes
> *W*ent *w*ide into the *w*orld
> *W*onders to hear.

And again:

> *P*atriarchs and *p*rophets,
> And *p*reachers of God's wordes.

In all these passages you will notice the music of the alliterations. In the first it is the letter *s* which does duty, in the second *w*, in the third *p*. These alliterations—three at least, and sometimes five in a single couplet—are imperative in the construction of the verse, and serve to supply that titillation to the ear which the taste of that day considered essential, in the absence of rhyme. The general effect seems to me to be pleasing."

"I very much doubt," said Lady Blessington, "whether such a structure of verse, pleasant as it is, would be acceptable to modern ears, and whether it would not be voted tedious and monotonous."

"Alliteration, in a moderate degree," said Mrs. Norton, "lends a peculiar charm to poetry, and serves to impress upon the memory any fine passage in which it may occur. The line in *Childe Harold*, where Byron, describing the battle of Waterloo, and the death of the Duke of Brunswick, says of the ill-fated hero that he

> Rushed into the field, and foremost fighting fell,

has always seemed to me to be productive of the finest possible effect."

In this opinion we all agreed. It was also conceded that the judicious use of alliteration added a charm to any otherwise fine passage in which it might occur. But no one was able to suggest a remedy for the poverty of the English language in rhymes, except in the compound rhymes, which are only permissible in mock heroics or in comic verse. In these the utmost limit of combination is allowed, as in the *Ingoldsby Legends*, which were then in the first flush of their early popularity, and afforded many excellent examples of the abounding capabilities of the vernacular English in this respect. The conversation afterwards turned upon the availability of the hexameter as a variation upon the comparative monotony of the old heroic ten-syllabic metre. But the hexameter met with but slight favour. The two ladies and Mr. Rogers were strongly opposed to it, and Mr. Macaulay had little or nothing to say in its favour.

"What," he asked, "can be more inconsistent

with the genius of English prosody than the following, among hundreds of others that might be cited at random, from Southey's *Vision of Judgment?*

> Toll, toll, through the silence of evening!
> 'Tis a deep, dull sound, that is heavy and mournful at all times;
> For it tells of mortality always. But heavier this day
> Fell on the conscious ear its deeper and mournfuller import."

"To my ear," said Mr. Rogers, "this is utterly discordant, and even painful. 'Evening' and 'import,' at the conclusion of the lines, are all very well, and are pronounced as they ought to be; but 'all times' and 'this day'—with a strong emphasis on 'this' and a slight one on 'day'—if they are pronounced according to the rhythmical necessities of the structure of the verse, seem to me to be utterly alien and inimical to the spirit of English poetry."

"To me, also," said Mrs. Norton, "the true hexameter of the English—if the word can be properly applied to what is not a hexameter—is the old ballad metre of fourteen syllables in a line, instead of twelve. The fourteen syllables are usually printed, for the convenience of the compositor, in two lines—one of eight and one of six—as in the fine old ballad of *Chevy Chase*, which

Sir Philip Sidney declared to stir his heart as with the sound of a trumpet:

The child shall rue that is unborn, the hunting of that day."

"I should like to know," observed Lady Blessington, " if any finer specimen of English versification has ever been given to the world than the ancient ballad of the *Nut Brown Maid*, which is written in that ancient metre. If there has been, I must own that I have never met with it or heard of it. Indeed, I doubt if, as mere versification, the English language can produce its equal in any poem of the same extent."

Mr. Macaulay at first thought he could cite some poems of the fifteenth or sixteenth centuries which might match it, but afterwards confessed that he was in error, and that the *Nut Brown Maid* was unique both for rhyme and rhythm. He held that it was vastly superior in every respect to the attempt of Matthew Prior in the eighteenth century to introduce it to a newer generation in a more classical garb. Not, he said, that Prior's poem would not have given pleasure to most readers, and even to many severe critics, if it had been first in the field, or if it had stood alone. But all comparison with the original, he thought, was fatal to the claim of its imitator.

The persons who thus discoursed upon the art of poetry, though they were all poets or versifiers, were not poets of the first rank—not even Mr. Rogers himself, or the Honourable Mrs. Norton. They both stood high in the second rank, and might even lay claim to genius, and have their claims allowed, though not perhaps very enthusiastically. But Lady Blessington and Mr. Macaulay were not even of the second rank, though Mr. Macaulay was a versifier of the very first order. The only one of the three who afterwards added to the poetic fame which they had previously acquired was Mrs. Norton, who, under happier circumstances than those in which her lot was cast, might have more than justified the title of the English "Sappho," which her admirers bestowed upon her.

The early life of this gifted woman was most unhappy. Lord Melbourne, who was himself one of the most agreeable as well as one of the most able men of his time, was fascinated more than he ought to have been by the conversation and society of Mrs. Norton, and passed in her company many hours, that, as Prime Minister, he ought to have devoted to the business of the nation. By this indiscretion—to give it no harsher name—which in other respects was perfectly innocent, he set the tongue of scandal in motion against himself and the lady, to such an extent as to lead his party opponents to imagine that they could damage him politically, and his administration along with him, by working upon the jealous weakness of her not very clever husband, one of the police magistrates of the metropolis, who owed his appointment to Lord Melbourne.

They did so with such mischievous effect that they persuaded, or rather incited, him to commence an action against the Prime Minister for criminal conversation with his wife. The base and cowardly plot succeeded but too well, and all London rang for several months with the scandal it created. The ill-judged action ultimately came on for trial, and resulted—to the satisfaction of all impartial people—in the triumphant vindication of the lady's character. But in such unhappy cases, as in that of Cæsar's wife, two thousand years previously, the mere suspicion, and the whispered calumnies that are certain to be built upon even smaller foundations, left their traces in the popular mind. For many long years the "unco' guid and rigidly righteous," affected to believe, to use their own language, that with so much smoke there must have been more or less fire.

The husband and wife only met again once as long as they lived; and that was at the grave of one of their children, more than a quarter of a century afterwards. Lord Melbourne provided handsomely, through his sister, Lady Palmerston, for the woman to whom his well-meant but unlucky attentions had done such great social injury, and settled upon her an annuity, sufficient in amount to maintain her in comfort, though not in splendour, and provide her with leisure to cultivate literature for the love she bore it, without being wholly dependent on the pecuniary rewards it might bring her. Her later years made amends, by the happiness they brought her, for the troubles she had endured in the first flush of her youth, her beauty, and her fame.

On her husband's death, she accepted the hand of the celebrated Sir William Stirling Maxwell, of Kier, the head of an illustrious Scottish family. He was known in Scotland as "Kier," a title of more than nobility in the estimation of all Perthshire. Sir William was not only a man of high rank, but was of the very highest eminence in literature. He had long known, admired, and esteemed Mrs. Norton. The marriage was one of mutual esteem and affection, as well as of worldly wisdom, and shed a halo of happy light over the autumnal years of a noble couple.

Lady Blessington was a general favourite in the male society of the metropolis; but was under a social cloud among the ladies, in consequence of her very peculiar and highly immoral relations with the handsome Count D'Orsay—" the glass of fashion and the mould of form." The Count was a man as fair to look upon as Antinous or Adonis must have been; but, as his life showed, as devoid of all moral principle as Jupiter, or any other god or demi-god in the Greek and Roman mythology. Their *salon* at Gore House, Kensington, was for many years the resort of all that was eminent in the literature and social life of the time, at least on the male side of both.

The Count was the recognised arbiter of the fashions of the day, the dandy *par excellence*, the very Prince or Pope of tailors, who not only competed for his custom, but furnished him with clothes, "free gratis and for nothing," in order that they might be enabled to make it known that the supreme "elegant," the "beau," the "masher," the "dude" of the day was supplied from their establishments. And not only the tailors, but the hatters, the glovers, the shirt-makers, and the boot-makers, were proud to supply him on the same terms, never sending him any bills, or, if they did, making him understand that he would never be asked for the money.

It has been said of poets that, in their youth, they

> Begin in gladness,
> But thereof come in the end despondency and madness.

So it might have been said of Lady Blessington and the Count D'Orsay. They began in gladness, and continued in gladness for a time; but the end was bankruptcy and ruin. They were compelled to leave London in 1849 or 1850, and, taking refuge in Paris, found a protector for awhile in the Emperor Napoleon III., who, in the days of his exile in London, had been a constant guest at Gore House, where the brilliant and hospitable but shameless couple resided. They both died in Paris, in comparative, if not in actual poverty, and in complete neglect, the Countess eking out her scanty means by ill-paid contributions to second and third-rate newspapers in London, which the Count did his utmost to sell for her—not always successfully. If truth must be told, the Countess was not at the best of times a very clever writer, and such little talent as she once possessed had become weakened in the days of her adversity. The Emperor Napoleon did all he could for the couple; for he was pre-eminently a grateful man, and never forgot, in the height of his power and glory, those whose friendship he had enjoyed in the days of his exile, when he was looked down upon by the highest society of London.

Breakfasts with Samuel Rogers.
No. IX.

It was in the summer of 1844, a few days after the interment in Westminster Abbey of Thomas Campbell, author of *The Pleasures of Hope*, and many other celebrated poems, that I received an invitation to breakfast with Mr. Rogers, to meet the Rev. Mr. Milman, the officiating clergyman on that solemn occasion. There were three other guests besides myself, the Rev. Alexander Dyce, well-known as a commentator on Shakspeare; Mr. Serjeant Talfourd, an eminent lawyer; Mr. Thomas Miller, originally a basket-maker, who had acquired considerable reputation as a poet and novelist, and as a hard-working man of letters.

Dr. Milman was at the time Rector of St. Margaret's, the little church that stands close to Westminster Abbey, and interferes greatly with the view of that noble cathedral. He was afterwards Dean of St. Paul's, and was known to fame as the author of the successful tragedy of *Fazio*, of many poetical volumes of no great merit, and of a *History of the Jews* and a *History of Christianity*, both of which still retain their reputation.

The conversation turned principally on the funeral of the poet, at which both Mr. Dyce and myself had been present. The pall-bearers were among the most distinguished men of the time, for their rank, their talent, and their high literary and political position. They included Sir Robert Peel, Lord Brougham, Lord Campbell, the Duke of Argyll, the Earl of Strangford, and the Duke of Buccleuch, the last named the generous nobleman —noble in nature as well as in rank—who had offered, when a lad in his teens, to pay the debts of his illustrious namesake, Sir Walter Scott, when the great novelist had fallen upon evil days in the full flush of his fame and popularity. A long procession of authors, sculptors, artists, and other distinguished men, followed the coffin to the grave. Many Polish exiles were conspicuous among them. As Mr. Milman pronounced the affecting words of the burial service, " dust to dust, ashes to ashes," a Polish gentleman made his way through the ranks of the mourners, and, drawing a handful of earth from a little basket which he carried, exclaimed in a clear voice, " This is Polish earth for the tomb of the friend of Poland," and sprinkled it upon the coffin. This dramatic incident recalled to my memory, as it no doubt did to that of other spectators, Campbell's unwearied exertions in the cause of Poland, and the indignant lines in the *Pleasures of Hope* :

> Hope for a season bade the world farewell,
> And Freedom shrieked when Kosciusko fell.

Mr. Rogers, reminded, perhaps, of a grievance by the presence at the breakfast-table of Mr. Milman, seemed to brood over an injustice that he thought had been done him with reference to the late poet. When Campbell, under the pressure of some pecuniary difficulty, complained of the scanty rewards of literature—and especially of poetry—Mr. Rogers was reported to have recommended him to endeavour to procure employment as a clerk! This was thought to be very unfeeling; but on this occasion Mr. Rogers explained to the whole company that he had been misunderstood, and that he had not meant any unkindness.

"I myself," he said, "was a clerk in my early days, and never had to depend upon poetry for my bread; and I only suggested that in Mr. Campbell's case, and in that of every other literary man, it would be much better if the writing of poetry were an amusement only, and not a business."

"No doubt!" said Mr. Dyce. "But men of genius are not always the masters of their own youth, and cannot invariably choose their careers, or make choice of a profession, which requires means and time to qualify for it. You, for instance, Mr. Rogers, when a clerk, were clerk to your father, and qualified yourself under his auspices for partnership in, or succession to the management of, his prosperous Bank. Mr. Campbell had no such chances."

"It is a large question," said Dr. Milman. "The love of literature in a man of genius, rich or poor—especially if poor—is an all-absorbing passion, and shapes his life, regret it as we may. Literature has rewards more pleasant than those of money, pleasant though money undoubtedly is. If money were to be the 'be-all and end-all' of life, it would be better to be a rich cheesemonger or butcher than a poor author. But no high-spirited, intelligent, and ambitious youth is of this opinion, or shapes his life by it. Sensitive youths drift into poetry, as prosaic and adventurous youths drift into the army or the navy."

"The more's the pity," replied Mr. Rogers, "as by drifting into poetry they too often drift into poverty and misery. I trust, however, you will all understand that the idle or the malevolent gossips did, and do me, gross injustice when they say that I recommended Campbell to accept a clerkship rather than continue to rely upon poetry. I never thought of doing so. I merely expressed a general wish that every man of genius, not born to wealth, should have a recognised trade or profession to rely upon for his daily bread."

"A wish that all men would agree in," said Mr. Dyce; "and that, after all, had no particular or exclusive reference to Mr. Campbell. He did not find the literature, which he adorned, utterly unprofitable. He made money by his poetry, and by his literary labour generally, besides gaining a pension of three hundred pounds per annum on the Civil List, and the society of all the most eminent men of his time, which he could not have done as a cheesemonger or a butcher, however opulent he might have become in those pursuits."

"These are all truisms," said Mr. Rogers, somewhat sharply, as if annoyed. "What I complain of is that the world—the very ill-natured world—should have spread abroad the ridiculous story that I recommended Mr. Campbell, in his declining years, to apply for a clerkship."

"I think no one believes that you did so," said Dr. Milman, "or that you could have done so. Your sympathy with men of letters is well known, and has been proved too often, not by words only, but by generous deeds, for such a story to obtain credence."

"Falsehoods," replied Mr. Rogers, still with a tone of bitterness, "are not cripples. They run fast, and have more legs than a centipede. I saw it stated in print the other day that I depreciate Shakspeare, and think him to have been over-rated. I know of no other foundation for the libel than the fact that I once quoted the opinion expressed of him by Ben Jonson, his dearest friend and greatest admirer. Though Ben Jonson called Shakspeare the 'Swan of Avon,'

> Soul of the age,
> The applause, delight, and wonder of the stage,

and affirmed that

> He was not for an age, but for all Time,

he did not hesitate to express the wish, in answer to one who boasted that Shakspeare had never blotted a line, 'Would to heaven that he had blotted a thousand.' Ben Jonson saw the spots on the glorious face of the sun of Shakspeare's genius, and was not accused of desecrating his memory because he did so. But because *I* quoted that very saying and approved of it, I have been accused of an act of treason against the majesty of the great poet. Surely my offence was no greater than that of Ben Jonson! If there were treason in the thought, it was treason that I shared with him who had said he loved Shakspeare with as much love as it was possible to feel on this side of idolatry."

"I think," remarked Dr. Milman, "that such apparently malevolent repetitions of a person's remarks are the results of careless ignorance or easy-going stupidity rather than of positive ill-nature or a wilful perversion of the truth."

"It is very curious," said Mr. Dyce, "how very few people can repeat correctly what they hear, and that nine people out of ten cannot repeat a joke without missing the point or the spirit of it. And what a widely prevalent tendency there is to exaggeration, especially in numbers! If some people see a hundred of anything, they commonly represent the hundred as a thousand, and the thousand as ten thousand."

"Not alone in numbers," interposed Mr. Rogers, "but in everything. If I quoted Ben Jonson's remark in relation to Shakspeare once only, the rumour spreads that I quoted it *frequently*. And so the gossip passes from mouth to mouth with continual accretions. Perhaps I shall go down to posterity as an habitual reviler and depreciator of Shakspeare."

"Perhaps you won't go down to posterity at all," said Mr. Dyce, with affected cynicism.

"Perhaps not," replied Mr. Rogers; "but if my name should happen to reach that uncertain destination, I trust I may be remembered, as Ben Jonson is, as a true lover of Shakspeare. But great as Shakspeare is, I don't think that our admiration should ever be allowed to degenerate into slavish adoration. We ought neither to make a god of him nor a fetish. And I ask you, Mr. Dyce, as a diligent student of his works and an industrious commentator upon them, whether you do not think that very many passages in them are unworthy of his genius. If Homer nods, why not Shakspeare?"

"I grant all that," replied Mr. Dyce. "Nay, more! I assert that many of the plays attributed to him were not written by him at all. And more even than that. Several of his plays were published surreptitiously, and without his consent, and never received his final corrections or any revision whatever. The faults and obscurities that are discernible even in the masterpieces of his genius were not due to him at all, but to ignorant and piratical booksellers, who gave them to the world without his authority, and traded upon his name; some, also, must be attributed to the shorthand writers who took down the dialogue as repeated by the actors on the stage. It is curious to reflect how indifferent Shakspeare was to his dramatic fame. He never seems to have cared for his plays at all, and to have looked at them, to use the slang of the artists of our days, as mere *pot-boilers*—compositions that brought him in money, and enabled him to pay his way, but in which he took no personal pride whatever."

"His heart was in his two early poems, *Venus and Adonis* and the *Rape of Lucrece*," said Dr. Milman; "the only two compositions, it should be observed, that were ever published by his authority and to which he appended his name. His sonnets, which some people admire so much, an admiration in which I do not share, were published surreptitiously, without his consent; and probably one half of them were not written by him. Some of them are undoubtedly by Marlowe, and some by authors of far inferior ability. Shakspeare's name was popular at the time; there was no law of copyright, and booksellers did almost what they pleased with the names and works of celebrated men; and, what seems extraordinary in our day, the celebrated men made no complaint, most probably because there was no redress to be obtained for them if they had done so. The real law of copyright only dates from the eighth year of the reign of Queen Anne (1710), or nearly a century after Shakspeare's death."

"But authors in those early days, even in the absence of a well-defined law of copyright," said Mr. Miller, "received payment for their works; witness the receipt of John Milton for five pounds on account of *Paradise Lost*, now in the possession of our host, and which we have all seen."

"But that was two generations after the death of Shakspeare," said Mr. Dyce; "and it does not appear that Shakspeare ever received a shilling for the copyright of any of his works. Perhaps he received gratuities from the Earls of Southampton and Pembroke and the other rich young men about town, for whom it is supposed that he wrote many of the sonnets. That he also must have received considerable sums for the representation of his plays at the Globe Theatre, is evident from the well-ascertained fact that he retired from theatrical business with a competent fortune, and lived the life for some years of a prosperous country gentleman."

As it has been asserted in my presence by an eminent literary man, within a month of the present writing, that Samuel Rogers systematically depreciated Shakspeare, and that he was above all things a cynic, I think it right, in justice to his memory, to repeat the conversation above recorded. Though it took place nearly forty years ago, I wrote down the heads of it in my note-book on the very day it occurred, and by reference to it I have refreshed my memory so as to be certain of its accuracy. Mr. Rogers doubtless said very pungent and apparently ill-natured things in his time; no professed wit, such as he was, can always, or indeed very often, refrain from shooting a barbed dart to raise a laugh, to strengthen an argument, or dispense with one; but there was no malevolence in the heart, though there might appear to be some on the tongue, of Samuel Rogers. To love literature and to excel in poetical composition were unfailing passports to his regard, his esteem, and, if necessary, to his purse.

One of the guests of the morning on which these conversations took place, and who bore his part in them, was a grateful recipient of his beneficence. Thomas Miller, who began life as a journeyman basket-maker, working for small daily wages in the fens of Lincolnshire, excited the notice of his neighbours by his poetical genius (or it may have been only talent), and their praises of his compositions filled his mind with the desire to try his literary fortune in the larger sphere of London. He listened to the promptings of his ambition, came to the metropolis, launched his little skiff on the wide ocean of literary life, and by dint of hard work, indomitable perseverance, unfailing hope, and incessant struggles, managed to earn a modest subsistence. He speedily found that poetry failed to put money in his purse, and prudently resorted to prose. When prose in the shape of original work, principally fiction, just enabled him to live from day to day, he took refuge in the daily drudgery of reviewing in the *Literary Gazette*, then edited by William Jerdan, an agreeable companion and friend, but a very bad paymaster. He had not been long in London before he made the acquaintance of Mr. Rogers, and, after a period of more or less intimacy, received from that gentleman the good, though old, and, as it often happens, the unwelcome advice that he should cease to rely wholly upon literature for his daily bread. As poor Miller could not return to basket-making, except as an employer of other basket-makers, for which he had not sufficient or indeed any capital, and as, moreover, he had no love for any pursuits but those of literature, he resolved, if he could manage it, to establish himself as a bookseller and publisher. Mr. Rogers, to whom he confided his wish, approved of it, and generously aided him to accomplish it by the advance, without security, of the money required for the purpose. The basket-maker carried on the business for a few years with but slight and decreasing success; and once informed me that he made more money by the sale of note-paper, of sealing-wax, of ink, and of red tape, than he had made by the sale of his own works or those of anybody else.

Mr. Rogers established another poet in the bookselling and publishing business, but with far greater success than attended his efforts in the case of the basket-maker. Mr. Edward Moxon, a clerk or shopman in the employ of Messrs. Longmans, who wrote, in his early manhood, a little book of sonnets that attracted the notice of Mr. Rogers, to whom they had been sent by the author with a modest letter, became, by the pecuniary aid and constant patronage of the "Bard of Memory," one of the most eminent publishers of his time. He was known to fame as "the poet's publisher," and issued the works not only of Mr. Rogers himself, but of Campbell, Wordsworth, Southey, Savage Landor, Coleridge, and many other poetical celebrities. He also published the works of Ben Jonson, Marlowe, Beaumont and Fletcher, Peele, and other noted dramatists of the Elizabethan era.

The friendly assistance, delicately and liberally administered in the hour of need by Samuel Rogers to the illustrious Richard Brinsley Sheridan, is fully recorded in the life of the latter by Thomas Moore. That which was administered, though under less pressing circumstances, to Thomas Campbell, has found a sympathetic historian in Dr. William Beattie. Rogers, in spite of the baseless libel concerning Shakspeare, had not a particle of literary envy in his composition. His dislike to Lord Byron was not literary but personal, and is adequately explained and almost justified by the gross and unprovoked attacks which Byron directed against him.

Serjeant Talfourd was an orator, not celebrated for his power over crowds, but highly distinguished in the senate and the forum. He did not speak often in Parliament or at public meetings, but when he did he was listened to with pleasure and attention. The scenes of his triumphs were the law courts, and especially the Court of Common Pleas, where he was the leading practitioner. He was noted at the Bar and among the attorneys for his power over the minds of jurymen, and his winning ways of extorting a favourable verdict for the client who was fortunate enough to secure him for an advocate. He had room enough in his heart both for law and literature, the law for his profit and his worldly advancement, and literature for the charm and consolation of his life. He was well known to and highly esteemed by the leading literary men of his time, and took a special interest in the law affecting artistic, musical, and literary copyright. He was largely instrumental in extending the previously allotted term of twenty-eight to forty-two years, and for seven years after the death of the artist, composer, or author. This measure put considerable and well-deserved profits into the pockets of the heirs of Sir Walter Scott, and was said at the time to have been specially devised and enacted for that purpose and for that only. This, however, was an error, which Serjeant Talfourd emphatically contradicted whenever it was hinted or asserted. It had incidentally that effect, which no one was churlish or ungrateful enough to grudge or lament, but was advocated in the interest of all men of letters, and of literature itself in its widest extent, and, if it erred at all, only erred on the side of undue restriction to so short a term as forty-two years. It ought to have been extended to the third generation of the benefactors of their country, and possibly will be so extended at a future time, when the rights of authors will be as strictly protected and will be thought of at least as much importance as the rights of landlords to their acres, or of butchers, bakers, and tailors to be paid for their commodities, or those of lawyers and doctors to be paid for their time and talents.

Mr. Charles Dickens dedicated to Serjeant Talfourd *The Posthumous Papers of the Pickwick Club*, the early work by which his afterwards great fame was established, in grateful acknowledgment of the Serjeant's services to the cause of men of genius, in the enactment of the new law of copyright. "Many a fevered head," he said, "and palsied hand will gather new vigour in the hour of sickness and distress, from your excellent exertions; many a widowed mother and orphan child, who would otherwise reap nothing from the fame of departed genius, but its too frequent legacy of sorrow and suffering, will bear in their altered condition higher testimony to the value of your labours than the most lavish encomiums from lip or pen could ever afford."

Serjeant Talfourd was raised to the Bench in 1848, being then in his fifty-third year. This promotion had the natural consequence of removing him from the House of Commons. He was a singularly amiable man, of gentle, almost feminine character, of delicate health and fragile form. He possessed little or none of the staid and stern gravity popularly associated with the idea of a judge, and looked more like the poet that he undoubtedly was, than the busy lawyer or the magistrate. He died suddenly in the year 1854, under circumstances peculiarly sad and pathetic. After attending divine service on Sunday the 11th of March, in the Assize town of Stafford, apparently in his usual health, he took his seat on the bench on the following morning, and proceeded to address the Grand Jury on the state of the calendar. It contained a list of more than one hundred prisoners, an unusually large number of whom were charged with atrocious offences, many of which were to be directly traced to intemperance. He took occasion, in the course of his remarks, to comment on the growing estrangement in England between the upper and lower classes of society, and the want of interest and sympathy exhibited between the former and the latter, which he regarded as of evil augury for the future peace and prosperity of the country. While uttering these words, he became flushed and excited, his speech became thick and incoherent, and he suddenly fell forward with his face on the desk at which he was sitting. He was removed at once to his lodgings in the immediate vicinity of the court, but life was found to be extinct on his arrival. Thus perished a singularly able and estimable man, universally beloved by his contemporaries.

Breakfasts with Samuel Rogers.

No. X.

Mr. JOSEPH PARKES, formerly an attorney in Birmingham, was a well-known character in the political and social circles of London; Lady Morgan was an industrious author, a sometimes brilliant writer, and a general favourite in certain influential social and literary coteries; Mr. Bernal Osborne was a wit, a man about town, and a Member of Parliament; and the Rev. Hugh Hutton was a Unitarian clergyman, well known for the leading part he took in all the philanthropic and humanitarian movements of the time.

The conversation at the breakfast-table of Mr. Rogers, where I met these people, was, as might have been expected from the composition of the company, each member of which was a good talker, varied and interesting, and never flagged, or ran exclusively in a single channel, or became a monopoly in the mouth of a single person.

Mr. Parkes and Mr. Hutton were both Birmingham men, who had acted together on a great historical occasion many years previously, but had never subsequently chanced to meet in London society. In the year 1830, the agitation for a reform of the Commons House of Parliament had attained a degree of violence previously unknown, in consequence, to a large extent, of the Paris Revolution of July in that year. Charles X. had been ignominiously hurled from the throne, and had taken refuge in the deserted palace of Holyrood in Edinburgh, and Louis Philippe reigned in his stead. Revolution was threatened in every European capital, and London was by no means unaffected by the general alarm and perturbation of men's minds. The prevalent excitement was greatly increased by the proposal of Mr. Attwood, a leading citizen and the most influential public character in Birmingham, to summon the people of that town, and of the midland and northern counties in general, to meet together to the number of 100,000 at least, and march, with guns, pikes, and other weapons, to London, to demand the Reform, which the Parliament, under the leadership of the great Duke of Wellington, obstinately withheld. As a preliminary to this threatened march, a public meeting of several thousand people had been held in Birmingham, at which Mr. Attwood had presided. The proceedings were opened by an impressive and very eloquent prayer, offered up to Almighty God, on behalf of the English people, by the Rev. Mr. Hutton, which had melted some of the audience to tears, and deeply affected Mr. Joseph Parkes, who was the real originator and mainspring of the demonstration. The proposed march on London never took place; but the mere possibility of it, and the evident earnestness of the men who were the leaders of the agitation, had its effect on the minds of the party chiefs in the metropolis, and caused them to reflect more seriously than they had previously done upon the dangers of unwise and protracted resistance to the people's demands. The conversation of Messrs. Parkes and Hutton, two of the principal actors in the scene, who now met for the first time after many years, turned naturally upon it.

"Have you ever heard," asked Mr. Parkes, "what became of the picture that Haydon undertook to paint, and actually commenced, of the great stand and the persons upon it, when you offered up your famous prayer? I know I sat to the artist several times for my portrait, and that I was instrumental in procuring subscriptions to the amount of several hundred pounds; near upon a thousand, if I remember rightly, to help him along during the progress of the work. Was it ever completed?"

"Never!" replied Mr. Hutton. "Every effort was made by his friends to procure him the money which he wanted, amounting to at least four times as much as he received. But all efforts, public and private, were equally fruitless; so, growing disheartened or disgusted, he laid the work aside for several years, locked it up in a lumber-room, and thought no more about it."

" Does it still exist ? "

" Perhaps it does ; but not in its original state. Haydon told me himself that, requiring the canvas for other purposes, and despairing of any further encouragement for the original work, he had painted a classical subject upon it; Curtius leaping into the gulf, I think, he said. I expressed my regret that he should have made such a sacrifice; but he only laughed at me for my pains. 'Who knows,' he said, 'but what some picture-dealer or cleaner of the future—a keen politician, thinking more of the heroes of Birmingham than of the heroes of Rome—may get hold of the canvas, and, rubbing away the second coating of paint, may awaken the original heroes to a glorious resurrection—you, Parkes, Attwood, and the whole lot of you!'"

"All Haydon's pictures," said Mr. Osborne, "were on too large a scale for commercial success. Nobody could hang one of them in his gallery, unless he built one specially for the purpose. He was continually involved in pecuniary difficulties from this cause. A person who wants a lap-dog in the drawing-room, and is content to pay a good price for the little animal, will not accept a dromedary or an elephant as a gift."

"It is odd," said Mr. Rogers, "that Haydon,

with his love for great size, and his incapacity for understanding or appreciating physical littleness, should have died of a little man after all."

"How so?" asked Lady Morgan.

"Do you not remember," replied Mr. Rogers, "the melancholy death of poor Haydon, by his own hand, caused by his disgust at what he considered the degraded taste of the public that crowded to a room at the Pantheon, in Oxford Street, to see Tom Thumb, an ugly American dwarf, and paid a shilling for the privilege, when in the very next room in the same building they might have seen a noble picture by Haydon for the same money? A thousand people visited the dwarf for one that visited the painter's masterpiece. The dwarf grew rich, the artist scarcely knew where to get a crust for the needs of the passing day."

"It was a great misfortune for Haydon," I remarked, "that he had no idea of size or space in his works. I know one of the ablest literary men of the present day, who suffers from a similar affliction, keeps himself down in the world in consequence, and prevents himself from obtaining the profitable work on the press, which he so greatly needs, and which he can perform so well. He has a thorough mastery of certain subjects, and there is not a newspaper in London that would not employ him to write on those topics, and pay him his own terms for doing so, but for the unfortunate fatality that he has no notion either of time or space. You ask him to write an article, say of two or three columns at the utmost, not because you would not gladly insert a larger quantity, but because the exigencies of the space at your command absolutely prohibit you from making use of more. He accepts the task, promises to comply with its conditions, and is grateful for the chance you have given him of earning a few honest guineas. You allow him three days to perform the task. To this he agrees also, and appears to be delighted. To your infinite annoyance he takes three weeks, instead of three days, for the stipulated work, and brings you a manuscript that would fill twenty columns of your journal, instead of the three to which you were compelled to limit him. What can be done with him? He demands payment for the larger quantity, which you do not require, and of which you cannot possibly make use, even if you had received it at the stipulated time. To prevent dispute and annoyance, you pay him what he asks, and resolve to employ him no more; a resolution which, for your own sake, you religiously adhere to. Haydon was a man of the same class."

"The story of Haydon," said Lady Morgan, "is a very sad one, which I had forgotten; but if his pictures were too large for the public to buy, they were not too large for the public to look at and admire. Their very size ought to have been an attraction, But then, as the crossing-sweeper says in the Adelphi farce, the public is a *hass*; not an *ass*, mind you, but a hass, with a strong aspirate. It does not want to be instructed. It does not care for pictures, or poetry, or high art. It only wants to be amused. It prefers Punch and Judy to Hamlet or Macbeth, or a wax figure of a murderer at Madame Tussaud's to the Venus of Milo, or to the Apollo Belvidere. *Que voulez vous?*"

"Yes!" interposed Mr. Hutton. "And in olden times it preferred Barabbas to Jesus, and would do so again if it had the chance."

"Then," said Mr. Osborne, "you don't believe that the *vox populi* is the *vox dei?*"

"Decidedly not! Conscience is the voice of God; but the crowd of all countries is deficient in conscience, or it has none at all."

"Conscience," remarked Mr. Osborne, "is common to all of us, and, indeed, may be said to be universal; but then, unluckily, though it whispers to us inwardly, we do not always listen to it. Its voice is as the idle wind which we regard not."

"You have lately returned from the highlands of Scotland; have you not?" said Lady Morgan, addressing herself to me. "My niece was on a visit to one of the Hebrides last month, and speaks with intense admiration of the beautiful scenery, and of the kind-hearted, simple people who inhabit the wild but lovely region. They are said to be of the same race and blood as my people—the people of Ireland; but I don't believe it."

"But they speak the same language—the Gaelic—and have been always held to be of the same stock," said Mr. Osborne. "What is the reason of your disbelief?"

"Because the Highlanders do not shoot their landlords, as they ought to do," replied Lady Morgan. "The Irish would not endure a hundredth part of the wrongs inflicted upon the poor Highlanders by the owners of the soil, without taking tithe of their lives. A poor Highlander cannot call his soul his own, and is scarcely allowed to have a right to his own body, or to an inch of earth to put his foot upon. The landlords think, because they own the land they own the people. My countrymen would soon teach them a different story. My niece tells me that a great Duke in the Western Isles, who owns every foot of ground in a tolerably large island, lately caused a notice to be affixed to the kirk door, to the effect that any tenant on the estate who paid less than thirty pounds of annual rent, who should *presume*—such was the very word he used—to drink, wine, whisky, rum, brandy, gin, beer, or any other fermented liquor, or give away to any of his guests any of the fermented liquors aforesaid, should be turned out of his farm at the next term or quarter-day. Would an Irishman, do you think, endure any such tyranny?"

"Tyranny! Pooh!" said Mr. Osborne, with a look of triumph. "I don't call that tyranny at all. The Duke is a cannie Scotsman, and it is only his cannie and very Scotch way of raising the rent upon his tenantry. If they pay less than thirty pounds per annum, the Duke is inexorable, but if they pay thirty-one pounds or upwards, they may do as they like!"

"I have been in the island alluded to," said I, "and have seen the efforts made by the Duke to prohibit or, at all events to check, whisky-drinking among the people. He will not allow the only inn-keeper in the place to provide a drop of whisky to his guests, or a drop of whisky to be sold on the island if he can help it. Strolling down the only street of the small village which considers itself the capital of the island, I noticed in the window of a grocer's shop several large bottles labelled 'Hair Oil.' As the Highland lasses and the elder women did not appear to me to pay much if any attention to their abundant tresses, but left them very much to Nature—which, on its part, had done all that was necessary to make them beautiful and attractive—I had the curiosity to enter the shop and inquire whether I could not be supplied with two or three pennyworth of oil. The buxom dame behind the counter smiled roguishly as she answered, 'Aye,

aye, Sir,' and straightway poured it out in a wineglass. It was whisky, and very good whisky, too—the real Talisker, or Mountain Dew. The Duke was none the wiser, and, as I should suppose, none the better or the worse for the libation I made."

"His conduct was none the less tyrannical," said Lady Morgan, "and could only be justified, if it could be justified at all, by the pleas put forward by the inquisitors of old, in vindication of their presumptuous meddlesomeness with the rights of conscience in matters of faith and doctrine. If it be my faith and my doctrine that it is a religious duty to drink a little whisky, shall an inquisitorial Duke prevent me, or torture me for my heresy? He would, if he could, I am sure."

"Ah! but you're a Radical, Lady Morgan, and haven't a proper respect for dukes," said Mr. Rogers. "By-the-bye, I have heard it said that you were the first woman who ever danced the waltz in England, and that you danced it with a Duke. Is it true?"

"Only partially true," replied Lady Morgan, who dearly loved to hear herself talk. "But I will tell you exactly how it happened. It was in the summer of 1812, I think, when I dined one day at the Duke of Devonshire's. After dinner, when the gentlemen joined the ladies in the drawing-room, the Marquis of Hartington, the next heir to the dukedom, offered to teach any lady present the new dance, which he called the 'waltz,' and which none of the ladies had ever heard of. The Marquis had just returned from St. Petersburg, where he had been on a diplomatic mission of some kind, and had passed through Germany, and made some stay there on his way home. None of the ladies volunteering to take a lesson, he addressed himself to me, paying me a pretty compliment, and said: ' Miss Owenson [that was my name before I married Sir Charles Morgan], will you not allow me to show you the steps? The dance is very easy to learn, and is certain to be popular this season.' I agreed at once, without making any fuss about it. But we were met at the outset by a difficulty that threatened to be serious. There was no waltz music in the possession of the Duchess (perhaps there was none in England at that day), and the Marquis was scarcely enough of a musician to show any lady present the true time and measure of the waltz movement, or how to adapt any well-known melody, even at the risk of spoiling it, to the necessities of the new dance. But the difficulty was at length got over, after a fashion, and the Marquis gave me my lesson. He said I was an excellent pupil, and needed but little instruction."

"Was the dance approved of?" asked Mr. Hutton.

"Very much disapproved of," replied Lady Morgan. "All the gentlemen were dead against it. The Duke of Devonshire said it was indecent, and declared that he would not like to see his wife, his daughter, his sister, or any woman that he respected, taking part in it. The ladies were not so positive, but, as I thought, looked favourably upon it. Byron's satirical poem, 'The Waltz,' which was published anonymously in the autumn of 1812, expressed the general opinion of the public on the subject. The waltz, in fact, was universally condemned, and universally popular."

"Because the ladies took it up," said Mr. Osborne. "The ladies can make anything they please popular. Witness the odious fashions which they every now and then adopt and maintain, in spite of abuse, in spite of ridicule, in spite of reason, in spite of everything, in fact, but their own dear selves, and their own dear will."

" 'Twas ever so since Time began," said Mr. Rogers, " and ever will be so till Time shall be no more."

Lady Morgan, though a great talker, was not an idle gossip. Her talk was worth listening to. People who wanted to talk themselves, complained, however that she would not, if she could help it, give them a chance of putting in a word; and Lord Macaulay, himself a great talker, was particularly disinclined, for that reason, to make one of any company of which she formed a part. Lady Morgan was somewhat rudely and unnecessarily outspoken in matters of religious belief, and often very indiscreetly, if not offensively, expressed opinions that in these days would not only have laid her open to the accusation of being a Positivist, or a Comtist, but which, in the less tolerant times in which she flourished, would have led people to designate her, point blank, as an Atheist, and consigned her to the stake, or the dungeons of the Inquisition.

Lady Morgan made no secret of her antipathy to Mr. Macaulay, and those who were acquainted intimately with both of them were careful to avoid bringing them together at their entertainments.

[NOTE.—It may be necessary to state that I have not relied wholly upon my memory for these records of the conversations of Mr. Rogers and his guests; but that I have derived them, for the most part, from the notes which I made of them in my common-place book, on the evenings of the days in which they occurred.]

CHAPTER X.

A CASE OF ARBITRATION.

THE late eminent composer, Michael Balfe, whose acquaintance I had the pleasure of making at Brighton a few years before his death, was the author of the *Bohemian Girl* and several other excellent English operas. The many pleasing melodies in the *Bohemian Girl* were more especially popular, and long enjoyed the favour of the musical few and the unmusical many. Mr. Balfe's publishers—as was natural—jealously guarded the copyright in these compositions, and showed no mercy to piratical members of the trade who brought out spurious and unathorised editions. They discovered, or fancied they discovered, in a song by the very popular composer, Mr. Henry Russell, an invasion of their rights, and commenced an action against him, either to stop the sale of the offending publication or to recover penalties for the injuries which they alleged they had suffered. The incriminated composer denied the charge of piracy, pleaded that he had never even heard Balfe's melody, and that the tune was entirely the production of his own genius. After a long series of futile correspondence and *pourparlers*, both parties ultimately agreed that the case should be submitted to arbitration. The arbitrator mutually agreed upon was an old Italian gentleman who occupied the post of musical librarian at Covent Garden Theatre. On the day appointed for his decision, the interested parties met in the librarian's room, and anxiously awaited his verdict. The old gentleman, when all the parties were ready, placed the library ladder against the shelves where all the musical books, in print or in manuscript, belonging to the theatre were duly ranged, and, after a search on the very highest shelf, took out an old volume. He slowly opened it in the middle, and flapping the two halves against each other to free it from the dust with which it was encumbered, and opening it at a page with which he seemed to be well acquainted, slowly drew his finger along several bars of a song, humming the air as he did so. The air bore a very striking resemblance to that of the two songs that were in dispute.

"Gentlemen," he said, in somewhat foreign English, "Mr. Russell did *not* steal from Mr. Balfe. Oh, certainly not! Mr. Balfe on his part did not steal from Mr. Russell. Oh, certainly not! The fact is they are both thieves, and stole from Cimarosa. Here is the air in Cimarosa's air-book published in his life-time. Judge for yourselves."

"Great wits jump!" said Mr. Balfe; "but I should like to know who Cimarosa stole from!"

And so the matter ended, to the mutual satisfaction of the rival composers, though not, perhaps, to that of the plaintiff publishers.

The "Daily News."

The *Daily News* was established in 1846, chiefly by the influence and exertions of Charles Dickens, its first editor, then in his thirty-fourth year. He was largely supported by many rich capitalists, who had great admiration for his genius, and great faith in the power and prestige of his name, sufficient, as they thought, to secure the prosperity of any periodical with which he might be connected. Unfortunately for themselves, they were oblivious of the hard fact that a daily London newspaper, to be successful, must secure the support of the great bulk of the plain unimaginative public, only to be gained by the importance and authenticity and earliness of its home and foreign news, by the soundness of its opinions on all political and commercial matters, and by the steady reliance of its readers on the political integrity of its conductors. I was personally acquainted with but one of the non-literary founders of the new journal—the late Sir William Jackson, who had made a considerable fortune as a railway contractor. That gentleman, many years after Mr. Dickens had ceased his brief connection with the paper, informed me, with a rueful countenance and a groan, that he had thrown away seven thousand pounds on the speculation. "Yes," he said, " seven thousand pounds in real *golden* sovereigns!" a way of putting it that might have led me to suppose, by the very strong emphasis he placed on *golden*, and by his melancholy iteration of the word, that he had actually counted out the money sovereign by sovereign, and not by cheques on his bankers. It was said at the time that the capital invested or ready to be invested in the concern was £100,000; but probably nobody knew the truth of the matter except the investors and Mr. Dickens himself.

I was in Glasgow at the time, engaged in editing the *Argus*, but was kept informed by Mr. Alexander Mackay, my former colleague on the *Morning Chronicle*, and then acting as London Correspondent of the *Argus*, of all that was known or knowable on the subject of the great new paper. It was expected by the quidnuncs that it was to snuff out the light of the venerable *Chronicle* and eclipse all the other London journals, even the *Times* itself, if money could do it. The conductors of the *Morning Chronicle* were particularly aggrieved, and even alarmed at the opposition, more especially as by the offers of higher salaries, in some cases fifty or a hundred per cent. in excess of what they were then receiving, some of the best men on the staff, whether as parliamentary reporters, or contributors of editorial or leading articles and reviews of books, were induced to abandon the old ship for the new.

Sir John Easthope, the chief proprietor of the *Chronicle*, affected not to fear the opposition, declaring that Mr. Dickens, anxious above all things to write political leaders for the *Chronicle*, had been found so wofully wanting in political knowledge and tact, as to have rendered it necessary to decline his further services in that capacity. Sir John affirmed to the end of his life that the brilliant author was so greatly offended with the *Morning Chronicle* for its want of judgment, that he set up the *Daily News* as a rival, and that if the conductors of the old journal had had a greater appreciation of the genius of the rising novelist the new journal would never have come into existence. Sir John, however, stood alone in this opinion.

Overtures were made to me to leave Glasgow and take part in the editorial management of the new journal, but I was bound by contract to stay where

I was for a certain period of which more than a twelvemonth had yet to run, and consequently declined the tempting offers. I agreed, however, to contribute twelve short lyrics on the political and social topics of the day, the first of which, entitled "The Wants of the People," appeared in the first number of the new paper, followed in due course by eleven others. One of these, "There's a Good Time coming, Boys," achieved an extraordinary, an unexpected, and, as its author has long thought and continues to think, an undeserved popularity as a literary composition. It was set to music by Mr. Henry Russell, the well-known vocalist, then in the meridian of his powers and the height of his celebrity, and sung by him, with much applause, in every city and great town of Great Britain and the United States, the audience invariable singing in the chorus, until its constant iteration, both as a song and a saying, became wearisome to the searchers after novelty. These lyrics were afterwards collected, and, along with many others of a like character and tendency, were published under the title of *Voices from the Crowd*, and went through four editions, from which the publisher derived a profit—though he denied it—and from which the author derived not a farthing, or a farthing's worth, unless in the shape of a few gratuitous copies for distribution among his friends. A fifth edition was agreed upon, from the sale of which

I was to derive a royalty of three-halfpence in the shilling for every copy disposed of; but unfortunately the publisher became a bankrupt before the work was issued. The stock, however, was purchased by the late Charles Gilpin, then a bookseller in Bishopsgate Street, and afterwards M.P. for Northampton.

In connection with the name of this much-respected gentleman—with whom I remained on terms of friendly intimacy until his death—I may mention the following circumstance as a part of the political history of the time. I had called on Mr. Samuel Morley, M.P., at his place of business in the city, and was engaged in conversation with him in his private room, when the card of Mr. Gilpin was handed in by an attendant. The attendant had informed Mr. Gilpin of my presence with Mr. Morley, and Mr. Gilpin had replied that he should be glad to see me also. Mr. Morley asked me if I knew him, and, on my answering in the affirmative, gave directions that Mr. Gilpin should be shown in. Mr. Gilpin expressed his pleasure to see two friends at once, as he had come to ask advice on a political matter of much importance to himself, and of some little interest, if not of importance, to the Liberal Party. Lord Palmerston, he proceeded to say, had asked him to join his administration and take office in connection with the Poor Law Board. Turning to me first as a writer for an influential Liberal newspaper, he asked me if I thought he would act wisely in accepting the offer.

"Lord Palmerston," I replied, "has, in my opinion, paid you personally a very high compliment, and shown a very laudable desire to conciliate the extreme or Radical section of the Liberal Party to which you belong. My advice, which I give only because you ask it, is that you should decidedly accept the offer, and be grateful for it."

"I quite agree," said Mr. Morley, when the question was put to him. "Lord Palmerston pays a tribute to your ability, shows his own discernment of character, and a just appreciation of his own position and duties as a minister in making you the offer. Accept it by all means."

Mr. Gilpin replied: "I am glad to have such support from two friends whose judgment I respect; the more so, as I had an interview with John Bright immediately before coming here. I put the case before him, and he answered me very rudely, as I thought, 'Rather go and cut your throat than serve under Palmerston!' and then abruptly changed the subject."

Mr. Gilpin accepted the office, offended no member of the Party, that I ever heard of, except Mr. Bright, acquitted himself entirely to the satisfaction of the Government, the House of Commons, and the public, and laid the sure foundation of still higher office, if the Government had remained in power and his life had been spared. But this is a digression, which has but slight reference to the *Daily News* or any connection with it.

Charles Dickens had had more than enough of night-work when engaged in the parliamentary corps of the *Morning Chronicle*, and found the partial renewal of late hours of work in the editorial room of the *Daily News* a little too much for his health and a great deal too much for his comfort. Accordingly, after but short trial of its inconveniences, he transferred his burden to the competent shoulders of his friends, John Forster of the *Examiner* and William Henry Wills, who had graduated in the office of *Chambers' Edinburgh Journal*. These gentlemen were followed in the work by the Messrs. Charles Wentworth Dilke, father and son. The elder Mr. Dilke was the proprietor and editor of the *Athenæum*, which he had purchased from its founder Mr. Silk Buckingham, and he converted its comparative failure under that gentleman to a very considerable success, both pecuniarily and socially. The younger Mr. Dilke took an active part in aiding the efforts of the Prince Consort to organize the great International Exhibition of 1851, and on the death of the Prince, in accordance with a wish expressed in a memorandum found among his papers, was rewarded by a baronetcy in lieu of a knighthood offered to but refused by him. The Dilkes were followed in the editorship by Mr.

William Weir, who was the editor of the *Glasgow Argus* a few years prior to my assuming the management; by Mr. Knight Hunt, author of an interesting history of the newspaper press under the title of *The Fourth Estate*. This gentleman retained the position until his death, after which I lost sight of the *Daily News* and its conductors.

The *Daily News*, which commenced its career as a cheap paper prior to the total repeal of the newspaper stamp duty, was not successful in its competition at twopence with its higher-priced rivals. After a struggle, its conductors judged it necessary to raise the price to a level with that of its morning contemporaries, and was believed not to have suffered to any considerable extent by the change, though it probably diminished its circulation. It was not until many years after the *Daily Telegraph* and the *Standard* had achieved a brilliant, and, until then, unparalleled, success at a penny, that the *Daily News* was induced to follow where these two papers had led, not without many misgivings that the fatal judgment of being "too late" would be pronounced upon it, alike by its supporters and its opponents. Doubtless the important step was taken "late," but not "too late," as the event has proved.

The "Illustrated London News."
(1848).

AFTER leaving Glasgow and re-establishing myself in London, I formed a connection with the *Illustrated London News*, which commenced early in 1848, and continued till 1860. I first made the acquaintance of Mr. Herbert Ingram, its spirited founder and principal proprietor, a few weeks before the outbreak of the French Revolution of February 1848, which drove Louis Philippe from the throne. At that time Mr. Ingram had made his arrangements for starting a daily morning newspaper, to be called the *Telegraph*, of which the specialty was to be the publication of a *feuilleton*, after the fashion of those rendered familiar by the Parisian press, and containing a succession of novels and romances. The first was to be written by Mr. Albert Smith, then rising into celebrity, and who held the office of dramatic critic for the *Illustrated London News*. The editor of the *Telegraph* was Mr. Thomas Hodgskin, an able writer, who, though very much my senior, had acted for some time as my assistant in the *Morning Chronicle* office. I was engaged by Mr. Ingram to contribute articles on foreign politics, Mr. Hodgskin confining himself to economical subjects, on which he was a reputed expert, while exercising a general supervision of the editorial columns. The new paper was not a success. Mr. Ingram, not contented with planting his acorn and trusting to Time and Nature to bring it to maturity, had expected it, like Jonah's gourd, to grow up in a night, or to develop itself into a lordly wide-spreading oak-tree in the "space of one revolving moon." The rapid growth of the *Illustrated London News* had accustomed him to success; and after sacrificing several thousands of pounds in the *Telegraph*, he lost heart and faith in the venture, and resolved to discontinue it.

Mr. Hodgskin reported that the disappointed proprietor, in his unreasonable and unreasoning wrath at the failure, accused him of being the cause of it, from his constant use of the word "bureaucracy," which, Mr. Ingram said, had occurred at least ten times in one week in the leading articles!

"Bureaucracy! bureaucracy!" he exclaimed in irate tones. "Such a word is enough to damn any newspaper, and it has damned the *Telegraph*!"

The *Telegraph* ceased to appear on the following morning. The name was afterwards adopted, on the repeal of the newspaper stamp duty, by Colonel Sleigh, who established the *Daily Telegraph*, without sufficient means to carry it on, and allowed it perforce to fall into more competent hands, who have made it one of the greatest successes of modern journalism.

On the stoppage of the *Telegraph*, Mr. Ingram invited me to write editorial articles for the *Illustrated London News*, and offered me a permanent engagement. Seeing the opportunities it afforded as an editorial medium, beyond those of the daily and ordinary weekly press, I endeavoured, as soon as I obtained the confidence of its proprietors, to extend its usefulness as a literary political and social exponent of advanced public opinion, without detriment to its pictorial speciality. There were two other proprietors besides Mr. Ingram, who were his brothers-in-law as well as his partners, namely, Mr. Nathaniel Cooke, who had married his sister, and Mr. William Little, whose sister he himself had married. But Mr. Ingram's authority in the concern was paramount and unquestioned. He was not an educated man, though not wholly illiterate. He had a clear head and good natural abilities, which had only needed proper cultivation in his youth to have fitted him to take higher rank in society than he was ever able to attain. His father was a butcher in Boston, Lincolnshire; and at a very early age, according to his own account of himself, he started in life as a "printer's devil," afterwards becoming a compositor, and finally a newsvendor and newsagent in Nottingham. While engaged in the latter business, he remarked that when Mr. Clements, the then proprietor of the *Morning Chronicle*, published in that journal a wood-cut engraving of any public event that excited more than ordinary interest, the sale of the *Morning Chronicle* was very largely increased. Turning the fact over in his mind, he came to the conclusion that a weekly newspaper that always contained " pictures " of the events and prominent persons of the week would command a large sale. He brooded over this idea for ten or twelve years, until he had acquired the means of making an experiment upon it. The *Illustrated London News* was the result of his cogitations. He started it in the face of many difficulties in 1842, and it became a financial success from the very beginning.

It was, when I assumed its literary management, a mere picture paper, appealing almost exclusively to the eyes of children and the great bulk of uneducated and semi-educated people, who were content with such amusement as it afforded. My desire was to give it a voice on all the political, social, and literary questions of the time, which I thought could be done without interfering with the pictorial illustrations of which it had the monopoly. On explaining my views to Mr. Ingram, he gave me *carte blanche* to do as I pleased. The result was, at the end of a few months, that the subscribers to the *Illustrated London News* discovered that they had something to read as well as to look at ; that its columns contained something more than the stale *crambe recocta* of the news which they had already seen in the daily journals; and that original opinions were set forth, in an independent and honest spirit, on all the current topics that occupied the public mind. In the course of a few months a perceptible increase, very gratifying to the proprietorial mind, took place in the circulation of the paper, which gradually rose in less than a twelvemonth from 40,000 to 60,000 copies.

Among the many more or less eminent literary men who contributed to the *Illustrated London News* during the time when I controlled it in all its departments, except the pictorial, which Mr. Ingram reserved to himself, were, in addition to John Timbs, the industrious sub-editor, author of a whole library of useful books, due to his solid judgment, his cultivated taste, and his ever busy scissors and gum-bottle, were the brothers Mayhew (Henry, Horace, and Augustus); George Hogarth and Charles Louis Gruneison in the musical department; John Abraham Heraud, author of *The Judgment of the Flood* and other epic poems, addressed to a non-epical age, who took the drama under his charge, in succession to Mr. Albert Smith; Thomas Miller the basket-maker and poet, friend and *protégé* of Samuel Rogers; Angus Bethune Reach, the versatile and accomplished, cut off in the prime of his promising days by overwork of brain and want of the necessary sleep which he denied himself; Professor D. T. Ansted the geologist; Mark

Lemon, the editor of *Punch*; Stirling Coyne, the dramatist; W. H. Wills, the partner of Charles Dickens in *Household Words* and *All the Year Round*; Douglas Jerrold, the greatest wit of the century (next to Thomas Hood and the Reverend Sidney Smith); his son Blanchard Jerrold; Lewis Filmore and George Clifford, of the *Times*; Miles Gerald Keon, the novelist (afterwards Secretary for Bermuda); Howard Staunton, the well-known chess-player, afterwards still better known as the editor of Routledge's excellent illustrated edition of Shakspeare; Henry Cockton, the author of *Valentine Vox* and other novels; Jonathan Duncan, a learned authority on currency questions and other kindred branches of political economy; two sporting writers, who concealed their real names under the pseudonyms of "The Druid" and "Harry Hieover"; Mr. Joseph A. Crowe, afterwards Consul-General of Great Britain in Germany; Alexander Somerville, who, under the signature of "One who Whistled at the Plough," had rendered good service to the Anti-Corn Law League; Richard Rowan Moore, one of the most eloquent of the orators who aided Messrs. Cobden and Bright in their agitation for the repeal of the Corn Laws; Mr. Bayle Bernard, the author of several successful plays, who, if he could have written as well as he talked, would, according to the testimony of Charles Dickens, have been one of the most deservedly popular authors of his time; and, among ladies, Miss Julia Pardoe, the Countess of Blessington, and her beautiful niece, Miss Marguerite Power.

Among the artists—without whose powerful aid such a journal as the *Illustrated London News* would, a quarter of a century ago, have been impossible of production—were John, now Sir John, Gilbert, the versatile, the prolific, the graceful, the imaginative—one might almost say, without being justly accused of exaggeration, the unrivalled and incomparable; John Leech, the most genial and gentlemanly of caricaturists, with a superabundance of wit, and without a particle of coarseness and vulgarity, whose contributions were, like angels' visits, "far between," but always welcome when they came; George Thomas, only second to Sir John Gilbert in his power of delineating modern life, but, in consequence of weak health, without his marvellous capacity for hard work; Birkett Foster, excellent in landscape; Samuel Read, equally excellent in architecture; William Harvey, a relic of a previous generation of artists on wood; Kenny Meadows, quaint and full of mannerisms, but full also of spirit and originality; Edwin Weedon, who had no equal in taking the portraits of ships; Benjamin Herring, renowned for his correct and unmistakable portraits of horses; Harrison Weir, as skilful as Benjamin Herring for the correct, spirited, and always natural drawing of all animals and birds, from a lion or a bull to a barn-door fowl or a sparrow; Edward Duncan, whose landscapes and sea-scapes were both of the greatest merit; and George Dodgson, weird, mysterious, gloomy, but always powerful and effective in the treatment of any subject on which he employed himself; and, last but not least, Louis Huart, a very able artist, wielding a most facile and industrious pencil, whom I had discovered in Belgium. I invited him over from Brussels in order to relieve Sir John Gilbert of a portion of the toil of drawing on wood, which he wished to exchange for the more agreeable task of painting. Mr. Huart proved himself worthy to succeed so eminent a predecessor, and rendered the partial secession of Sir John Gilbert less felt and marked than it might otherwise have been.

In the summer of 1852, Mr. Ingram proposed to me to take a month's holiday with him in Switzerland and the Rhine country, offering to pay all the expenses. He did not think—although he had great faith in his own luck and "pluck," as he called it—that he could manage to enjoy a trip on the Continent all alone; especially as he said he only knew three words in any foreign language: "*eau chaude,*" which would procure him hot water when he wanted to shave; "*mangez,*" when he wanted to eat; and "*dormez,*" when he wanted to go to bed.

The worthy man would no doubt have managed to traverse Europe in comfort, from south to north, and from west to east, with or without these words, inasmuch as it is rare in any of the great Continental hotels to find a waiter who cannot speak a little English; but, having an eye to business, even when taking his pleasure, he required a more copious vocabulary in negotiating with any artists whom he might discover in the cities through which we passed, for the purchase of sketches of public buildings, scenery, or events, that might be useful to the journal with which his fortunes were bound up. He confessed as much; and, having no objection to help him, and liking the idea of the trip, for personal reasons, the necessary arrangements were speedily completed, and we started together for Antwerp, Brussels, and Cologne.

I have no intention to describe the journey, and only mention it that I may narrate an incident that occurred to us at Chamouni, which, remembered in the lurid light thrown upon it by a subsequent tragical catastrophe, has ever since exercised a powerful influence on my imagination. The large windows of our room at the hotel commanded a magnificent view of the Valley of Chamouni, the great glacier, and the sources of the infant Aveyron, with the giant bulk and snow-clad summits of Mont Blanc, truly the "Monarch of Mountains," of which we had caught the first faint glimpses at Lyons, nearly a hundred miles distant, and again at Saint Martin, in fuller majesty, more imposing even than he seemed to be when seen from his very feet at Chamouni.

Suddenly, soon after 11 o'clock, as we were thinking about retiring to rest, a loud thunder-burst was heard, echoing and re-echoing on the sides of the mountain, almost immediately succeeded by a vivid flash of lightning, and the loud pattering of large rain-drops at our window-panes. Another peal and another flash after a short interval, the peal still louder and the flash still more vivid than the first. To me the scene appeared indescribably grand and sublime, and filled my mind with a rapture, not, perhaps, unmingled with terror; but, if terror there were, with a delight that overpowered, overmastered, and almost extinguished it.

In the fervour of the awful kind of joy which thunder-storms have, since my early childhood, always excited in my mind, I rushed to the window and threw it wide open, that I might have a less-impeded view of the elementary commotion, and watch the masses of snow, that were loosened, either by the concussion of the thunder or by the direct stroke of the fiery bolts of heaven, and rolled down the mountain-side in harmless avalanches. Without looking at my companion, I called to him, and exclaimed rather than said, "Come here,

Ingram! This is too magnificent to be lost! It has been sent on purpose for us!"

A faint voice replied, "Don't say so! It is wicked!" and, looking round, I saw Mr. Ingram crouched on the floor in a corner, his face pale, and his hair on end with terror. In less than a minute he rolled flat on his back, unconscious, and apparently lifeless. I rang the bell for assistance. Before it came I endeavoured to administer to him a glass of neat brandy, with the idea that the stimulant would revive him; but his teeth were clenched and his mouth impenetrable. At last assistance, both male and female, arrived, and the housekeeper or mistress—I don't remember which it was—having some experience of similar cases among her own sex, applied such restoratives and means as she knew how to use with good effect, and in less than ten, or possibly five, minutes, we all had the satisfaction of witnessing the signs of revival.

On the complete return of consciousness, after the storm had totally subsided, Mr. Ingram told me that he always, ever since he could remember, was possessed by this unaccountable terror of a thunder-storm; that he had often endeavoured to reason himself out of it as an absurd and unmanly weakness, but that all his efforts were in vain, and would probably continue to be so as long as he lived. The more he struggled to subdue his terror, the more violently it affected his whole being, body and soul alike, and he declared that he had never previously witnessed so frightful a storm as this had been.

Eight years afterwards, the unfortunate gentleman, when on a visit to the United States, was on board of the steamship *Lady Elgin*, on Lake Michigan, with two or three hundred passengers, on their way to Chicago. There was a ball in the saloon that night, and the dancers, fatigued with their festivities, had most of them retired to rest, at one or two hours after midnight; but a portion of them were still keeping up the dance, when a sailing vessel, called the *Augusta*, bore suddenly down upon the steamer with a tremendous crash. The music and the merriment ceased immediately, and the passengers, who were asleep in their berths—among whom were Mr. Ingram and his eldest son, a lad of fifteen or sixteen—rushed up on deck, where at least three hundred people, many of them ladies in ball-dresses and in full feminine finery, were already congregated, panic-stricken, the men shouting, the women shrieking, and some preparing to jump overboard in desperation, or with faint hopes that rescue might possibly come to them in the waves, but none if they remained on board. In less than half-an-hour, during which a violent thunder-storm burst over the lake, the ill-fated *Lady Elgin* sank to the bottom, and crew and passengers, amounting in all to four hundred souls, were precipitated into the water.

The body of Mr. Ingram, clinging with his right arm to a broken spar of the vessel, was washed ashore five hours afterwards, still so warm that the people of a little village sixteen miles from Chicago, who had gathered on the beach at the early dawn, on the first news of the catastrophe, thought that life was not extinct, and endeavoured in vain to restore animation. When I afterwards learned the full particulars, and that the unfortunate man had been alive in the water, battling for his life, during five miserable hours, amid a furious storm of thunder and lightning, the remembrance of the scene at Chamouni was brought vividly to my mind, on which it has ever since been painfully impressed.

The long weary agony amid the pitiless waves, helpless as a floating straw, and apparently of as little account amid the whirl and rush of waters, would have been a concentration of bodily and mental agony almost equivalent to the accumulated miseries of a long life, to a mind constituted as Mr. Ingram's was, without the superadded horror of the elemental war in the heavens, dull, dark, and black, except when the lightning-flash threw a momentary gleam upon the waters, and the pallid, appealing face of the drowning man. Such was the death of poor Mr. Ingram, unexpectedly cut down in full health and vigour, in the hopeful maturity of his prime, with fame, fortune, and honour all apparently within his grasp. "Vanity of vanities—all is vanity!"

It may be interesting to superstitious people, and noteworthy to those who are not superstitious or inclined to believe in the marvellous, if I record the fact that, on the very morning when Mr. Ingram perished thus miserably in the waters of Lake Michigan, a large bird was observed to perch on the beautiful tower of St. Botolph, in Boston, of which town Mr. Ingram was a native, and of which he was at that time the representative in Parliament. The strange bird attracted the notice of the sexton or door-keeper by its unusual size, and, with the thoughtless cruelty of the average Englishman, both of high and low degree, he no sooner beheld it than he had a desire to kill it. He accordingly fetched a gun, and took steady and deadly aim at the luckless bird, which fell fluttering to his feet in the churchyard. The strange fowl was found to be a cormorant, or, in the Lincolnshire parlance of the townspeople, a "scart," which is declared in the Old Testament to be unclean, and ominous of grief and desolation.

The local journal, in its next issue, in recording the circumstance, laid particular stress on the character attributed to the bird on such high authority, and represented that its appearance on the church-tower, where no cormorant had ever been seen before within the memory of the "oldest inhabitant," was held by many of the people of Boston to presage some great impending misfortune, that would befall either the town or one of its principal citizens, or even the noble old church itself. When in due course the news of the death of Mr. Ingram arrived, occurring as it did on the very morning that the "scart" appeared on the high church-tower, all the old women of both sexes in Boston were confirmed in their superstitious belief, and convinced that the departed spirit of the late Member had sped four thousand miles, from Lake Michigan over the Atlantic, and entered the body of the "scart," and seen with physical eyes, for the last time, the town he loved so well, and with which his name and interests were so intimately connected.

Making the Best of it.

The editor of a London newspaper, whom I shall designate only as G——, a very excellent man, but of imperfect education, of little talent, but of much vanity, self-esteem, and overweening conceit, and author of several books of personal gossip about the parliamentary, literary, and other notabilities of his day—was most severely reviewed in the *Times*. A more truculent piece of criticism —though well-merited—had rarely been seen, and the whole town rang with it for two or three days. G—— affected to be pleased with it, and asserted that a spiteful critique always did an author good, and helped the sale of his book. When he met a friend or an acquaintance in the street, he stopped him and asked, "Have you seen the article in the *Times* pitching into me? It is very clever, and has done me a power of good. Though I paid for its insertion, and found it very expensive, I don't regret it, as I am sure to be the gainer in the end!" And so he went on his way, apparently rejoicing; but relieving his wounded feelings, whenever he had to quote the *Times* in the columns of his own paper, by refraining from mentioning it by name, and only alluding to it as a "scurrilous contemporary"!

CHAPTER XI.

PATRIC PARK AND CELEBRATED MODERN SCULPTORS.

I HAVE since my youth been fond of the art and the society of sculptors. My earliest friend in that high department was Mr. E. H. Bailey, to whom the world owes the graceful statues of "Eve at the Fountain" and "Eve listening to the Voice," two of the noblest examples of the beautiful and pure nude which the chisel and the imagination of man have ever produced. I was also acquainted, at a somewhat later period, with Mr. Lough, whose fine ideal statue of "Satan" excited much admiration, and which, when it temporarily failed to find a purchaser, suggested to the Rev. Sidney Smith the idea that the best thing for the sculptor to do with it would be to present it to the Reform Club, to be set up in its noble hall, for the reason "that the Devil was the first Reformer, and came to grief in Heaven for the too great zeal, indiscretion, and untimeliness with which he agitated the Reform question!"

A third sculptor with whom I was more or less intimate, was Mr. M. Cotes Wyatt, by whose invitation I lunched, with Dr. Richardson, of the *Times*, and eight or nine other gentlemen, at his foundry in Dudley Grove, Paddington, in the capacious belly of the great bronze horse which, with the counterfeit presentment of the Duke of Wellington on its back, was afterwards set up at Hyde Park Corner, on the arch opposite Apsley House, and formed for many years—until so recently as 1883 or 1884—the most prominent and painful monumental eye-sore in the metropolis. The guests on this occasion were somewhat cramped for elbow-room, but the host was all that a host should be; the viands were unexceptionable, the claret and champagne plentiful, the mirth and eloquence abundant.

The much-maligned statue did not really deserve the jibes and jeers that were levelled at it, and, had it been placed on a level with the ground, as I first saw it, or on a pedestal not above three or four feet high, would have been recognised as a fine work of art, which it undoubtedly was. But to place a bronze horse high up in the air was a mistake. The horse is a graceful animal, when seen on a level with the eye of the beholder; but, when seen at a high altitude, when its belly and legs appear to be its most prominent parts, or from the top of an omnibus, when its back is more conspicuous than the remainder of its body, it does not impress the senses with any idea of beauty of outline. Placed on the summit of the arch, whatever intrinsic beauty the statue possessed was totally lost, and presented, from every point from which it was possible to view it, a spectacle of "hideosity." This word is not yet recognised English, but it expresses my meaning more strongly than any synonymous expression, and I therefore use it, with many apologies to any reader whose severe taste may feel offended at it.

I have paid friendly visits to the studios of Matthew Noble (whose fine busts of Richard Cobden and Oliver Cromwell stand in the hall of the Reform Club), of Foley, the sculptor of "Ino nursing Bacchus," and of Calder Marshall—still among us (1885)—destined, it is to be hoped, still to produce many fine specimens of the art which he adorns. But my two most particular and dearest friends among sculptors were Patric Park and Alexander Munro, both natives of Scotland, with both of whom I lived for many pleasant years in familiar intercourse.

Patric Park was one of the great unappreciated geniuses of his time. He was a man of powerful intellect, as well as powerful frame, a true artist of heroic mould and thought, who dwarfed the poor pygmies of the day in which his lot was cast by conceptions too grand to find a market. He concealed under a somewhat rude and rough exterior as tender a heart as ever beat in a human bosom. Had he been an ancient Greek his name might have become immortal. Had he been a modern Frenchman, the art in which he excelled would have brought him in not only bread but fortune. But as he was only a portrayer of the heroic in the very prosaic country and time in which his lot was cast, it was as much as he could do to pay his way by the scanty rewards of an art which few people understood and which still fewer appreciated; and to waste upon the marble busts of rich men who had a fancy for that style of portraiture the talents, or rather the genius, which, had encouragement come, might have produced epics in stone to have rivalled the masterpieces of antiquity.

He was born in Glasgow in 1809, and I made his acquaintance in the *Morning Chronicle* office in 1842, when he was in the prime of his early manhood and five years my senior. He came to request the insertion of a modest paragraph in reference to a work of his, which had found a tardy purchaser, to be erected in the cemetery of Stirling. The paragraph was inserted, not as he wrote it, but with a kindly addition in praise of his work and of his genius. He came to the office the next day to know the writer's name; and, when the writer avowed himself, a friendship sprung up between them which suffered no abatement during the too short life of the grateful man of genius, who for the first time had been publicly recognised by the humble pen of one who could command in these minor matters the columns of a powerful journal.

Park's nature was broad and bold, and scorned conventionalities and false pretence. George Outram, a lawyer, and editor of a Glasgow newspaper, author of several humorous songs and lyrics upon the odds and ends of legal practice, among which the "Annuity" survives in perennial youth in Edinburgh and Glasgow society, and brother of the gallant Sir James Outram of Indian fame, used to say of Park that he liked him because he was not smooth and conventional, and had all his "corners" about him. "There is not in the world," he said to me on one occasion, "another man with so many delightful "corners" in his character as Park. We are all of us much too smooth and rounded off. Give me Park, and genuine nature!"

Park had a very loud voice and sang Scotch songs, perhaps with more vehemence than many people would admire, but with a heart and appreciation that were pleasant to listen to. It is related that a deputation of Glasgow Bailies came up to London, with Provost Lumsden at their head, in reference to the Lock Katrine Water Bill, for the supply of Glasgow with pure water, which was then before Parliament, and that they invited their distinguished townsmen to dine with them at the Victoria Hotel, Euston Square. After dinner, Park was called upon for a song, and as there was nobody in the large dining-room but one old gentleman, who, according to the waiter, was very deaf, Park consented to sing, and sang, in his very best style, the triumphant Jacobite ballad of " Hey, Johnnie Cope, are ye wauking yet ? " till, as one of the Bailies said, "he made the rafters ring, and might have been heard at St. Paul's." The deaf gentleman, as soon as the song was concluded, made his way to the table, and, apologising for addressing a company of strangers, turned to Park, and said, with extraordinary fervour and emotion, " May God Almighty bless you, Sir, and pour His choicest blessings upon your head ! For thirty years I have been stone deaf and have not heard the sound of the human voice. But I have heard your song, every word of it. God bless you ! God bless you ! "

Upon one occasion when we were travelling together in the Western Highlands, the captain of one of the Hutcheson steamers was exceedingly courteous and attentive to his passengers, and took great pains to point out all the picturesque objects on the route to those who were making the delightful journey for the first time. At one of the landing-places, the young Earl of Durham was taken on board with his servants, and from that moment the captain had neither eyes nor ears for any other person in the vessel. He lavished the most obsequious and fulsome attentions upon his Lordship, and when Park asked him a question, cut him short with a rude and snappish reply, and went on with his toadying. Park was disgusted, and expressed his opinion of the captain in a manner more forcible than polite. As there was a break in the navigation in consequence of some repairs that were being effected in one of the locks, the passengers had to disembark and proceed by omnibus to another steamer that awaited their arrival at Loch Lochy.

Park mounted on the box by the side of the driver, and was immediately addressed by the captain, "Come down out of that, you Sir! That seat's reserved for his Lordship!"

Park's anger flashed forth like an electric spark. "And who are *you*, Sir, that dare address a gentleman in that manner?"

"I am the captain of the boat, Sir, and I order you to come down out of that."

"Captain be hanged!" said Park. "The coachman might as well call himself a captain as you. The only difference between you is that he is the driver of a land omnibus and that you're the driver of an aquatic omnibus."

The young Earl laughed, and quietly took his place in the interior of the vehicle, leaving Park in undisputed possession of the box-seat.

His contempt for toadyism in all its shapes and manifestations was extreme. There was an eminent engineer of some repute in his day, with whom he had often come into acrimonious contact, and whom he especially disliked for his slavish subservience to rank and title. This gentleman, meeting Park one day in the street, said, "Mr. Park, I wish you not to talk about me. I am told that you said I was 'not worth a damn.' Is it true?"

"Well," replied Park, "it may be; but if I said so, I underrated you. I think you are worth two damns; and I damn you twice!"

On another occasion, when attending a soirée at Lady Byron's, he was so annoyed at finding no other refreshment than tea, which he did not care for, and very weak port-wine negus, which he detested as an unmanly and unheroic drink, that he took his departure, resolved to go in search of a stronger potation.

The footman in the hall, addressing him deferentially, said, "Shall I call your carriage, my Lord?"

"I'm not a lord," said Park.

"I beg pardon, Sir. Shall I call your carriage?"

"I have not got a carriage. Give me my walking-stick. And now," he added, slipping a shilling into the man's hand, "can you tell me of any decent public-house in the neighbourhood where I can get a glass of hot brandy and water?"

Park resided for a year or two in Edinburgh, and procured several commissions for the busts of medical, legal, literary, and other notabilities of the place, and, what was in a higher degree in accordance with his tastes, for a few life-size statues of characters in the poems and novels of Sir Walter Scott to complete the Scott Monument in Princes Street. But funds were wanting to pay the artist for all the statues that were required, and the work ceased. Park's statuettes, though worthy of the honour, were never erected, for what reason I have never thoroughly understood, though I believe that in after years, when funds were forthcoming, new artists were employed who wanted all the money for their own works.

Park also executed, without a commission, a gigantic model of a statue of Sir William Wallace, for whose name and fame he had the most enthusiastic veneration, with the idea that the patriotic feelings of the Scottish nation, would be so far excited by his work, as to justify an appeal to the public to set it up in bronze or marble [he preferred bronze], on the Calton Hill, amid other monuments to the memory of illustrious Scotsmen. But the deeds of Wallace were too far back in the gloom of bygone ages to excite much contemporary interest. The model was a noble work, eighteen feet high, and wholly nude. Some of his friends, especially Mr. Alexander Russel of the *Scotsman*, suggested to him that a little drapery would be more in accordance with Scottish ideas than a figure so nude that it dispensed even with the customary fig-leaf. Park revolted at the notion of the fig-leaf. "A cowardly obscene subterfuge," he said. "To the pure all things are pure." There is nothing impure in nature, but only in the mind of man. Rather than disgrace my statue with the fig-leaf, I would dash the model to pieces." " But the drapery ? " said his friends. " What I have done I have done, and I will not spoil my own design. Wallace was once a man, and if he had lived in the last century, and I had to model his statue, I would have draped it or put it in armour as if he had been the Duke of Marlborough or Prince Eugene. But the memory of Wallace is scarcely the memory of a man, but of a demigod. Wallace is a myth, and as a myth he does not require clothes." "Yes, true," said the goodnatured friend ; " but you are anxious to procure the public support and the public guineas, and you'll never get them for a naked giant." " Then I'll smash the model," said the indignant and disspirited artist. And he did so ; and a great and beautiful work was lost to the world for ever.

At the time of our first acquaintance Park was somewhat smitten by the charms of a beautiful young woman in Greenock, the daughter of one of his oldest and best friends. The lady had no knowledge of art, and scarcely knew what was meant by the word sculptor. She asked him one day whether he cut marble chimney-pieces. This was too much. He was *desillusionné*, and the amatory flame flickered out, no more to be lighted.

Park and I and the late Alexander Mackay, and three or four friends, were once together on the top of Ben Lomond, on a fine clear day in August 1846. The weather was lovely, but oppressively hot, and the fatigue of climbing was great, but not excessive. At the summit, so pure was the atmosphere, that, looking eastward, we could distinctly see Arthur's Seat that overlooks Edinburgh, and the Bass Rock in the Firth of Forth, twenty miles beyond. Looking westward, we could distinctly see Ailsa Craig in the Firth of Clyde, and the whole diameter of Scotland. By a strange effect of the atmosphere, the peak of Goatfell in Arran, separated optically from the mountain by a belt of thick white cloud, seemed to be preternaturally raised to a height of at least 20,000 feet above the sea. I pointed it out to Park. "Nonsense!" he said; 'why Arran would be higher than the Himalayas if your notion were correct." "But I know the shape of the peak," I replied. "I have been on the top of Goatfell at least half-a-dozen times, and would swear to it, as to the nose on your face." And as we were speaking the white cloud was dissipated, and the Himalayan peak seemed to descend slowly and take its place on the body of Goatfell, from which it had appeared to have been dissevered. "Well," he said, "things are not what they seem; and I maintain that it was as high as the Himalayas or Chimborazo while the appearance lasted."

The sun was at this time in its noon-tide glory, and Park, inspired by the grandeur of the scene, preached us a very eloquent little sermon, addressing himself to the sun, on the inherent dignity and beauty of Sun worship, as practised by the modern Parsees and the ancient Druids. He concluded by a lament that his own art was powerless to represent or personify the grand forces of Nature, as the Greeks had attempted to do. "The Apollo Belvidere," he said, "is the representation of a beautiful, a divine young man. But it is not Apollo. Art can represent Venus, the perfection of female beauty, and Mars, the perfection of manly vigour; but Apollo, no! Yet I think I would have tried Apollo myself, if I had lived in Athens two thousand years ago."

"A living dog is better than a dead lion."

"True," said Park, "I am a living dog. Phidias is a dead lion. I have to model the ugly faces of cheesemongers, or grocers, or ironmasters, and put dignity into them, if I can, which is difficult. And when I put the dignity, they complain of the bad likeness; so that I often think I'd rather be a rich cheesemonger than a poor sculptor."

Park modelled a bust of myself, for which he would not accept payment. He found it a very difficult task to perform, and I had to sit to him at least twenty times or oftener, before he could please himself with his work. On one occasion he lost all patience, and swearing lustily *more suo*, dashed the clay into a shapeless mass with his fist. "D——n you," he said, "why don't you keep to one face? You seem to have fifty faces in a minute, and all different! I never but once had another face that gave me half the trouble."

"And whose was the other?" I inquired.

"Sir Charles Barry's (architect of the Houses of Parliament at Westminster). He drove me well-nigh to despair with his sudden changes of expression. He was a very Proteus, as far as his face was concerned. And you're another! Why don't you keep thinking of one thing while I am modelling, and why can't you retain one expression, for at least two minutes?"

It was not till fully three months after this outburst that he took courage to begin again, growling and grumbling at his work; but determining, he said, not to be beaten, either by Sir Charles Barry or myself. "Poets and architects, and painters and musicians, and novelists," he said, "are all difficult subjects for the sculptor. Give me the face of a soldier," he added. " Such a face as that of the Emperor Napoleon. There is no mistake about *that* ; or, better still, Sir Charles James Napier! If there is not very much variable soul, so called in the faces of such men, there is a very great deal of body ! "

Park was commissioned by the Duke of Hamilton to model a bust of Napoleon III., and produced, perhaps, the very finest of all the fine portrait busts which ever proceeded from his chisel. The Emperor impressed Park in the most favourable manner, and he always spoke of him in terms of enthusiastic admiration, for the innate heroism and tenderness of his character. "All true heroes," he said, "are tender-hearted ; and the man who can fight most bravely has always the readiest drop of moisture in his eye, when a noble deed is mentioned or a chord of sympathy is touched."

The bust of Napoleon was lost in the wreck of the vessel that conveyed it from Dover to Calais ; but the Duke of Hamilton commissioned the sculptor to execute a second copy from the clay model, which duly reached its destination, and is now in the South Kensington Museum.

I called at Park's studio one morning, and was informed that he every minute expected a visit from the great General Sir Charles James Napier, for whose character and achievements he had the highest admiration. He considered him by far the greatest soldier of modern times, and had prevailed upon the General to sit to him for his bust. Park asked me to stay and be introduced to him, and, nothing loth, I readily consented. I had not long to wait. The General had a nose like the beak of an eagle, larger and more conspicuous on his leonine and intellectual face, than that of the Duke of Wellington, whose nose was familiar in the purlieus of the Horse Guards, and procured for him the title of "Conkey" from the street urchins. I recognised him at a glance as soon as he entered. On his taking a seat, for Park to model his face in clay, the sculptor asked him not to think of too many things at a time, but to keep his mind fixed on one subject. The General did his best to comply with the request, with the result that his face soon assumed a fixed and sleepy expression, without a trace of intellectual animation. Park suddenly startled him by inquiring, "Is it true, General, that you gave way, retreated in fact, at the battle of —— ?" (naming the place, which I have forgotten). The General's eyes flashed sudden fire, and he was about to reply indignantly, when Park quietly remarked, plying his modelling tool on the face at the time, "That 'll do, General. The expression is admirable." The General saw through the manœuvre, and laughed heartily.

The General's statue in Trafalgar Square is an admirable likeness. Park was much disappointed at not receiving the commission to execute it.

Patric Park died before he was fifty, and when to all appearance there were many happy and prosperous years before him, when, having surmounted his early difficulties, he might have looked forward to the study and completion of the many noble works, to which he pined to devote his mature energies, after emancipation from the slavery of what he called "busting" the effigies of cheesemongers. He had been for some months in Manchester, plying his vocation among the rich notabilities of that prosperous city; when one day, emerging from a carriage at the railway station, he observed a porter with a huge basket of ice upon his head, staggering under the load, and ready to fall. Park rushed forward to the man's assistance, prevented him from falling, steadied the load upon his head by a great muscular exertion, and suddenly found his mouth full of blood. He had broken a blood-vessel! and stretching forth his hand, took a lump of ice from the basket and held it in his mouth to stop the bleeding. He proceeded to the nearest chemist's shop for advice and relief, and was forthwith conveyed to his hotel, delirious. A neighbouring doctor was called in, Park beseeching him for brandy, which was refused, but ought to have been given according to to the opinion of his own medical attendant in London, who had been summoned by telegraph and came down by the next train. But he arrived too late. The noble, the generous, the gifted Park, was no more, and his attached young wife and family and hundreds of friends were left lamenting.

Park married Robina, the daughter of Dr. Robert Carruthers, of the *Inverness Courier*. He met the lady first at my house, and the marriage was one of unalloyed happiness. A small and beautiful bust of Mrs. Park, executed by her husband, adorns the collection of the Royal Scottish Academy in Edinburgh, where it appears under the title of "A Highland Lassie."

Alexander Munro was of less heroic genius than Patric Park; but his works were of an equally high order in a softer mood. He was of frail build and delicate organization. But the spirit was strong though the flesh was weak. The sword within the scabbard was finely tempered, and of the truest metal. He was a native of Inverness, and while in his early teens, during my frequent visits to the Highlands, I was often shown by Dr., then Mr., Carruthers, little miniature heads, exquisitely carved out of slate pencils by the clever boy, whose skill was the admiration of all the teachers and pupils at the Inverness Academy, as well as of most of the intelligent inhabitants of the town. His future fame as an artist was fondly predicted, and it was thought highly desirable that the promising boy should be sent to London to study art. But poverty's "unconquerable bar" prevented, and it was not until his twentieth or twenty-first year that the means were found, with great difficulty, among his many humble friends and admirers, to pay his expenses to London, with a small sum in his pocket to enable him to wait and look about him for a chance of bettering his fortune. He arrived, armed with two letters of introduction, one to the late Duchess of Sutherland, mother of the present Duke, and the other to myself at the *Morning Chronicle* office. The letter to the Duchess was fruitless of good results, but that to myself proved ultimately to be of service. I introduced the ambitious young man to Mr. E. H. Bailey, the sculptor, whom I have already mentioned, who received him kindly, praised his slate-pencil heads, gave his good advice in his art, and allowed him to frequent his studio, to familiarise himself with the mechanism of the profession to which he had resolved to devote his life. Mr. Bailey afterwards introduced him to Sir Charles Barry, the architect of the new Houses of Parliament, the exteriors of which were at that time not wholly completed. He was soon employed by that gentleman at mechanic's wages, to carve in stone many of the small heads, which are to be seen by those who care to look, or have patience to examine the somewhat filagree walls of that edifice. He remained at this work for more years than I can remember, paying his way, living humbly, incurring no debt, and not only instructing himself in his art, but endeavouring to complete his literary education by diligent study in his leisure hours. He had imagination as well as skill, and produced several statuettes, which he was enabled to exhibit in the inadequately filled sculpture-room of the Royal Academy, where they excited little attention. But he was not to be discouraged, and his appearances at the exhibition during successive years ultimately attracted the notice of a few wealthy and influential lovers of art, among others of Lady Marian Alford, and Mr. W. E. Gladstone, then rising fast into fame and importance, and aspiring to the post of Prime Minister. Both of these personages gave him commissions, that acted as "pot-boilers" when pot-boilers were sorely needed. At this period Munro appealed to me at the *Illustrated London News* office, with the hope that I would exert my influence in his favour, to procure the insertion in that paper of an engraving of one of his statuettes. This I had all the will but not exactly the power to do, and his wish remained ungratified until the following annual exhibition of the Royal Academy, when an unforeseen and lucky chance did that for his advantage, which solicitation might have failed to accomplish, and for which interest might possibly have been excited in vain. It happened that Mr. Ingram, the proprietor of that influential journal, which had not then degenerated into a mere picture-sheet, without political, literary, artistic, or any other authority, asked me to accompany him to the private view. We had gone the round of the pictures of the year, and proceeded to the sculpture-room, when Mr. Ingram's attention was attracted by a group of nude children, very beautifully executed, when he turned to me and said, "I think we must have this for the paper. Who is the sculptor?" I turned to the catalogue and found it was by Munro. As fate, or luck, or predestination would have it, I caught sight of the artist himself at no great distance from us, watching our movements, preparatory to addressing me. I beckoned to him to come forward, and then and there introduced him to Mr. Ingram. Mr. Ingram expressed his approbation of the work, and, with the instantaneous decision which was a principal feature of his character, gave the delighted sculptor, before we left the room, a commission to execute in marble a group of his three infant children. He paid him on the following day half the stipulated honorarium for the work, according to the usual custom, and Munro thought that his fortune was made. And such ultimately became the fact. Mr. Ingram was so pleased with the work when completed, that he became a fast friend of the artist, and never lost sight of an opportunity to advance his interests. Munro's career from that time forward was a continuous and steady if not a brilliant advance, and he rose by slow but sure degrees to a high rank in his profession. Mr. Ingram was twice elected to Parliament for his native town of Boston in Lincolnshire, which he represented until his untimely death by accident in Lake Michigan in America, which I have already recorded. The sudden close of his promising career excited much feeling in the country, especially in Boston, where he was so highly esteemed, and the prosperity and amenity of which his ungrudging munificence and public spirit had done so much to promote. It was resolved by the grateful citizens to erect a statue to his honour in the market-place by public subscription. His widow, however, determined to erect the monument at her own expense, and commissioned Munro to execute the work in bronze. This was the most lucrative commission with which he had ever been entrusted, and the grateful sculptor wrote me a letter on the occasion, though I had no direct concern in the business, in which he quoted a line from a well-known poem of Leigh Hunt—

> This also do I owe to thee.

The statue is not only an excellent likeness of the man whom it commemorates, but a fine specimen of the sculptor's art, and was erected at a cost, I believe, of upwards of three thousand pounds.

Munro, like Patric Park, married a daughter of Mr. Carruthers, of Inverness. He died when he was a little above forty, to the great grief of those who esteemed him most and loved him best, and who knew but too well the delicacy of his constitution, and how frail was the thread that held him to life. His devoted wife, who nursed him during his long illness, did not long survive him. The late Mr. Tom Taylor, the well-known dramatist and editor of *Punch*, the executor of his will, reported him to have died worth ten thousand pounds—a considerable fortune to have acquired in so short a career in art, and which was a proof, not only of the public appreciation which he enjoyed, but of his careful and economic management of his resources.

CHAPTER XII.

THEODORE VON HOLST.

THEODORE VON HOLST, an Englishman of German extraction, as his name implies, was an artist of whose future fame many hopeful prognostications were made by his friends, but of which his early death prevented the fulfilment. He was introduced to me by Patric Park, as one who greatly admired my then recently published poem of the *Maid of Mora, or the Salamandrine*, founded upon the wild Rosicrucian fancies of the Count de Gabalis. Mr. Von Holst had made some sketches, which he wished me to see, of its opening cantos. The sketches were afterwards developed into finished pictures, and were of great beauty and merit. They were intended at the time to be published by the late Mr. Martin Colnaghi, in a handsomely-illustrated edition of the poem. The intention, however, was not fulfilled, in consequence of a change of mind on the part of Mr. Colnaghi, on the ground that he was a print-seller, not a book-seller, and that the work might suffer in his hands.

I was not fortunate enough to become the purchaser of the whole series of Von Holst's designs, though I managed to secure possession of two of the best of them. I saw much of him during the time he was occupied on the poem, and learned to appreciate his genius, and to take pleasure in his companionship. His imagination was highly poetical and graceful, though often wandering into the wild, the grotesque, and the fantastic, with a tendency, I thought, to degenerate into the extravagant, the ultra-romantic, and the supernatural. He was eccentric but picturesque in his costume, and often suggested to my mind, as I looked upon him, what his erratic predecessor, Blake, must have appeared in the eyes of his contemporaries, when the semi- or demi-semi fits of his highly poetical lunacy were upon him.

He was the owner of a human skull, mounted with a silver rim, which he used as a punch-bowl, and out of which he often, he said, drank ale or wine, and punch, when he was grimly convivial among his Bohemian comrades. He became possessed of the relic by exchanging one of his pictures, or "pot-boilers," with his friend and commercial agent, Mr. Ovenstone, noted in his day as a dealer in old curiosities and bric-a-brac, and especially in the rare articles that had a charm in the eyes of the libidinous, and the admirers of such obscenities in art as are to be found in the Hotel Cluny at Paris, and the Museum of Antiquities at Naples.

Poor Theodore was unwisely enamoured of a young woman who stood to him as a model in the nude for eighteen-pence an hour, and whose form he declared to be absolutely faultless, and as exquisite as that of Aphrodite herself when she rose from the sea-foam in immortal loveliness. He ultimately married this paragon, whom he sometimes called the "Mother-of-Pearl Lady." Her mental graces were by no means equal to those which her fascinated lover saw in the transcendent beauty of her incomparable nudity, and their connubial life was believed among his friends to be not of the happiest. The lady refused to pose for him in the nude after she was married, and preferred to be taken in character, as a tragedy Queen, with the skull, supposed to contain poison in one hand, and her dagger in the other, her eyes "in a fine frenzy rolling." I am not aware that her husband ever painted her in this character, though he very possibly did so; but, if he did, a very noble picture was doubtless the result.

The chief purchaser of Von Holst's "pot-boilers" was the Mr. Ovenstone already mentioned, his friend in need, his prop in the adversity of which, during his short life, he had more than an adequate share, and which, superadded to the ill-health which he owed to a more than usually delicate constitution, tended to shorten his days and extinguish prematurely the light of his genius.

Ovenstone was a remarkable character in his way, well known in his time to the fashionable Aspasias, Phrynes, Lesbias, and Anonymas, by whose temporary but wealthy "protectors" he was extensively and profitably employed in furnishing secluded villas for their occupation. He had a very remarkable time-piece in his private sanctum at the back of his shop, which he highly prized, which was not for sale, and the hidden mysteries of the mechanism of which he only revealed to a chosen few, after much solicitation, and as a very particular mark of his favour.

The circumstances under which he became possessed of the article were interesting. Many years previous to my knowledge of him—in the days when he was a young man and I was but a schoolboy, when George IV. was king, and his brother, the Duke of York, was commander-in-chief of the British army—Ovenstone happened to be passing across the Parade in St. James's Park on his way to Whitehall, when his foot kicked against an obstruction on the road. On stooping to see what it was, he discovered a bulky and rather shabby pocket-book, of which he forthwith possessed himself. On opening it at his leisure, after his return home to Great Titchfield Street, he found it filled with letters, all opened, that were addressed to the Duke of York, most of them marked "private and confidential," the great majority of them being written in a female hand. A hasty glance at some of them convinced the finder—who confessed to himself that he ought not to have read them—that they were of a delicate and highly compromising character.

He at once sealed up the packet, and wrote a letter to the Duke—which he would not trust either to the Post Office or to a private messenger, but delivered himself, the same day, at the office of the commander-in-chief at the Horse Guards. He informed His Royal Highness of the "waif" he had found, requesting him to name an hour and place when and where he could wait upon him, and deliver the pocket-book and its contents into the hands of the lawful owner. The Duke was absent from town, and Ovenstone remained for two days without an answer to his message. On the third day, a hackney coach—there were no cabs in those days—drove up to the door of the old curiosity-shop; and the coachman, descending from the box without fear of the docile horses becoming aware of the absence of his controlling hand. Entering the shop, he requested that Mr. Ovenstone would step out and speak to a gentleman in the coach outside.

Mr. Ovenstone obeyed the summons, and immediately recognised his visitor, whom he knew by sight, as the Duke of York in *propria persona*. The Duke invited him to step into the vehicle, which Mr. Ovenstone did, after a preliminary visit to his writing-desk, in which he had safely secured the precious pocket-book, with its contents complete and unharmed. The Duke on receiving it was profuse in the expression of his thanks, and pressed the finder to accept of a hundred pound Bank of England note, as a reward for his honesty and the care and trouble he had taken in the matter. Mr. Ovenstone declined the proffered gratuity, either as a reward or a mere acknowledgment, much to the Duke's surprise.

"You are a very honest man," said His Royal Highness. "Will you do me the favour to shake hands with me?"

The favour was granted. Mr. Ovenstone descended from the vehicle, made a low bow to the Duke, who merely said to the coachman, "Put me down where you took me up," and drove off to his destination, wherever that may have been.

About a week afterwards, Mr. Ovenstone received a haunch of venison from the Duke of York, and a large case, very carefully packed, which, on being opened, was found to contain the superb antique time-piece, of which mention has been previously made, and of which the new owner continued to be proud as long as he lived. The mysterious interior—seldom displayed to anybody, especially to those whom Mr. Ovenstone designated as "the profane"—revealed two exquisite figures in ivory, representing a nude Adonis and a nude Venus, or, as Mr. Ovenstone stated, an Adam and an Eve recumbent in a bower in Paradise before the Fall. The workmanship was chaste, but the idea of the artist was unchaste in the extreme, and of a nature to find no favour except in the eyes of a vulgar and obscene sensualist. In his late years Mr. Ovenstone came to grief, and was tried at the Central Criminal Court for an attempt to murder, and acquitted on the ground of insanity.

END OF VOL. I.

London: Printed by W. H. Allen & Co., 13 Waterloo Place. S.W.

www.ingramcontent.com/pod-product-compliance
Lightning Source LLC
Chambersburg PA
CBHW022123290426
44112CB00008B/791